MORE Than me

MORE Than me

Step Out of Yourself and Into Humanity

Kelly Jo Eldredge
and
Eric L. Mott

Copyright © 2010 Kelly Jo Eldredge and Eric L. Mott
All rights reserved.

ISBN: 1-4563-4300-9
ISBN-13: 978-1456343002

*To all of the inspiring people we interviewed for
the MORE Than me project.
Thank you for showing us that true joy begins
with an outstretched hand.*

Contents

Preface	ix
Chapter 1: It Happened One Night	1
Chapter 2: Finding Myself by Searching for Others	6
Chapter 3: Wise Women	13
Chapter 4: All in the Family	19
Chapter 5: Two Guys Named Jim	34
Chapter 6: Small Steps, Big Rewards	41
Chapter 7: Staying Local	50
Chapter 8: Going Global	63
Chapter 9: Stepping Out of Your Comfort Zone	87
Chapter 10: Creating a Legacy	114
Chapter 11: Hobbies Help	132
Chapter 12: You've Got Skills	149
Chapter 13: Answer the Call	165
Chapter 14: Empowering Opportunities	185
Chapter 15: It's in Your Job Description	215
Chapter 16: Volunteers Matter	227
Chapter 17: Follow Your Passion	238
Epilogue	255

Preface

IT'S MID-SEPTEMBER, A HOT, SUNNY DAY IN THE WESTERN UNITED STATES. A gold dome gleams against a brilliant blue sky. Under the watchful eye of the state capital, traffic shuffles around the exterior of a small but stately park. From a painter's perspective, the park provides a beautiful landscape of large, old trees, crisscrossed walkways, and bright red and yellow flowers planted in neat rectangles of earth.

But look more closely.

A thin, young man kneels down to pet his tiny Chihuahua. The man's hat is not out of place in this cowboy town, but closer inspection reveals shabby, dirty clothes, no socks, and worn out shoes. The knapsack slung over his shoulder holds everything he owns.

A few feet away, Chuck Wagner wheels slowly from the public library to the southeast corner of the park under the shade of a few large oak trees. His eyes scan the sidewalks. Then he sees them—two familiar faces toting a bunch of sacks and a card table.

Chuck smiles. He can always count on Randy and Jerry…and Ryan, Dave, Tony, and John. They'll be showing up soon, too. For the last six months, Chuck has met at least three of these guys in the park every Tuesday and Friday without fail.

The men shake hands, and soon a couple of college students join the group, running up the sidewalk with grins and a few more bulging bags.

The cowboy picks up his dog and ambles over to the gathering.

One by one, previously unnoticed (or possibly ignored) people of a variety of ages start to hover around the guys with the bags and the card table.

What kind of club is this?

What could this disparate group of people possibly have in common?

Out of the bags come more bags—brown paper sacks filled with peanut butter and jelly sandwiches, fruit, and granola bars.

"Brother, can I get you a sandwich today?" Jerry smiles broadly at his friend, Chuck.

"Thanks, Jer," Chuck grins and plops the sack lunch on his lap. This might be the only meal he gets today. Randy smiles and tosses his friend a bottle of water to wash it down.

Within twenty minutes, eighty lunches, two cases of water, and forty pairs of new socks are gone.

The man in the cowboy hat asks for communion. He kneels with his dog and gives the Chihuahua a taste of the bread dipped in grape juice before he crosses himself and partakes.

"God loves all creatures, great and small, right?" Ryan winks.

Chuck's eagle eye catches a disheveled woman lumbering across the park toward their group. She has a look of panic in her eyes. She's a few minutes too late.

"Hey," Chuck motions to one of the college students. "Here."

He passes his lunch and bottle of water to the college student to give to the woman as she arrives panting and hopeful. A huge, toothless smile spreads across her face.

Chuck is fifty-six years old. He broke his leg in two places last spring when he slipped on the ice. Chuck grew up right here in the Capital Hill area. He has lived within a few miles of this spot ever since he was eight years old. It has been quite an interesting life. Not very long ago, Chuck was laid off and ended up on the streets—too young for retirement and too old to be hired in a stagnant economy.

The guys with the card table helped Chuck find a low-income apartment for $31 a month, but Chuck is not quite sure he'll be able to come up with rent next month.

Civic Center Park can be a dangerous place at night, so he's grateful to have a room to sleep in for now. Chuck is not short on common sense. He knows to steer clear of the drug addicted and mentally unstable on the streets if he wants to survive. He has become, for the most part, skeptical and mistrustful—hard. Life hasn't always been kind, and sometimes Chuck feels like he's just waiting for the next blow.

But on this beautiful September afternoon, Chuck chooses to forget about his grumbling stomach, the bad luck he has recently experienced, and his fears about the future. He smiles at the woman walking away with his lunch.

1

It Happened One Night

If you want to lift yourself up, lift up someone else.
—Booker T. Washington

JUST A FEW BLOCKS AWAY AND A FEW MONTHS EARLIER, A MAN AND WOMAN smiled at each other across a cozy booth snuggled in the back corner of a dimly lit restaurant. She sipped a cup of peppermint tea; he nursed a glass of amber beer. The couple wasn't old, but they weren't young either. They talked about life in the middle.

They had only known each other for a little over two years, but they shared a startling list of similarities. Both were raised in middleclass families in the middle of the country.

Not exactly the start of a gripping adventure story, is it?

But these two people enjoyed quite a spectacular and privileged upbringing. It had nothing to do with their parents' incomes, the neighborhoods where they lived, or the schools they attended. They shared one very precious advantage—growing up in a culture of volunteerism. Their parents instilled in them the importance of helping others and modeled every day how volunteering made their lives happier and more interesting.

When the man and woman grew up and moved away from their respective towns in the middle, they rediscovered the power of volunteerism. In quite separate instances, before they ever met each other, they found out that volunteering could transform their lives—it may have even saved their lives. How could that be true?

The couple talked passionately about their transformations, as the rain poured down outside and sent people scattering on the Sixteenth Street Mall. They talked with breathless excitement, as if they had unlocked one of the great mysteries of life. They compared notes, and every story yielded the same conclusion—helping someone in need changed them in magnificent and unforeseen ways. Simple acts of kindness carried great power for the giver as well as the receiver. What if they could harness that energy? What would the world look like if citizens everywhere rushed to volunteer locally and globally? What would this couple's parents think of their epiphany?

The pair laughed in unison. Their parents would tell them they hadn't discovered anything new. What they were experiencing was the power of being part of a greater humanity. We are not meant to travel this road alone.

If that is true, why do so many of us try to make it a solo journey?

That couple in the middle was us—the authors of this book—on a date night in downtown Denver nearly a year ago. Our conversation on the power of volunteerism didn't end that night. In fact, quite the opposite happened. It turned into more than forty interviews with people all over the world.

An intimate conversation between a husband and wife has now become a mission with a simple slogan: Volunteer. It will change you. We belong to humanity, and we must strengthen our connections instead of put up barriers that isolate us.

In order to demonstrate the power of stepping into humanity, we started with our own families and looked for examples of the benefits of volunteerism. Then, we branched out to friends, acquaintances, and random people we met on Twitter and through various other Internet connections. A wonderful web spun its way from Denver to parts of the world we've never visited and people we have never met before. One story led to another, and soon we had a pile of case studies to prove our slogan.

We asked the same basic list of questions:

- When did you first discover the joy of volunteering?
- Was there a specific person or event that inspired you to volunteer?

- Do you have any stories to share about how volunteerism has shaped your life?
- Have your volunteer activities improved your quality of life? If so, how?
- Would you say that helping someone in need has changed you in any way?

We received a wide variety of answers, but the ultimate conclusion matched our slogan 100 percent: volunteering changes people.

What do you think of when you hear the word volunteer? Mother Theresa? Homeless shelters? Selfless martyrs? Maybe you experience a slight bit of guilt. You think you should probably do some volunteer work, but you can never find the time. Instead, maybe you hastily send a check to your favorite charity on December 31 for the tax write off.

What often gets lost in the idea of volunteering is the fact that the giver is transformed through the act of helping someone else, and it doesn't have to be something as big as changing your house into a homeless shelter. Any act of kindness, no matter how small, has a positive effect on both the giver and the receiver.

The most healing and powerful thing any person can do is place the concerns of another human being above their own. It's not something we "should" do to be good people. It's something we must do to be part of this world. Plus, the benefits are amazing!

One doesn't have to look very far to see examples of despair today. Times are tough, and everyone could use a little help. The unemployment rate in the United States has hovered around 10 percent for most of 2010, according to the Bureau of Labor Statistics of the U.S. Department of Labor. Job losses, foreclosures, and bankruptcy lead the headlines, and the word depression describes more than just the economy. The United States is in need of a serious makeover, and citizens are experiencing it on a very personal level. It's hard to look in the mirror when the future is so dim. The truth isn't very pretty.

What will it take to feel good again? The New York Times Best Sellers list is sprinkled with books about getting one's winning edge back, but most individuals don't have any spirit left to light the fire of success. They simply feel ragged, listless, and sick of continually being asked to cut back instead of enjoying abundance.

The days of excess were fun, but now they are a hazy memory. Celebrity examples have demonstrated that popping pills have fatal consequences, so that's no longer a valid escape route. A vacation is a ridiculous pipe dream unless it takes place in a tent in the backyard. Expensive plastic surgery, liposuction, and psychotherapy are out of the question if funds are low. Even a manicure or pedicure is hard to justify when one's home is about to go into foreclosure.

The present-day picture looks very gray, and many people don't see any sunshine in the forecast. But there is a solution. Brighter days do lie ahead. In fact, it is possible to start a personal transformation right now. The answer is simple: do something for someone else.

> *It is one of the most beautiful compensations of life, that no man can sincerely try to help another without helping himself.*
>
> —Ralph Waldo Emerson

Most self-help solutions deal with just that—the self. But the real key is to look outside of self. Each individual on this planet is part of a powerful and dynamic humanity, and connecting with others is the key to true happiness and fulfillment. This book will encourage the reader to step out of self and into humanity, to discover that there is *MORE Than me*.

Our project started with a dinner conversation and moved on to a few personal stories from family and friends about the benefits of volunteerism. Soon we were interviewing people around the world about random and not-so-random acts of kindness. There is power in this, a force for change that cannot be discounted. Read about the people we interviewed in these pages. Let them inspire you to take action. Selfless acts are not completely selfless. They transform us all.

In every community, there is work to be done. In every nation, there are wounds to heal. In every heart, there is the power to do it.

—Marianne Williamson

FINDING MYSELF BY SEARCHING FOR OTHERS **2**

Eric's Story

I SURVIVED MY DIVORCE BY GETTING LOST.

I have never understood the concept of needing to find oneself. In my opinion, that phrase gives a troubled person an excuse to look inward and withdraw from life. In times of personal hardship, the opposite should occur: one should get lost—lost in the possibilities of life-altering change.

The transformative nature of a broken marriage takes place whether you desire change or not. I was not looking for change the day my ex-wife called me home early from the office and suggested we get divorced. Change found me instead. I didn't know it then, but that uncomfortable moment set me on the path to a rich, mature life.

Too many people give in to self-pity at times such as divorce. If only we could all appreciate the gift that the opportunity to start over represents. My wife, Kelly, calls that a re-boot. I re-booted my life and found myself lost in the wilderness of grand new activities and adventures. More importantly, I re-booted and got lost in the world of service to others. I survived my divorce by discovering volunteerism.

Too much good came out of my first marriage to have any regrets about those seven years. Long before we decided to honor our love for each other by letting each other go, my ex-wife told me to get out of the house. She didn't mean go live somewhere else, she meant go do something. Her intuition told her something that mine did not: life was more than television and video games.

I remember fondly the day she drove me to The Home Depot and told me to buy as many woodworking tools as I wanted. That must be every husband's dream come true. I also remember when I signed up for martial arts classes, driving dutifully to the dojo twice a week after work with many of my officemates, whom I convinced to come with me.

That was a good start; I will be always grateful to my ex-wife for pointing me in the direction of getting lost. Her words in a recent email to me summed up my current feelings on our divorce perfectly. *I hope you believe now that getting divorced was a good thing for both of us—that we are both in a better place.*

I couldn't have said it better.

The Next Step

Woodworking is a fine hobby. I love creating useful items out of a blank piece of wood. I have several creations of mine around our house: a quilt rack and a bookshelf, for example. However, in the early days after my divorce, I realized I would not find ultimate fulfillment from drilling random holes in a stubborn piece of pine.

Even though woodworking technically got me out of the house, I never got past the garage. I spent hours and hours out there making sawdust and praying my neighbors didn't mind the noise at ten o'clock at night. My poor car required a daily trip to the wash to remove all the dust I generated.

Aikido lessons didn't do much for me in the end, either. I participated for a solid year, though, enjoying my exposure to Japanese culture and language. But the bruises on my arms never went away and my back never stopped hurting. Martial arts were not the answer to my quest for getting lost.

I eventually joined the Colorado Mountain Club. The CMC is a hiking and mountaineering group based in Golden, Colorado. It offers plenty of activities and classroom experiences for the novice hiker. Through CMC education opportunities, I learned how to use a topographical map and a compass in the wilderness. That gave a whole new meaning to the phrase *finding oneself.*

I finally got out of the house.

Dating Again

I made a lucky intuitive leap soon after I became single again. I realized that in order to avoid the mistakes I made in my marriage, I needed a new master plan in life, or else any new relationship I formed would be destined to end up like my failed marriage. That was a hard lesson learned; I wouldn't wish divorce on anybody.

The compelling urge to reenter the dating world and find that elusive soul mate provided just enough motivation for me to improve the man I was. I discovered introductions and first dates went much better if I actually had something to talk about. That didn't happen until I began participating in life, and volunteerism was the key. The key to thriving as a well-rounded, mature person had nothing to do with me, and had everything to do with others. Without volunteerism, I am just not that interesting. Life is more than me (thank goodness).

Find Your Inspiration

Deciding to become a volunteer was the easy part; deciding where to volunteer was much harder. I took over a year to find a good fit. My one criterion was a tough one: whatever I decided to do, it needed to *inspire* me. An archaic definition for the word inspire is to infuse with breath—as in life-giving. I think that is a beautiful definition. Everything we do should breathe life into us. If only that were true!

During my search for the perfect volunteer opportunity, the story of Terry Schiavo hit the national news. Terry was the grievously injured Florida woman living in a permanent vegetative state. Her ex-husband wanted to remove her feeding tube and let her pass quietly away, while her parents wanted to keep her alive on the slim hope she might recover. The drama surrounding the public argument over her fate was tragic and undignified. As far as I could tell, nobody on either side had Terry's best interests at heart. Whether she lived or died, I ached for her to be at peace. The story moved me deeply and led me to find Hospice of Metro Denver.

What can be a more lonely experience than having a terminal illness? Spending time in friendship with a fellow human being at the end of life is one of the most sacred acts of compassion I can think of.

That inspires me! My time with HMD was rewarding and fulfilling. Most people reacted with shock when I told them I volunteered for a hospice. "How can you do that?" was the typical response. I think death intimidates people.

"Try it, once," was my simple reply. I will never be the same.

My time with hospice was short but memorable. I treasure many rich, moving memories of people I befriended there. For example, I spent just one evening with a man who had been one of the founding members of the historic Negro Baseball League. The sweet, confused soul kept asking me if I had read his book. What book? I went out to his atrium and found hundreds of copies of a book written about him, his life, and his career as a baseball player. I read it that night sitting by his bedside. His daughter was so impressed that I did so that she gifted me a copy. I believe he died shortly after my visit, but I have that precious memento to remember a great human being.

I'll never forget another time I went grocery shopping for a woman in hospice care. She gave me money and told me to buy, among other things, premium frozen orange juice. She didn't want a generic brand because she was dying and wanted to "live it up" in the time she had left—with orange juice, of all things. The weight of that concept crashed down upon me while I was at the store, and I cried openly in the frozen foods section while holding the beloved woman's twenty dollar bill in my fist...a sacred, transforming moment. I hope she enjoyed her orange juice; she died soon after that.

One of my favorite hospice friends, Knut, was a merchant marine from Norway who told me over and over again how it took him two years to immigrate to America because he swam the whole way *and boy, did my arms get tired.* I went shopping for juice on his behalf, too. Prune juice. Evidently the morphine he took to mitigate his pain made him constipated. He never tired of pointing to his calendar and showing me the big red X's marking the days the prune juice did its job.

I loved visiting Knut in his tiny one-room apartment in the care facility and listening to his stories of the old country. My long legs could barely fit in the small space between his one chair and his bed. I dreaded the moment when he might catch his oxygen tube on my big feet, trip, and fall. He loved to tell me about Norway. One day he tried to point out Oslo to me, but he oriented the map upside down and didn't realize that he was fingering South Africa, instead. I fell on the floor laughing—another sacred moment. That was the last time I saw him alive.

My dear friend, Knut—I miss you.

Rescued by Search and Rescue

As much as hospice did for me, I concluded it was not my ultimate volunteer experience. I had found a little part of myself with hospice, but I was still lost in opportunities. My search resumed.

During that time, I was learning plenty of outdoor survival skills in the Colorado Mountain Club. Each time I took a class from that organization, my backpack got larger and heavier. Soon I felt I was prepared for anything.

I wasn't prepared to a sleep overnight outdoors without a tent.

One weekend, my fellow CMC survival class students and I stayed overnight in the forest, learning how to bivouac. My shelter was impressive; I was like the Martha Stewart of the wilderness. I built a log cabin from branches gathered far and wide. If I had been truly lost or injured, I probably would have perished from exhaustion.

Without filling the gaps between the loosely stacked branches, my Taj Mahal did nothing to keep me warm from nightly breezes. I felt surely I was going to freeze to death and nearly fell into my morning cup of coffee when the instructor told us the overnight temperature had only fallen to forty-eight degrees. I think he had slept in his car.

My biggest inspiration during survival class came when a member of Alpine Search and Rescue gave an evening classroom lecture on safe wilderness trip planning. Search and Rescue! That sounded interesting and noble, a way to spend time having fun outdoors in the service of others. The seed was planted.

Meanwhile, my hiking adventures continued. If you want to raise some eyebrows, show up in a suburban state park for a day hike carrying a forty pound backpack, a map, and a compass. Numerous people stopped to ask me for directions, as I must have looked quite official. I had seen a black bear in the park that day, so most of my advice included, "Go wherever you want, but watch out for the bear." Very helpful.

If every lost person I met was going to ask me for directions, I figured I might as well do it for a (volunteer) living. I soon found Douglas County Colorado Search and Rescue; I had finally found my true volunteerism inspiration.

Being a member of a search and rescue team is at once both an exhilarating and humbling experience. The training never stops; the learning never ends: search theory, safety, technical rope systems, wilderness medicine, incident command and management, and avalanche scenarios fill our evening and weekend sessions. Our smallish group of fifty-odd men and women volunteer over ten thousand hours and drive over one hundred thousand miles on personal vehicles per year. That's an impressive commitment, if I do say so myself. I think the citizens of Douglas County should be proud.

We live for the moment the pager goes off, no matter how inconvenient or unexpected that moment might be. When the moment arrives and the butterflies come and go, we race off into the unknown eager as can be—eager to put our skills and training to use. I am humbled by the depth and breadth of skills my teammates bring to the table—way more than I did. Many members have been involved in search and rescue for decades and are involved in SAR at both the state and national level. I have so much to learn from them.

I have gained much already, such as leadership and crisis management skills, how to rappel off a cliff, and how to tie a double sheet bend knot in a rope. Great stuff! Greater yet is the moment the pager beeps and we realize a rescue is at hand—the opportunity to save a life. Those moments come far and few in between.

I feel privileged to have been a part of just such a rare moment in the fall of 2007 when we were called upon to rescue a hiker suffering from a heart attack deep in Pike National Forest south of Denver.

The man was three miles from the nearest road. That meant carrying all our gear for that distance over rugged terrain before even beginning to think about the trip out while carrying him. We were exhausted by the time we arrived on the scene. Then we still had to load him into the litter and return. That mission was the longest carryout in terms of round trip foot mileage in team history.

We got him out with the help of a neighboring SAR team and local EMT crews, and he lived to hike another day. The pain in our legs and arms meant nothing, our searing lungs of no consequence. My knees were sore for weeks after, but I counted it as no cost at all.

I never thought I would have the chance to be a member of a team that saved a life. However, I will always remember that misty, moonlit evening in the forest as the night I was rescued. I had found my calling, something that gave me purpose beyond my own existence. I found myself by searching for others.

When I got divorced, I could have become absorbed in self pity. Rather, I looked outward when I realized life was more than me. I wish I could take credit for that concept, but instead I believe it was the hand of God leading me. There are so many opportunities to give back to humanity. So many that one could get lost in the multitude of ways to serve other human beings. I guarantee the one thing you will find is yourself.

Get lost.

3

Wise Women

Kelly's Story

I GREW UP IN A CULTURE OF VOLUNTEERISM. MY PARENTS WERE always involved in volunteer activities through church, the universities, and hospitals where they worked, or community organizations. My brother, Thad, and I were often taken along for the ride and expected to dig in and participate in these activities. It wasn't exotic or noble. It was a very ordinary part of our lives. In fact, I don't remember thinking much about it as a child or as a young adult. Volunteerism was just part of life, like getting a haircut or going to the grocery store. I never fully appreciated the power of being of service to others until my mid-thirties. That's when I experienced what it's like to be on the receiving end of aid.

A wise woman once told me, "When your life gets complicated, there are really only three things you should consider every day: what you are grateful for; what you can do for yourself; and what you can do for someone else." I'm fairly certain she didn't come up with that brilliant saying, but it doesn't matter. When I heard her speak those words in an AA meeting, they struck a chord deep within me that hasn't stopped resonating.

I'm an alcoholic. When I was deep into my disease, drowning in a bottle and unable to see anything clearly, I could hardly stand myself. I knew that there was a bright light that still flickered deep within me, and I knew it was in real danger of being snuffed out. I hated myself for letting that happen. I was powerless over alcohol. It had taken over my life, and I was letting it stomp out any good I had left in me. Eventually, it started to take my health along with everything else, and my days were numbered.

I had been slowly losing pieces of me for years, and it had gotten to the point where I didn't even recognize the hollow person staring back at me when I looked in the mirror. That girl was so filled with shame and remorse. She was a shell...without substance, without life.

You need help. I whispered to myself from somewhere deep within.

I remember thinking in a moment of self-centered self-loathing that if I died, if I really managed to drink myself off this earth, that the world wouldn't miss me much. What had I done for anyone lately? What had I done for myself lately? Nothing.

Shortly after the silent conversation with myself in the bathroom mirror, I dipped my toe in recovery by attending a few AA meetings. My first impression was, "What the heck do these people have to be so happy about? Aren't they supposed to be drunks, like me? Am I in the right place?"

For some unknown reason I stayed. (It might have been because my mom dropped me off, and I was stuck there for the next sixty minutes.) I listened to this crazy group of unlikely friends talk very candidly about what it was like for them when they were drinking, what happened as a result of their drinking, and what it's like now that they are in recovery. There was hope there—and a lot of laughter. I wanted to laugh like that again, so I stuck around.

How did they do it? That was my burning question. I knew by the way these alcoholics talked that they had been where I was. They weren't faking. They knew the pain I was experiencing. But they were changed. How? I kept going to meetings to find out.

I found a sponsor a few months into sobriety, and I couldn't wait to sit down and talk with her. She wasn't much older than me, but in my eyes she was a very wise woman. She was happy, healthy, confident, a successful businesswoman—everything I wasn't. I couldn't wait for her to give me the secret to her success.

This wise woman had a different task in mind. She told me to get a service position.

"A what?!"

"A service position," she repeated.

I had a number of choices: setting up chairs at meetings, making coffee, greeting people when they came to a meeting, or taking baked goods to an upcoming retreat.

"What?!"

My wise sponsor ignored my sudden deafness. She didn't care which one of those choices I decided to take on; I just had to get into service work IMMEDIATELY. She called it a "suggestion," but she looked at me with a certain steadiness that made it a dare.

Did she understand that I was hurting here? What did setting up chairs have to do with my recovery? I was the one who needed help!

She didn't let up, either. As soon as I put together a few consecutive days of sobriety, she had me going to rehab centers to conduct meetings. The last straw was when she talked me into maximum security prison meetings—on Friday nights. I could think of a lot of things I would prefer to be doing on Friday nights, and none of them had anything to do with traveling all the way across Phoenix to a maximum security prison to take a meeting to a bunch of women who scared the hell out of me. I would rather have spent my time on Match.com or eHarmony.com finding the man of my dreams. It was time to stop hanging out with losers and start dating! I mean, I had a full six months of sobriety under my belt at that point. I was cured. My oh-so-wise sponsor was totally cramping my style.

Then a really odd thing happened—well, two really odd things happened. First, I showed up for the prison meeting. I actually followed through on a commitment. It had been a little while since I had been a person someone could count on, so that was a shock to me (and to my sponsor).

Second, I walked out of that ugly, hot complex of buildings and barbed-wire fences two hours after the prison doors clanged shut behind me, and I swear I was floating several feet above the ground. I almost asked my sponsor to grab onto my shoelaces, because I was about to drift away in giddy gratitude. I felt indescribably good! I almost didn't recognize the feeling at first. It had been a long time since I had experienced it.

So what was going on here? I did something I thought I would hate, and I left feeling wonderful. That one prison AA meeting snowballed into many trips to the prison. I met some incredible women and heard some heartbreaking stories. I learned that I could have just as easily been wearing an orange jumpsuit and languishing behind bars if I had been apprehended when I was under the influence. I also learned that I'm a little gullible. They had a lock down once when we were there, and my sage sponsor told me that we were probably going to have to spend the night. I totally believed her for a few terrifying minutes. (She messes with me sometimes.)

A strange thing happened during that first year or so of going to prison meetings and doing a bunch of other service work. I began looking at myself in the mirror again. I was making real friends in and out of AA, and they could count on me when they needed help. I could count on them, too. Wow. Someone or something relit that pilot light that burned deep within me. I was no longer stuck in self-destruction mode. I had rejoined humanity.

I discovered that I was far from alone. My wise sponsor had a wise sponsor of her own; and that smart lady confided in yet another clever chic. We were creating an unbreakable chain of support, and soon I realized that I was going to be okay. Life was not so bad. In fact, it was starting to look pretty darn wonderful. We went to women's retreats in beautiful Rio Rico, Arizona and shared our burdens and our laughter. We had pillow fights, and we shopped for unusual, artsy trinkets in neighboring Tubac. We never stopped being of service to others, and because of that, we grew. No, we thrived!

Then, a true miracle occurred. I didn't feel like having a drink. I have no idea when the obsession left me. I guess I was busy at the time. I've been sober a little over six years as I write this, and believe me, I was just as shocked as anyone when I picked up my six-year chip. The women and men of AA saved my life, and it is my goal now to pay it forward every chance I get. I sponsor women now, and while they might not consider me "wise," at least I'm passing along a message of hope, strength, love, and most of all service to others. Today, I get the privilege of seeing a teenager pick up her one-year chip. I've watched her transform this year; I've seen her pilot light come back on. She is beautiful.

My service work is not confined to the rooms of AA. I am now free to be part of my community and my world. I've gotten involved in lots of different projects that lend a hand to someone in need, and each one of them leaves me with that same giddy, weightless feeling of joy, that inner bubble of satisfaction that fuels me for days.

I am a slow learner, though. I think I'm just now starting to internalize what that wise woman said in an AA meeting a long time ago. If I really want to do something wonderful for myself, I should start by reaching out to someone else. When I take action and help someone in need, I end up being incredibly grateful for my own life. It's a circle that gets stronger and stronger with every simple act. The more often I give a little of myself to someone else, the more I become intertwined with humanity, and the better this life gets. The big question now is: how much happiness can one girl handle?

We're all connected. We are meant to share this experience of life and help each other along the way. I gave up in my struggle with alcoholism. I surrendered to God and admitted I was powerless to overcome it by myself. Then, I let someone help me, and it was the most powerful step I have ever taken.

The symbol of AA is a circle enclosing a triangle. The circle represents the whole world of AA. The three sides of the triangle represent Recovery, Unity, and **Service**. Service is not the only route to recovery, but it is part of the foundation. The service of others quite literally saved my life, and I intend to give back with gratitude at every opportunity. It's now my responsibility to be there when someone reaches out for help.

I have the privilege every day of strengthening the circle. I start by asking myself three questions:

- What am I grateful for?
- What have I done for myself?

- What have I done for someone else?

It's so simple it makes me want to cry—and laugh at the same time.

4

ALL IN THE FAMILY

IT ONLY TOOK A FEW WEEKS OF INTERVIEWS—STARTING WITH OUR OWN family—before a wonderful metaphor for humanity began to materialize. Humanity is like the rings of a strong tree. The center ring is the self, and the next ring that radiates out from that center is family. Family does not necessarily have to be blood relatives, but it is a core small group that is responsible for nurturing the person in the middle. It is also the first group that the self reaches out to in order to reciprocate love and support and strengthen the bond.

The next ring in the tree is friends. It is a wider, more loosely knit circle, a bit further from the center, but still familiar and comfortable. It has the potential to be very influential on the self. And the final ring on the outside is humanity—the large and beautiful spectrum of beings that make up the human race.

One of the first people we interviewed, Jeff Lamontagne (we'll get to his story later), has a theory that each of these rings represents a level of human development, and as a species we are always moving outward toward an understanding, compassion, and connection with a greater humanity. We start with our own selfish needs as infants, and then we reach out to our small family unit. Eventually, we branch out even further to interact with friends; and the final stage of development is when we become aware of the all-encompassing humanity that makes up this world. A connection to humanity is the final powerful stage in our development. It is awe inspiring to think of a world where every human being is linked in meaningful ways to this greater humanity.

We told you a little about the center of our circles in the previous two chapters. What does the center of your tree look like? Grab a journal, a notebook, or open a new document on your computer and describe yourself—your history, your passions in life, your fears, and your dreams for the future. What is your essence? Take some time and write about you. The description you create is the center circle of your tree.

> *Other things may change us, but we start and end with family.*
>
> —Anthony Brandt

Next, we looked at the family circle. We sat down to interview our parents and siblings and were not surprised to find out how many of our own values and beliefs grew directly out of our family tree—especially when it came to lending a hand to others.

We were surprised, however, to discover the multitude of things our family members do for those in need. Acts of kindness are not typical subjects of family conversation, so we had no idea just how much our parents and siblings stepped out of themselves and into humanity until we asked them directly. It was shocking to discover what they've been up to.

When we interviewed our parents, the most difficult part of the interview was that they didn't think most of the things they do for others could be classified as "volunteerism." In fact, they almost bristled at the word. In their minds, volunteerism is a word that describes serious stuff like missionary work, the Peace Corps, or signing up to work with a large organization like Habitat for Humanity. The incredible amount of time and talent they offer to their churches, 4-H clubs, PEO clubs, Music Man Square, Boy Scouts, the Ronald McDonald House, and a host of other organizations were just "what you do." They didn't think they should get credit for any of it.

It took us awhile to explain that we were interested in hearing about anything they did that reached out to lend a hand to someone in need. Everything counted—and we really weren't keeping score anyway. We just wanted to know how much of their time is spent serving others and what kinds of things they do on a regular basis to step out of self and into humanity. We are well aware that our family members live full and happy lives, and we had a hunch that their level of service work had something to do with their overall enjoyment of life.

All four of our parents credited our grandparents and extended family members to explain their actions. Gary Mott (Eric's father) remembered how their house filled with family shortly after his younger sister was born. Aunts, uncles, and cousins all swarmed into their home to cook and clean and even wallpaper a room or two. The kids were not exempt from the activities, either. They hauled items back and forth and performed a variety of small tasks to help out. They all knew that a young family would need a little extra help, and they were right there to provide it.

Carolyn Mott (Eric's mom) remembered that her mother was very active in church, and that is probably why she is today. She has been a member of UMC Women for most of her adult life and has served on committees, taught Sunday school, ushered, and stepped into a multitude of tasks that need to be done in the life of the church.

Janis Eldredge (Kelly's mom) talked about how active her parents were in 4-H. She explained to us that her parents taught, not just their own four children, but hundreds of children in the community how to take care of animals and sew and cook—things that were essential to farm life in northern Ohio.

Cliff Eldredge (Kelly's dad) pointed out that he didn't grow up in a wealthy home, but there was always a feeling that you did what you could to pitch in and help your neighbor. He remembers vividly one event when he was a young boy. His mother bought an extra turkey and all of the fixings right before Thanksgiving and took it to a needy family. Cliff was only about seven years old at the time, and he remembers hiding behind his mother as they walked up to the door. A woman answered the door, and several children peaked back at Cliff from behind her skirts. Unfortunately, the woman's stove was broken, and she had no means to cook the turkey, so Cliff's mother went home, cooked everything, and brought it back to the family in time for Thanksgiving dinner.

Cliff's dad often took care of a neighbor's home, checking to make sure the furnace was running and collecting the mail every day for three or four months, while the neighbor was in Florida. He never expected anything in return. That's what you do. His mother also took several elderly women in the neighborhood for groceries and to their doctors' appointments, because they could no longer drive.

In fact, helping the elderly was a common theme in both of our families. Our parents and grandparents regularly sought out people in the community who needed extra help with everyday chores, and they reached out to them. Carolyn took Eric with her when he was just a "tot" to deliver Meals on Wheels. Janis eventually centered her graduate studies at the University of Iowa on ways to care for the increasing elderly population. Gary helped an elderly woman in the grocery store parking lot who locked her keys in her car. He called AAA for her, bought her a cup of coffee, and waited with her until they came. Cliff mowed the lawn at the gravesite of a widow's beloved husband, because she didn't think the grass was trimmed well enough.

We could go on and on about all of the things our parents did and do currently in their communities. Nevertheless, throughout the interview, our parents kept telling us that they didn't volunteer that much. It was no big deal. It was what you do. You help out; you pitch in; you make someone else's life easier. It's nothing special. It's just part of being human.

We learned that our grandparents volunteered at schools; they were part of election boards; they were Boy Scout leaders, 4-H leaders, and very active members of churches. It's no wonder that our parents picked up the same values. From the time they could walk, they were hauling groceries for old Mrs. Goldy and Mrs. Teetz and helping take buckets of nails to workers when a cousin down the road was building a barn.

"I don't remember our parents ever saying, okay, now you're going to do some volunteer service work here," Janis told us.

"Our parents just had that altruistic set of values that you do things for people," Cliff added. "It was part of their whole life fabric."

"It's part of the culture we grew up in," Gary explained. "We didn't call it volunteerism. We just pitched in when somebody needed help."

"In Sunday school class we learned the verse that says 'to those whom much is given, much is required,'" Carolyn reminded us. "I do these things for others because I can. I'm capable of helping out, so that's what I should do."

All right! We get it! Just do it.

The concept of *MORE Than me* has been part of their social fabric from day one. That's why they have such a hard time classifying it as something separate from everyday life. How cool is that? And they passed that set of values on to us without us even realizing it. We are incredibly lucky to have grown up this way. We were able to experience all four rings of the tree immediately, and it has allowed us to pass back and forth between these circles without thinking about it much.

That does not diminish the gift of lending a hand to others. We learned about it from our parents' example, and our lives are infinitely better when we practice it daily.

After a mind-boggling number of stories about our grandparents, aunts, uncles, and cousins, we finally got around to what our immediate family members are up to these days.

Gary is the ultimate Good Samaritan. He is a retired teacher, so he has always been geared toward helping others, but the real gem in his actions lies in random acts of kindness. We already mentioned how he helped the elderly woman who had locked her keys in her car. That's only one in a long list of Good Samaritan acts. He feels as though he and Carolyn have been overly blessed with a wonderful life, and now it's payback time.

"I'm not sure we could ever possibly give back all the good that has been bestowed on us," Gary said. "We are now in the payback period of our lives. I would be very unhappy if I couldn't do these things for others."

Gary notices everything, and he reaches out to help without hesitation. He stops to help people who are stranded on the side of the road; he offers to take pictures for tourists; he steps in to stop a fight at Burger King; he grabs up a child in a parking lot who has wandered away from his mother and is about to be hit by a car. Gary is involved in many organized volunteer activities at church and throughout the community, too, but he told us that nothing compares to the quiet feeling of satisfaction you get when you help someone in need on the spot. He says that it gives him an inner glow that lasts for days.

Carolyn loves to be a resource for people. Her college degree in health and nutrition has given her a number of very useful skills in cooking, crafts, and administrative work that are essential for the many organizations in which she is involved. She is one of those multitalented women who can be counted on to come in and organize the books—or bake cookies for a church function—whatever is needed. Eric and his sister, Sarah, remember coming home from school often to the smell of fresh-baked brownies, but they always had to ask, "Is this for us, or is this for church?"

Usefulness is a pretty terrific gift, and Carolyn enjoys having the necessary skills to help out wherever she can. She recognizes that her skills are valuable, and she gives them away freely and often. We didn't know that she cooked a roast for a friend who didn't have money for food and took it over to her without hesitation. It was one of those acts that went unspoken.

We also were moved to hear about when Gary and Carolyn welcomed a troubled student into their home for dinner one night. The student was suicidal, and they took her in (after calling her parents to let them know where she was) and offered her a hot meal and a non-judgmental ear. That former student still keeps in touch with them.

Recently, Gary and Carolyn drove from Iowa to Colorado to help Sarah move into a new home. They spent weeks painting and cleaning and helping to fix things up. When we asked them about it, Carolyn couldn't help but smile.

"It was way more fun to help Sarah with her home than it is to do our own fix-it jobs!" she grinned. "There is just a bigger sense of satisfaction. It felt good to be able to help out."

Janis shares Carolyn's feeling of joy in helping her children. One of the most rewarding jobs Janis and Cliff have these days is taking care of their twin grandchildren, Kate and Sam.

"My mother offered to babysit my brother's and sisters' children when they were at work. I grew up playing with my nieces and nephews," Janis said. "It was only natural that I would offer to babysit my own grandchildren now. I love to do it, because I get to know my grandchildren better."

We should mention here that all four of our parents are just about the coolest grandparents ever. They get right down on the floor and play with their grandchildren; they don't care if there are Cheerios all over the living room and Popsicle stains on the coffee table; and they offer endless hugs and kisses. What a wonderful circle for Jessica, Grady, Kate, and Sam to grow up in! I think Janis summed it up perfectly when we asked if volunteering as a babysitter for her grandchildren has changed her life at all.

"Well, that's easy," Janis beamed. "Just to hold a child in my arms again and feel that soft, warm little body close to me is thrilling beyond words. They look up into my face with such trust and love, and they speak to me now with so much conviction that it tickles me and makes me laugh, yet they know so little about the world. I feel a strong desire and need to protect and nurture them and to help them learn to love life and not be afraid. I felt that way with my own children, too, but now (for a short time) I have the reward of a second chance, and it's just as strong and fulfilling because they are my grandchildren. Friends have told me that when I speak of Kate and Sam, my face lights up and I become very animated and joyful. I guess I can't deny that. Yes, they are a commitment in time and energy, but I have time—I'm retired from the workforce now. As for energy, I think they boost my energy level and help to keep me young and active!"

Janis has always been active in church and the community. She is a retired dental hygienist who did extensive work with the elderly while working toward her graduate degree. She also taught dental hygiene at the University of Iowa. There are hundreds of volunteer activities that Janis has taken part in, from making Thanksgiving baskets at Abiding Hope Lutheran, to singing in the choir, to volunteering at our schools when we were young, to being a 4-H leader, to participating in a 5K walk with family members. But one of the volunteer activities she mentioned was particularly interesting, because we knew little about it. When our family lived in Honeoye Falls, New York, Janis joined the garden club. She thought of it as a "fluff" volunteer job, because she loves to work with flowers anyway, but it taught her some valuable lessons. One of the things they did was plant flowers around town and in the parks.

"I learned so much about flowers by doing that," Janis told us. "I learned to beautify our own home just by participating in the garden club."

Cliff is a retired hospital administrator and physical therapist. He has had a prestigious career in healthcare, but he always comes back to one thing when asked about his greatest accomplishment—the Ronald McDonald House. One of Cliff's duties as a hospital administrator at the University of Iowa Hospitals and Clinics was to oversee the building of a Ronald McDonald House. It was such a rewarding experience that Cliff and Janis both volunteered there often. It wasn't the biggest project he ever worked on, but it was the most impactful, because he really got to know the people who benefited from it. Cliff and Janis spent New Year's Eve at the Ronald McDonald House and celebrated with families who were in serious need of a little joy as they dealt with life-and-death issues. He saw how that house made their lives easier, and that left a very strong impression on him.

Currently, Cliff is active in a fly fishing club that gives him opportunities to learn new skills and give back some of his own knowledge at the same time. The club often works with physically challenged people from a VA hospital. Cliff is able to utilize his skills as a physical therapist and also learn about fly fishing techniques and become more aware of environmental concerns. He is quite active in church activities and a multitude of other volunteer opportunities, but he made a point toward the end of our interview to mention one new way he and Janis have learned to lend a hand.

"I think there is one big thing we have today that is different than our parents, and that's money," Cliff said almost apologetically. "So in addition to service work, we have been able to create scholarships for college kids and give monetarily to organizations as well as having the hands-on experience. It's nice to have the financial ability now to do that. When we receive a letter from a student we were able to help financially with their education, it's a great feeling."

Would they do anything differently?

"The biggest dilemma I have now," Cliff said, "is using my skills to their maximum potential. I'm retired, but I have some very useful professional skills, and I am always looking for ways in which I can use them to help others."

Gary and Carolyn also often work as a team in their volunteer activities. They have become very involved in the huge task of cataloguing items at Music Man Square in Mason City, Iowa. This multi-million dollar complex celebrates the life and music of Meredith Willson and also the rich musical heritage of Mason City. Thousands of items are donated to this museum, and Gary and Carolyn help to catalogue them all. They even donated one of their computers so that there would be a computer available in the cataloguing area of the museum.

And what about our siblings?

> *Siblings are the people we practice on, the people who teach us about fairness and cooperation and kindness and caring—quite often the hard way.*
> —Pamela Dugdale

We had no idea what our siblings were up to, either. We're close, but we never talk about these kinds of things. We found out that they have kept that fabric of giving in their daily lives, as well. They've done a ton of things to carry on the legacy that has been handed to us by our parents.

Eric's sister, Sarah, gave us a beautiful example of this legacy. Recently she was at church with her children, and her six-year-old daughter, Jessie, was diligently helping her load the big industrial dishwasher in the kitchen. Sarah turned away from the steam of the dishwasher and had a flashback. She could remember an almost identical scenario in a church kitchen back in Mason City, Iowa, when she was helping her mother.

She had to giggle when she was relaying the story, because she hadn't thought about just how closely she was following in her parents' footsteps.

"I never thought I would end up on a church committee," Sarah laughed. "But here I am. Somebody called me out of the blue and asked me if I would be on the Children's Education Committee, and I said okay. This was our month to serve refreshments at church, so that's what we were doing."

Sarah said yes to the Children's Education Committee before she even had a chance to think about it. She responded to the call for help, because that's what she saw modeled by her parents throughout her entire life. She never planned to be on the church council; she never sought out the chance to become a Sunday school teacher; but there she was, following what her parents modeled and providing an active example of giving to her own daughter.

Sarah talked about many examples of how her parents' willingness to help spilled over into her own volunteer activities at a young age. But when she was in high school, she started to discover her own passions for volunteering and decided to be a counselor at a camp for exceptional people. She spent six weeks every summer from eighth grade through high school at this camp where she was a buddy to a different developmentally disabled adult each week. It's one of her happiest young-adult memories.

"I loved it!" Sarah told us. "It wasn't about me. It was about them. I tried a couple of camps that were for me, and I absolutely hated them, but this camp was the greatest."

Other kids her age may have been going to band camp or hanging out at the mall, but Sarah became a one-on-one buddy for a special needs person. She thoroughly enjoyed the camp and looked forward to it every year. In fact, Sarah says that experience ultimately guided her to a career in occupational therapy.

Later in high school, Sarah worked for Parks and Recreation in Mason City in their special kid's summer program. One day, she decided it would be fun to take a group of special needs kids fishing as part of that program. Who did she call to help coordinate the activity? Gary and Carolyn, of course!

"We took three of them fishing that day," Sarah recalls. "I can always count on Mom and Dad for help, whether it's taking three special needs kids fishing or picking up a friend from the airport."

Sarah is now a lead case coordinator at Spalding Rehabilitation Hospital in Denver. Her job focuses much more on the big picture, coordinating everything a patient and their family need to recover. Last year, her employer encouraged her to take part in a professional community program called Leadership Aurora. In this program, she had an opportunity to network with people in all sorts of different professions. They worked together on various projects and learned about the thriving community in which they live. Through this program, Sarah got to ride in a jet that conducted a mid-air refueling mission; she donned a Michelin Man suit and let herself be attacked by police dogs; she coordinated fundraisers; and in general she gained an incredible understanding of the many different people and organizations that play important roles in society. Those exhilarating experiences gave her insight into the needs and issues in her community, and they also introduced her to some local heroes.

She explained to us that the real power of the experience was in the personal connections she made with people in her community and how they were all able to bring their unique professional skills to the table. One of the most rewarding projects they did was to build a dog run at a women's shelter. One of the people on the team was a victim's advocate for the Aurora Police and had many personal experiences with women in shelters. She knew that leaving a family pet behind was often a barrier to exiting a dangerous family situation. Another member of the team was a contractor and had the tools and supplies available for them to get the job done. In one afternoon, this group descended on the women's shelter and built the first dog run at a women's shelter in the country! No one had thought of that need before this group put their heads together and brainstormed about ways they could help. They had so much fun working together that when they finished the dog run early, they stuck around and did some landscaping before they left. They received such fabulous feedback from the people at the facility, it inspired them to continue to connect with their community.

"I got so much more out of it than I put into it, no doubt," Sarah said. "The connections that I gained out of that program, out of that group of people coming together, are so valuable to me. And you don't get that by not reaching out and by not volunteering. It is such a no-brainer."

Kelly's brother, Thad, shares many similar experiences with Sarah. He enjoyed spending his vacation time as a young adult in unique ways, too. We found out in our interview that in college Thad spent spring break at an Indian reservation helping the residents with their taxes. Not exactly a trip to the beach, but the experience was empowering to Thad. He was able to use the skills he learned in college to help people in need. It was an experience that fueled him from the inside out for a long time.

Thad is now living his dream. He's a father of twins, a husband, and the owner and manager of Carvers, a ski, snow board, and sport shop in Breckenridge, Colorado. He enjoys every opportunity he has to use Carvers as a tool to reach out to the community. Just about any local fundraiser who walks through the door at Carvers seeking a donation for a silent auction or other event will walk out with a smile on their face. The certificates and merchandise Thad donates each year amount to thousands and thousands of dollars.

Thad doesn't talk about it, but we've heard from many of his employees and locals in Breckenridge that he's a silent source of personal strength, too. He often lends an empathic ear, offers a ride, or helps those in need whenever the opportunity arises. He can be counted on as a source of help and understanding when life gets tough.

A few years ago, Thad received a letter from a homesick soldier in Iraq who was wishing he was snowboarding in the Rockies. The letter really touched him, and he wanted to find some way to reach out and thank the guy for his service to our country. Instead of a letter, Thad mailed a snowboard to Iraq! The surprised soldier was thrilled and got together with his buddies to develop a new sport—sandboarding! In their down time, the soldiers tied the snowboard to the back of a Humvee and glided across the hot sand in Iraq for a momentary diversion. Every member of that platoon signed the snowboard and sent it back to the shop as a thank you. It hangs in Carvers today as a tribute to those who are willing to risk their lives for our country.

Thad's wife, Michelle, is right there with him when it comes to reaching out to those in need. She recently chaired a huge fundraiser in Fargo, North Dakota for her friend Holly, who was suffering from a rare and deadly lung disease. Holly was in dire need of a transplant, and the event raised over $40,000 to help pay for the precious gift of life even before the doctors found a match. That fundraiser was aptly named "Hope for Holly," and it showed Michelle's friend in a very concrete way that she had support and love from her friends and family. She wasn't alone. Holly's prayers were recently answered. In early 2010, she received her transplant at the Mayo Clinic and is recovering beautifully, surrounded by the support of her circles of family and friends.

Michelle's experience with volunteerism started at a very young age. She was a member of an outstanding gymnastics team in her hometown of Fargo from age eight through high school, and every year her team volunteered to help with the Special Olympics. They assisted athletes with their routines, handed out ribbons and medals, and provided all sorts of support.

"The athletes and their families were awesome," Michelle recalled.

Michelle recognizes what a gift it was to be part of that gymnastics team. It not only taught her about the sport and the rigors of training, but it also gave her an opportunity to help others. She is currently in the process of starting a scholarship fund with another family for the gymnastics team, and she looks forward to making sure that legacy continues to thrive.

It was hard for us to pry stories out of our siblings—maybe even harder than it was to extract them from our parents. They share the same sentiment as our parents—helping others is just what you do. What's the big deal? It is part of everyday life. They did admit, though, that being of service to others makes them happy. That's not why they do it, but they think of service to others as a no-brainer, and they surround themselves with people who share the same values. They help others because that's what you do! It's as simple as that.

Here are a few final gems from our parents as we concluded the interview:

> *People are just great!*
> —Gary Mott

> *It's really fulfilling to be part of what's going on around you.*
> —Cliff Eldredge

> *The biggest thing is to take that first step and get out of the house.*
> —Janis Eldredge

> *I still don't think of myself as a volunteer.*
> —Carolyn Mott

These stories from our family circle make a very important point. When you surround yourself with people who look out for one another, who give freely and laugh often, you will have a better life. During the interviews, one memory dovetailed into the next until we were surrounded by warm recollections. We could have sat there all night talking about what a joyful experience it is to reach out to someone in need. Our families have surrounded us with positive people throughout our lives—interesting, happy, giving people who nurture us and show us by example how important it is to put the concerns of others before our own. We want that legacy to continue and grow. It's an incredible way to live!

We were both very fortunate to have been born in the middle—in the middle of a very strong circle of family. Our family tree has deep roots and branches that bear much fruit. What have you learned from your family? How does your family circle nurture your life today? What do you do to strengthen that priceless bond?

If you don't feel like your family circle is very strong, it's not too late to make a change. Do it right now. Reach out to your family; encourage them; help them; learn from them; consider their needs before your own. Don't waste any time. Of course, if your family environment is toxic or abusive, it's probably not a good idea to stay within a bad situation. You may need to surround yourself with a surrogate family that understands the power of creating positive, healthy connections with each other and a greater humanity.

In Chapter 5, we will take a look at the next circle—friends. You can improve your life immensely by picking great playmates. You choose the people who enter this next circle. Are the people you currently hang out with interested in stepping out of themselves and into humanity?

Two Guys Named Jim   5

AFTER SPENDING A NUMBER OF HOURS WITH FAMILY MEMBERS, WE DECIDED to branch out and talk to two friends who exemplify volunteerism in action. These guys are two of the happiest people we know—and they do a ton of volunteer work. Is there a connection? We think so. Here's their story:

Two guys, both named Jim, throw an awesome party once a year. Friends, family, and co-workers gather in their backyard for a day of fun that usually lasts long into the night…and even into the early morning hours.

How is this party different from any other get-together? It is the kick-off for a much tougher journey. A large glass bottle placed off to the side of the festivities slowly fills throughout the day with change, bills, and checks, all to raise money for multiple sclerosis. Both Jims will spend the next few months testing their mettle as they bike through the Rockies for MS.

Jim Francis and Jim McKeever are great guys who are heavily entrenched in humanity. The hundreds of people who show up in their backyard once a year are proof of their multifaceted approach to community involvement. Their bash last summer was a crazy cross section of family members, people from work, church members, volleyball team members, friends from volunteer organizations, and neighbors—aging from infants to the elderly—crowded into their backyard toting lawn chairs and broad smiles for the annual event. This is not your average party. People actually plan their summer vacations around this day.

Last summer, the party included a demonstration from their "solar guy" in the garage. Yes, the Jims are environmentally conscious, too. They recently installed a PV system (or photovoltaic system—it turns sunlight into electricity) on their roof, and it is working beautifully and saving them lots of money. It was quite amazing to see a dozen or so people cram into their steamy garage for a demonstration of this alternative energy source.

Jim...and Jim moved into their house the year before they started taking part in Bike MS. The first party was just a house warming, but it was so much fun that they decided to make it an annual event. It was Jim Francis' idea to make the next party a combination social/fundraising event for MS. It was a huge hit. People came for the party, but they ended up learning about what the Jims were doing. They were impressed by the number of miles they logged to train and participate in Bike MS, and ultimately most of them contributed to the big glass bottle by the end of the night. All it took was two great guys with great friends and an awesome idea.

The following is an excerpt from our interview with Jim McKeever and Jim Francis:

When did you first discover the joy of volunteering?
Jim M: My first volunteering activity was when I was about seven years old. Interfaith Taskforce (now Interfaith Community Services) held an annual twenty-five mile fundraising walk, and we made it a bit of a family affair. My mom, sister, and I all trained and walked together the first few years. Then when I got older, I walked with my friends. Looking back, sacrificing my time to train and actually do the walk was an easy and rewarding way to help others who were less fortunate than I was. I especially remember one girl who was nine years old. She had lost a leg to cancer. She did the whole walk and was truly an inspiration.

Jim F: I only have one memory of a volunteer activity when I was a kid. (I was in the Boy Scouts, but I can't say that had a huge impact on me.) But when I was in the sixth grade, my brother and I did a bike ride to raise money for some heart disease charity. It was fun, and we totally overdid it by riding the route two full times. I remember two things about that experience: I cramped up really badly on the drive back home in my mom's car; and the neighbors who had pledged by the mile yelled at us. It seems they only expected us to ride fifteen miles. They were a little put out that we did the route twice, and they owed us for thirty miles.

I think volunteering became more personal for me in the mid-1980s, when I had friends who were dying of AIDS. That's when I got involved with different AIDS charities. It was more personal then. It hit closer to home.

What types of volunteer activities have you been involved in over the years?
Jim M: Growing up, I was often involved in various church-related activities, including church mission trips. As an adult, I have been one of the top fundraisers for the Dumb Friends League's Furry Scurry for many years. I have also volunteered as a tax preparer for the Denver Asset Building Coalition for the past three years. (That is an organization that offers free tax preparation for low-income individuals and families.) We have worked on all of the Habitat for Humanity houses that St. Andrew United Methodist Church has sponsored. And of course, 2010 will be the sixth year that we have ridden in Bike MS.

Jim F: Well, let's see, so there were the AIDS walks in the 80s. Then, I spent a lot of time being very self-centered. It wasn't until I got involved at St. Andrew United Methodist that I started volunteering again.

We are planning for the fifth year of our company Bike MS team, which will be the sixth year that McKeever and I have ridden in the event. We have also taken part in IHN (Interfaith Hospitality Network). I walked in the Susan G. Komen 3-Day for the Cure a few times, too.

Habitat for Humanity has been an amazing experience. For some reason, it felt more like real volunteering than taking part in fundraising activities. Also, Jim M. and I are both Stephen Ministers, which is truly an intense volunteer position.

We are always looking for new opportunities to volunteer with causes that we feel strongly about. Earthworks Expo was a one-time experience that helped us become more familiar with environmental concerns. It led us to buy the PV system for our house.

Was there a specific person who inspired you to volunteer?
Jim M: Not really any one person, but the stories I have heard and seen, either personally or through the media, have really helped me to realize that my life is very full and blessed. Because of this, I find it pretty easy to give of myself to help those who truly have a difficult time.

Jim F: Not really. It wasn't until I got involved at church, and really with Jim M. beside me on most of the volunteer activities, that I have learned what it means to give to others from the abundance that I have been blessed with in my life. And that doesn't mean just donating money, because I feel that doing is more in the spirit of volunteering than *giving*.

Tell us more about why you chose to get involved with Bike MS.
Jim M: This particular opportunity was just dumb luck really, as neither Jim F. nor I probably would have ever done anything like this on our own. Our friend Bill Shoaff had been involved in the ride for several years and was starting a St. Andrew team to participate one year. He hit me up, either at choir practice or on a Sunday morning, and the rest is history.

I have always really enjoyed cycling anyway, and while the training that first year was HARD, after we made it through, we realized that it wasn't nearly as bad looking back as it seemed at the time. Once we got involved with the ride, then we would talk about it with others. Invariably the response was, "Oh, really? I know someone with MS." Or sometimes they would even say, "Thank you so much! I was diagnosed with MS a number of years ago."

I think that has been one of the keys to sticking with the ride. It personally affects us, and the people we know. We can see the devastating effects of the disease, and this helps us realize how important it is to find better treatments and eventually a cure.

Jim F: I echo what Jim M. said. I was a once or twice a year bike rider, and it wasn't until we were invited to ride in Bike MS that I really started looking at the impact MS has on the lives of people I know and work with.

There is a personal component, as well. When you are training for a 150-mile bike ride, when you are actually pedaling all those miles, you face a lot of personal mountains. It is tough to train, and you hit walls and want to stop. All sorts of thoughts go through your head.

On team training rides, I have ridden alongside other team members who hit a wall and broke down crying, because they pushed themselves too hard. Unless you are a professional cyclist, I think everyone faces those tough moments. What helps me get up the next hill...and the next...and the next is knowing that I am riding to raise money for the National MS Society. Their sole focus is finding a cure for a painful, crippling disease. It is humbling to think of the pain people with MS suffer daily, and I am complaining about my legs after a steep climb on my bike?

Do you have any specific stories you would like to share about how Bike MS has shaped your life?

Jim M: I think just about anyone who rides Bike MS will tell you that their life has been transformed immensely by participating. The fellowship that happens on Saturday night builds a real sense of camaraderie, as do the "competitive" activities for best jersey, best team tent, and so on.

It's not all about having fun, though. Persons living with MS and staff from the National MS Society give presentations that really drive home why we ride. The first year we rode, the founder of the Sugar Bees team spoke, and seeing her there in her wheelchair, cheering us all on, made it very worthwhile. On Sunday at the finish line, not only do family members line up to welcome everyone as they complete the race, but many people living with MS are there as well, thanking riders as they cross the finish line. They put a face on the disease.

Jim F: Again, I echo McKeever's comments. I think one of the things that has changed me since I got involved with Bike MS is that I have become less self-centered. I am more aware that there are people out there that I should be helping. Even if their struggles don't affect me directly, I am more aware that I can help them. I can do something about it.

Have volunteer activities improved your quality of life? If so, how?

Jim M: Oh, yes! I think Jim F. and I do a pretty good job of recognizing how fortunate we are. But everyone gets down sometimes, and being involved with helping others really helps you to say, "Hey, what am I complaining about? Look at what other people deal with EVERY DAY." Furthermore, recognizing this makes it much easier to give up whatever to help those who are facing difficult times or who are unable to do very much for themselves.

This applies not only to the ride but also to the other organizations I am involved with. The Furry Scurry directly benefits homeless animals who cannot speak for themselves. The tax preparation work I do lets me see immediately how one person CAN make a difference. To see someone come into the site with literally nothing more than the shirt on his or her back, because they lost their job, and then to get that person several hundred or even a thousand dollars...it's indescribable. People have broken down in gratitude for what we do, because our work means that they will be able to pay their rent or feed themselves and their families for a little while longer. More than anything, though, I think it gives them hope and restores their faith in humankind, at least a little bit. I think that's really what it's all about—HOPE.

Jim F: I can't add to what Jim M. said. There is no doubt that helping others is a selfless act that makes you feel differently about yourself and "others." Getting involved breaks down the walls that separate us and lets us feel like we are all connected. Suddenly, those "others" start to feel like family, and who would turn down a family member in need?

Two great guys let their pedals test their mettle each year when they take part in Bike MS. It is obvious that they are knee-deep in humanity with numerous volunteer activities that fill their lives year around.

One of the things that kept coming up in their interview was the word abundance. If you met the Jims, you would see by the smiles on their faces how they create an abundant life each and every day. Their abundance continues to expand and multiply with everything they do to reach a hand out to someone in need. Party on, Jims!

6

SMALL STEPS, BIG REWARDS

SO FAR, WE'VE COVERED THREE OF THE FOUR RINGS IN THE TREE OF HUMANITY: self, family, and friends. Now, we would like to step into the final ring—humanity as a whole—and dedicate the next chapters to highlighting different ways that people all over the world choose to lend a hand to those in need. Our intention is to inspire and mobilize. These aren't just nice stories; they're opportunities. We hope that you will collect ideas from these personal accounts. Let them inspire you to take action. Step out of your front door and into humanity. The rewards will be astounding.

> *I think there is something, more important than believing: Action! The world is full of dreamers, there aren't enough who will move ahead and begin to take concrete steps to actualize their vision.*
>
> —W. Clement Stone

We would like to introduce you to two young men: Frank L. Banks and Zach Hirsch. One is from the St. Louis area; the other is from Illinois. Both of these men had the courage to take one small step out of their comfort zone, and their actions snowballed. They stepped into humanity and found that it opened up a whole new world of opportunities for them—and they haven't even reached their twentieth birthdays yet. These young men have already learned many of the lessons we are putting forth in this book, and we felt privileged to interview them both.

Frank L. Banks

At Trinity Catholic High School in his hometown of St. Louis, Frank L. Banks began an incredible journey into humanity. He was nudged along his way by an interesting school rule: in order to graduate from Trinity Catholic High School, every student is required to contribute 100 hours of community service—a brilliant move on the part of the leaders of that school.

During Frank's sophomore year, he decided to log in a bunch of his service hours at once with a week-long mission trip to South Bend, Indiana on his spring break. He took one step—signing up for the trip, which was sponsored by a Catholic youth group called Vincentian Marian Youth. Every day, Frank's mission group experienced a different form of volunteering. They helped at a local homeless shelter, cleaned up parks and public areas, spent time with abused children, visited with senior citizens, and even went door to door to collect donations.

Frank's eyes opened to the joy of service to others during that trip. He realized how many people in the world need help. Frank saw humanity all around him, and he was inspired to reach out and connect even more. His first step created an urge deep within Frank to make this world a better place in his own way.

When Frank returned from his trip, he did what few others do: he launched into further action. You see, Frank wasn't just participating as a volunteer that week; he was closely observing the staff of all of the various volunteer organizations the mission group supported.

"I can do that," he said to himself.

The mission trip got Frank thinking. There was a need in his own community for someone to step up and shed some light on the difficult issues of homelessness and poverty, and he was certain he could inspire other young people just like him to take action.

Frank wasted no time in mobilizing. He started the Frank L. Banks Foundation at the advanced age of seventeen, because he didn't want to wait to help the lowest of the low. At the time of our interview, Frank was about to turn nineteen and had helped over

1,700 people through the Frank L. Banks Foundation. He had recently engaged over 600 individuals to donate to a clothing drive and mobilized over 375 volunteers to help him with his efforts. In total, over 4,000 clothing items had been donated to Frank's foundation when we talked to him, and the numbers continue to rise.

Frank refused to let the clothing drive to be a one-time deal. The needs of the homeless are continuous. He turned his inspiration into a monthly clothing and food drive. Frank personally delivers the clothing, toiletries, and food to Lucas Park—a popular location for the homeless in downtown St. Louis.

"I started the drive because hundreds of shelters, families, and non-profit organizations have been drastically affected by the current economic crisis," Frank told us. "The first drive started off small, and then over the course of a few weeks, everything took off. I've helped thousands of homeless individuals in the downtown St. Louis area. Currently, I help over 200 homeless individuals a month."

The advantages of having a young person lead a foundation are tremendous. Frank has the bright, fiery enthusiasm of youth. He doesn't know what he can't do, so he focuses on what he can, and great things happen. Frank has used social media to get the word out, and through that forum, he has generated thousands of clothing items including shoes, shirts, pants, and jackets. He collects them all and then gives them to the homeless each month during his clothing drive.

Frank's small steps are turning into big rewards for the homeless in downtown St. Louis. He has become a local celebrity throughout the community for his philanthropy, and dozens of radio and news stations have done stories on this kid who lit the fire of change. Frank's work has even become the subject of a few blogs. All you have to do is Google Frank L. Banks, and you will see what a firestorm he has created—and his mission is not complete. Frank has visions of his foundation expanding to cities like Chicago, L.A., New York, and Washington, D.C.

"I don't want to only help the people in my community," Frank stated. "I want to help as many people as I can."

That's the kind of attitude that creates change.

Where does Frank's empathy for the lowest of the low come from? Is it learned from his parents, or is it an innate part of his being human? It doesn't really matter. The point is Frank is not hiding in his room playing video games all afternoon. He's out in the community connecting, learning, giving, and creating hope. He is experiencing the fourth circle—humanity—on a daily basis and his life is richer because of his actions.

"I realized that there was a void, and when I volunteer, I am being used to fill that void."

Just to give you an idea of how Frank thinks, the following is a story he told us that demonstrates how helping others has shaped his life:

> One of the places I volunteer is a place called The St. Louis Crisis Nursery. It's an independent, non-profit agency funded by donations and committed to preventing child abuse and neglect by providing short-term emergency shelter for children who are twelve years old and younger. It really hurt me to see these young children who had been abused and neglected. Lots of them didn't know where their next meal was coming from. The children just wanted someone to interact with them.
>
> My parents were always there for me to talk to and play with when I was a child. These children have never had anyone like that in their lives. This experience taught me to be thankful for what I have and not complain when something doesn't go my way. I realize that there are lots of people who have it worse than me. Now, I try not to complain about the simple things—like having to eat Pizza Rolls instead of going out to eat with friends. In the back of my mind, I think about the people who go days without eating.

Frank L. Banks would have known nothing about those neglected children if he hadn't walked into The St. Louis Crisis Nursery to volunteer. He stepped into humanity, and his eyes were opened to ways in which he could help others and improve their lives. Frank is always thinking big. How many high school kids do you know who start their own foundation? But much of his success is built on small steps, single actions.

"We don't always realize the effects that volunteering can have unless we directly experience it," Frank told us. "Throughout the world, there are so many people in need. Volunteering of any kind gives you the chance to change lives. I never knew simple things like cleaning out gutters, shoveling mulch, and having a conversation could have so much impact on someone else's life. I realize now that downtrodden individuals are uplifted when they see that there are people in the world willing to help them. Not only does volunteering bring happiness to people, it also gives them hope."

Frank gives us hope. He is a shining example of our next generation of leaders. Frank had the courage to step out of himself and into humanity, and in doing so he discovered a world of interesting people and experiences that he never would have seen if he had stayed closed up in his smaller circles of family and friends. When Frank stepped into humanity, he discovered opportunity.

Zach Hirsch

Zach Hirsch is a kindred spirit to Frank L. Banks, even though the two young men have never met (to our knowledge). Zach also took one small step that ended up changing his life.

He was a star athlete and popular senior at St. Charles North High School in Illinois , when an average day in the school cafeteria turned into a life-changing experience. Zach decided to take one small step out of his comfort zone. He sat down to eat lunch with Graham Jackson, a fourteen-year-old freshman diagnosed with a form of autism called Asperger's Syndrome.

Zach explained their first meeting to us:

> Initially when I saw Graham, it never even occurred to me to sit with him. As the days passed, though, I realized that no one

ever sat with him. I knew that he was the cousin of my friend Dave Johnson, and Dave told me that Graham suffered from autism. Not knowing much about the disorder, I didn't really know how Graham would react if I were to introduce myself to him. One day, I chose to go for it. I figured I could mention my relationship with Dave if there wasn't anything to talk about. Luckily, he knew who I was because he attended all of our basketball games.

The story speaks well of Zach's humble nature—he was a local sports hero, but he was worried that Graham might not know who he was. Yes, Graham knew exactly who Zach was. He was a huge sports fan, whether it was high school sports or following his favorite professional teams—the Chicago Cubs and the Boston Red Sox—and Zach was a star athlete on the high school basketball and baseball teams. Graham probably knew more about Zach's sports statistics than Zach did himself. Zach didn't know it before he sat down, but he found out soon that they had a lot in common. The pair hit it off immediately.

When Graham got home from school that day, he told his mother that he had lunch with Zach Hirsch.

Her first words were, "Yeah, right."

But she eventually found out that Graham wasn't making it up. The boys were becoming close friends.

Zach and Graham continued having lunch together every day from that point forward, talking mostly about sports but also touching on school subjects and life in general. Zach found out that Graham has an incredible memory. He would remember aspects of Zach's basketball game from the night before that Zach had lost when he was caught up in the moment. Zach learned a lot from Graham's insights.

Graham became a big influence in Zach's life; and the impact Zach has had on Graham was nothing short of a miracle. One of the major hurdles of individuals with Asperger's is severe difficulty in social situations. Graham was shy; he didn't like crowds, loud noises, or physical contact. A few short months after Zach and Graham became friends, Graham started to change. Graham's parents watched in disbelief as their young son joyfully threw himself into a crowd of celebrating players when the basketball team won regionals. Graham went on to become the team helper for the varsity baseball team, sitting in the dugout with the players and proudly wearing a St. Charles North jersey.

Graham's mother, Melissa, is a program supervisor for Mid-Valley Special Education Cooperative in St. Charles. Her professional background and her experience as Graham's mom have made her very sensitive to the herculean issues Graham faces every day with autism. She can hardly contain her excitement when she talks about the incredible progress Graham has made as a result of his friendship with Zach.

"Zach is truly one of the most extraordinary people I have ever had the privilege to know," Melissa told us. "Graham continues to develop in so many wonderful ways, and we can trace so much of it back to the decision that Zach made to join us on the road of Graham's life."

One of the key aspects of their friendship is that each young man has grown and benefitted from the experience. Their relationship is not the least bit one sided. Zach feels that Graham has taught him very valuable lessons about life and the importance of reaching out beyond his regular circle of friends. Graham's intelligence and patience has rubbed off on Zach, too.

There were two specific stories that Zach wanted to share with us about his friendship with Graham:

> The first was after a baseball game when we beat our high-school rival, St. Charles East. Before this moment, Graham and I would give each other fist bumps or high fives, because I learned that sometimes physical contact makes him uncomfortable. But after this game, Graham gave me a big hug. It made me realize what kind of friendship we have, and it seemed to make it even stronger.

The second story happened when I recently came home from college for Christmas break. We were eating at one of Graham's favorite places, the Colonial Café, along with our friend Travis Misner. Out of nowhere, Graham put his winter hat over his face like he was a monster and said, "Zach and Travis, I'm going to eat you!" While it was a had-to-be-there moment, it was also the first time he ever made a joke like that. It just reaffirmed my thoughts on how much Graham has grown as a person in just one year.

Zach graduated from high school in 2009 and is currently at the University of Nebraska on a baseball scholarship, but that has not diminished his friendship with Graham. They email often and get together whenever Zach is home on a break. Their friendship has blossomed far beyond the high-school cafeteria.

We wanted to learn more about Zach to find out what made him follow through on his impulse to sit down with Graham that day. Hundreds of kids must have noticed Graham sitting alone in the cafeteria. What made Zach decide to take action?

We learned that Zach has always been one to reach out and lend a hand. Even as a kindergartener, he would help kids up to the drinking fountain if they couldn't reach it.

"I think one small act is how it all gets started," Zach said. "I've just always felt it was important to give back to the community or anyone who needs help."

We asked Zach if there was one person in his life who inspired him to reach out to others, and his told us that person is his mom.

"She's extremely caring and generous and one of the most genuine people that I have ever met. She sets a great example for how I should try to live my life."

Both mothers could not be more proud of their sons. Their joy was obvious when they had a chance to join Zach and Graham on the Today Show in December, 2009 for the popular Everyone Has a Story segment. It was a tender example of how family circles nourish individuals and give them the strength and courage to reach out to humanity.

Zach believes that his friendship with Graham has indeed shaped his life.

"I have realized even the smallest acts can make an impact on someone's life," Zach told us at the end of the interview. "While I have started to do a little more community service this past year, I think it was just a great experience for me to learn firsthand that you can make a difference anytime, and that in itself is gratifying."

Maybe reaching out to humanity is learned; maybe it's innate; maybe it's a combination of both. What makes Frank L. Banks and Zach Hirsch unique is the fact that they took action. They had an inner impulse to reach out, and they followed it. It's as simple as taking one small step. The next time you hear your inner voice urging you to reach out to someone in need, don't ignore it. Remember Zach and Frank—and go for it.

Staying Local

7

Sometimes you don't have to go far to find inspiring opportunities to lend a hand to someone in need. For this chapter, we interviewed a few people who concentrated their volunteer efforts in their own backyard. They built strong connections in their communities by reaching out to humanity and creating change right where they live and work.

We're All the SAME

When Libby and Brad married in 1998, they immediately carried on a culture of volunteerism their parents had instilled in them by volunteering together at a soup kitchen where they lived in Peoria, Illinois. They really enjoyed making meals and serving them to people who found themselves in bad situations. Handing over a smile and some nourishment felt like a powerful opportunity to connect and offer a bit of hope.

But there was a downside. Brad and Libby didn't exactly love what they were serving. The food was not very good quality. It seemed like they were always digging through bags of slimy, half-rotten lettuce to pull together something halfway decent for the people to eat.

"It was such a disconnect to us that people in poverty were basically being told you only deserve to eat this half-rotten stuff," Brad told us. "In the back of our minds, we wanted to address that somehow."

Brad and Libby also noticed that there was a population that wouldn't—or couldn't—walk into a soup kitchen or a shelter for a meal. Even though they desperately needed food, they just could not bring themselves to walk through the doors, because they were scared or embarrassed. This population consisted of students, single parents, elderly persons, and those who were trying to survive on a low income. They were in desperate need of a healthy meal at an affordable price, and they didn't seem to have any alternative to soup kitchens.

Libby was a teacher at the time, and she applied for a job in Colorado to work at a school for gifted children. She got the job and the couple moved out to Denver, which ended up being a great thing, because Brad's sister already lived in the area. Everything fell into place, and soon Brad found a new job in his field of IT, as well. Life was cruising along just fine, but Brad and Libby couldn't shake their desire to create a place where people could come and get a good meal even if they had fallen on hard times. That's when they started to form the concept for a restaurant called the SAME Café—So All May Eat.

> *What should young people do with their lives today? Many things, obviously. But the most daring thing is to create stable communities in which the terrible disease of loneliness can be cured.*
>
> —Kurt Vonnegut, Jr.

This café would not be a soup kitchen; it would be a regular restaurant; anyone would be welcome. They would serve one meal a day—during the lunch hours—and instead of a cash register, there would be a donation jar. There would be no set price for the meal—people would pay only what they could afford. The restaurant would also offer an exchange program for individuals to volunteer for a couple hours in exchange for a free meal. But no one would be turned away from a meal, even if they didn't choose to volunteer.

Libby and Brad continued to work in their full-time jobs, but in their off hours, they started to turn their dream of the SAME Café into a reality.

"We did it gradually," Libby said. "Our parents are pretty, I wouldn't call them conservative, but they're just very level-headed, grounded people. So convincing them that we were just going to jump ship and put all of our money into something crazy like this would never win them over. We did it as soundly as we thought we could. The first year and a half, we both still had our other jobs. Brad's company allowed him to work part-time evenings, so he would be at the café all day cooking and serving, and then he would leave at 3:30 and run to his IT job until 8:00. Then I would go to the café from school and do everything for the next day for him, so that when he got up to go to the café in the morning, he would have some stuff done. It was quite a year and a half!"

The SAME Café was a hit in the neighborhood, and soon Brad and Libby realized something had to give or they would burn themselves out. Luckily, their hard work had paid off, and the café was on solid ground financially. The board approved a salary for Brad, and he quit his IT job and went to work for the SAME Café fulltime. He took a $40,000 pay cut, but that didn't matter much to Brad and Libby. The tradeoff in realizing their dream of helping others and connecting with an incredibly diverse cross section of their community was priceless. A year later, Libby left her job, too, and now they both work fulltime at the café.

What Brad and Libby like most about their café is that it gives them a chance to build a strong community. They don't like the term giving back. They prefer being part of the neighborhood. They are constantly building relationships with people who come by for a meal, and those relationships are quite powerful.

"I would say we know by name probably between 65 and 70 percent of the people who walk through the door." Libby beamed just thinking about the friends they have accumulated in their four short years of existence. "We know their names. They are normally, I mean, they are people that we would never know otherwise and we would never have talked to otherwise. Most of the people who walk through the door I would call my friends now. It's kind of like having a dinner party every afternoon. All of our friends come over to eat and hang out, and we visit with them. I think the most interesting part about this particular setup is that it's an open kitchen, so we get to talk with everybody."

Speaking of the kitchen, what about the food? Brad and Libby first came up with this idea because they were not happy with the quality of food in many soup kitchens.

If you poll anyone who has enjoyed a meal at the SAME Café, they will all tell you the food is awesome. Brad and Libby work hard to serve high quality, healthy, organic dishes. They remember what it was like to sift through those bags of rotten lettuce, and they know they can do much better. They believe people experiencing poverty simply do not deserve to eat crappy food; that is not honorable in any way. Brad and Libby have made a conscious effort to serve the highest quality food that is available to them. If that means they have to pay $5.99 a pound for something that is normally $2.99 a pound, they do it without a second thought.

The spring and summer months in Colorado are particularly good for the SAME Café, because Brad and Libby have access to local produce. One woman who supplies vegetables for the SAME Café tends her garden less than a mile from the restaurant.

"Sometimes we have carrots from her that, I mean, they were pulled out of the ground less than an hour before someone eats them," Libby laughed. "She brings us the sweetest, most awesome, delicious vegetables."

When Brad and Libby buy local produce, they are building a double community bond by also supporting the micro-economy of local growers. In addition to the vegetables, they get cheese from Boulder, chickens from a farm east of town, and they are always looking for more opportunities to support local vendors.

Recently, when the economy took a downturn, they saw the prices of some food items climb.

"The cost of olive oil went through the roof," Brad said. "And olive oil is essential for our pizza dough."

"We looked at each other, took a moment, and then said, no, we value this," Libby added. "We will find the money somewhere. It's important that we buy the highest quality."

And that's exactly what they did. Brad and Libby have not backed down on their promise to honor their patrons with the highest quality food they can find. As a result, the SAME Café fills to capacity most days.

How do they survive when they spend so much money on food and only accept donations? There are similar restaurants in other parts of the country that follow a safer model, where they have a suggested meal price and a cash register, but people can still opt out to pay less if they have to.

Libby didn't hesitate with her answer. "We are not going to shame people into doing the right thing. I believe they're going to do the right thing—no matter what—and if they don't do the right thing now, then they'll do the right thing some day. It'll come back, you know. Maybe they don't have $11.50 for a meal today. My duty is not to make them feel bad for that. My duty is to make sure they get something good to eat. Maybe someday they'll have $11.50 to put in the box. I don't care."

That attitude of giving without expecting something in return, of paying attention to the person behind the poverty, is what really inspired us when we talked to Brad and Libby. They are interested in creating connections with people—real and lasting connections. That's what matters; that's what feeds Brad and Libby.

We asked the couple what their parents think of their café idea now.

"My dad cries every time I talk to him on the phone," Libby smiled, a tear or two welling up in her eyes. "He's proud of us."

He's not the only one.

Libby and Brad both come from working-class families in Illinois. Libby's father was one of eleven children, and he had to fight for everything while he was growing up. When he started his own family, he felt incredibly lucky that he didn't have to struggle as much as his parents did. It was that traditional Irish-Catholic mentality of each generation making a better life for their kids. He instilled in his children a feeling of gratitude and showed them that it's important to give back some of what has been freely given to them. They were not wealthy, if you're talking about dollars and cents, but the values their parents gave them were priceless.

Both Brad and Libby recalled that some of their earliest family memories are of taking part in volunteer activities with their parents and siblings. Volunteerism was a regular part of their lives, and it drew them closer together. Brad mentioned that the church his family went to was very active in a variety of volunteer efforts. Many of the members were missionaries, but Brad's parents made a conscious decision to do things a little differently.

"They decided that they wanted to volunteer locally instead of going out," Brad recalled. "My aunt and uncle were missionaries, and my sister went to the Dominican Republic for a year, but as I was growing up, I remember a culture of volunteerism that was close to home. Volunteering in our community was just part of how we were raised."

Brad and Libby learned about the importance of lending a hand at a very young age, and they also learned about building community. On a typical day at the SAME Café, Libby, Brad, and up to fifteen volunteers prepare the meal in an open kitchen, and lively conversation bubbles up around the pots and pans and throughout the room.

They ask one woman how her job interview went; another gentleman walks in, and they make sure to find out how is mother is doing. They have a personal friendship with most of the patrons, and that feels really good.

"We want them to know that somebody cares about them and genuinely wants to know how they are doing," Libby said. "I think that makes a difference. You know, when somebody knows your name, a totally different connection happens there. That person recognizes you as a human being rather than, you know, a lot of these people get ignored on the street. People pass them and look down instead of looking them in the eye and recognizing them. We look people in the eye here, and that's empowering."

"Yeah, we have a completely different outlook on life now because of it," Brad added. "We don't wake up and go to work anymore. We wake up, we come here, we cook, we serve, and we hang out with people. It's not a job; it's a totally different mindset.

Getting to meet so many different people enriches our lives. We've made new sets of friends. For example, we go out to see a lot of local bands now, because many artists and musicians come through here. We get to see them perform all around the city. We've been exposed to a lot of different stuff, things we never would have done otherwise."

The SAME Café attracts a huge variety of people. It's close to the capital building in downtown Denver, so it's not unusual to see the mayor's chief of staff hanging out for lunch and talking with a yoga instructor, a musician, or a single parent. Everyone is the SAME; and Brad and Libby have one other rule: everyone participates in the conversation. This is a place to make connections, not hide in the corner. It has even become a great place to brainstorm new ideas. Recently, a group of young people who hang out at the SAME Café came up with a plan to start a free school. They all had different talents, and they thought it would be cool to share them. The free school is now in full swing. One day a yoga instructor conducts sessions; the next day there is a class on crocheting; a few days later their might be guitar instruction; and the idea was born around a table at the SAME Café. Speaking of the tables, at the SAME Café the tables form a sort of horseshoe around the kitchen area, so that the whole place is set up to be just what Brad and Libby hoped it would be—a great, big dinner party.

We asked Brad and Libby if they had any particular memories of their first four years that they would like to share, and they both recalled a man who had a huge impact on their lives. He had been a regular volunteer at the SAME Café for some time, and when he signed up for a volunteer shift, he never missed. In fact, if the kitchen was full and he couldn't get in to volunteer right away, he refused to eat until he donated a few hours of his time.

Brad and Libby got to know this man very well, and one day he didn't show up to volunteer. They started to worry about him when they didn't see him for a few days. He had become a friend, and they were concerned about what happened to him.

A few days later, the man showed up again at the café, and their first instinct was to run up to him and give him a huge hug. The man is an alcoholic, and he had fallen off the wagon, but he told Libby and Brad that he knew they would take him back without judgment. He got back on track, because he knew someone out there was worried about him and cared whether or not he lived or died. He came back to the café; he got in touch with his AA sponsor again; and he got back to living instead of dying. He said he came back because he didn't want to let Brad and Libby down. He's staying sober now partly because the SAME Café is counting on him. The café has become a venue for accountability and a place of hope.

They told us about another volunteer at the SAME Café who had quite a different background. The man was a pastor of a nearby church, and he signed up to volunteer as part of his service work in the community. At first, this pastor was very uncomfortable with the open kitchen concept. He was a middleclass guy who assumed he would be serving nothing but dirty, homeless people. The thought was frankly a little scary to him. He always offered to wash dishes or do whatever task was the furthest removed from the customers. Face-to-face contact with such a variety of people was uncomfortable.

But after a few weeks, the pastor began to transform. He started listening in on the conversations and then gradually moving closer and closer to the patrons. Suddenly, poverty had a face. It wasn't just a smelly, nameless man sleeping in the park. It was an elderly man on a fixed income named Joe or a single mother named Tracy who was trying to go back to school and struggling to make ends meet. The pastor's misconceptions fell away one by one, and eventually he was right up front, talking and laughing with people he had gotten to know. Now, he is encouraging other people in his church to come and volunteer at the SAME Café. He wants them to experience that same transformation.

The SAME Café is able to run with about fifteen volunteers a day in addition to Brad and Libby. About 40 percent of those volunteers are in need of a meal; and 60 percent of the volunteers are just looking for an opportunity to volunteer. The statistics for the patrons are about the same, but in reverse: about 60 percent of the patrons are people living in poverty and in need of a meal, and 40 percent are people who are just coming to support the community endeavor and get to know one another. It's pretty close to a fifty-fifty split, and the resulting dynamic is quite powerful. Brad and Libby consider it one of the perks of their jobs to watch people from all walks of life sit down and share a meal. They have even had some long-lost friends reconnect at the SAME Café.

Finally, we asked Brad and Libby what they would tell someone who was unsure about volunteering, and they had terrific advice:

"Volunteering doesn't have to be scary," Brad laughed. "Go where you love what they're doing. If you like to cook, volunteer at a place that serves food. If you like to cut hair, then go do that. It will take the edge off if you pick a volunteer opportunity that you already enjoy. Then you're not doing an unfamiliar task in an unfamiliar place. You already feel comfortable if you're doing something you enjoy. If you like books, go to the library. If you like museums, volunteer there."

"Yes, if you're going to volunteer, do something you enjoy!" Libby agreed. "I remember a couple of volunteer things I did not enjoy. I thought I'm never doing that again."

"Yes," Brad added. "That's our own personal theory: if it doesn't inspire you, you won't keep coming back."

What makes a good volunteer in their kitchen?

"Someone who's flexible and friendly," Brad said simply.

They can teach the rest.

Creating and sustaining the SAME Café is not easy. Brad and Libby currently work about sixty hours a week—and that's for a restaurant that's only open three hours a day. An incredible amount of planning and preparation goes into each meal. But judging from the relaxed and joyful conversation we had with this couple, it's all worth it. They saw a need and filled it. They are making sure that everyone who walks through their doors gets a chance to eat healthy food, no matter how much money they have. They empower people and build connections in their community every day, and it shows on their faces—the broad smiles and lack of stress lines. Brad and Libby are living the good life!

A Hands-On Experience

ReGina Dobson of Atlanta, Georgia is another inspiring person who is hard at work building community connections. She utilizes volunteerism as a way to balance the stress of her career in software development. ReGina is firmly entrenched in fast-paced corporate America, but she likes to rid herself of that stress by getting out and get her hands dirty with a group called Hands on Atlanta.

ReGina isn't a stranger to volunteerism. The first volunteer experience she can remember was in Bremerhaven, Germany. Her mother ran a daycare center when their family lived there, and one spring day ReGina donned an Easter Bunny suit and entertained the children. She remembers that it was fun; it cost her nothing but a few hours of her time; and the smiles on the faces of the children gave her much more in return.

She, too, grew up in a culture of volunteerism. ReGina's parents often volunteered as coaches for their kids' sport teams and leaders with the Girl Scouts, and there were lots of opportunities for the entire family to lend a hand through events at church.

In the fall of 1993, ReGina was working and living in Atlanta and looking for a new opportunity to get involved in her community. She read an article about Hands on Atlanta in the *AJC* (*Atlanta Journal Constitution*) and decided to give it a try. The first project ReGina signed up for was at Benteen Elementary, and every year since that day, her efforts with Hands on Atlanta have grown right along with the plants she put in the ground around that school. She has gone from a volunteer participant to a project coordinator to a citizen volunteer to the Hands on Atlanta Day logistics Chairman to winning the Presidential Service Award in 2003.

"I think Hands on Atlanta is now in my blood," ReGina joked.

Many inspiring projects came to mind as ReGina recalled her eighteen years with HOA, but one of the most memorable was in the mid-1990s when she became an emergency project coordinator for a day. The project was at Brook Run, which is a ninety-eight-acre facility in Dunwoody—just north of Atlanta. Brook Run is home to 326 mentally retarded and severely disabled individuals. The goal of the project was to beautify the campus for the residents to enjoy.

As soon as ReGina got the project rolling, she asked the facility manager to tell her more about Brook Run and how it served the community. He gave her a wonderful tour of the facility and explained in detail the services provided at Brook Run. The project was a success, and ReGina learned something new about the good things people were doing around Atlanta—things she didn't know existed prior to the project. She walked away with sore muscles and a real feeling of satisfaction. Even more importantly, ReGina felt a growing connection to the people of Atlanta.

Another project that stood out in ReGina's memory took place in the Dixie Hills community just west of Atlanta. It was there that ReGina met community activist Pearl Johnson for a Martin Luther King Service Summit project. Dixie Hills is a beautiful little community filled with mostly retired and elderly individuals. They needed help painting their homes and cleaning up the neighborhood. The volunteers who came together were a diverse group of people from all around the metro area. Their enthusiasm energized ReGina as she joined forces with them and went to work. Pearl provided the group with a list of homes that needed repair or paint jobs, and the group also cleaned up trash and cut back overgrown bushes and trees.

ReGina described what it felt like when they were done. "Hands on Atlanta always gives its volunteers a sense of a job well done, but this time we really felt like we could see it and feel it. This project was truly *hands on*."

ReGina keeps coming back for more, because Hands on Atlanta allows her to have some fun, blow off a little steam, meet great people, and constantly learn about her community. She looks forward to finding out what's on the new volunteer calendar every year. So far ReGina has cleaned up after hurricanes, operated phone banks, painted, planted, picked up trash, and even helped design the volunteer training manual.

"There is really nothing like volunteering," ReGina said. "The smiles on the faces of exhausted volunteers and the end of a project make it all worth it. The people in the community—or the children at the various schools—fall all over themselves to thank you over and over again. Volunteering allows one to feel like part of the community and meet people from diverse and interesting backgrounds."

ReGina has also volunteered outside of Hands on Atlanta, but she really enjoys the way HOA brings together diverse volunteer groups throughout the metro area. She believes they have even more power to ignite change when they combine resources.

"A Hands on Atlanta volunteer truly *gets* more than they *give*," ReGina explained. "My most recent project was during Hands on Atlanta Day 2009 at Wadsworth Elementary Magnet School. The enthusiasm and commitment from parents, students, and staff helped us pull this project off. The largest volunteer group traveled twenty miles across town to make a difference in a community that was completely unrelated to them. It was such a great feeling to see people working side-by-side planting azaleas and crepe myrtles around the school. We all learned how we can make a difference when we work for a common goal."

ReGina told us that she also had the opportunity to work on a church in the projects that had been set on fire because members of the church reported a nearby crack house to the police. The pastor refused to give up on that community and was committed to rebuilding in the same location. When people who lived in this neighborhood saw Hands on Atlanta volunteers working on the church, they came out to lend a hand. Many of them ended up meeting their next-door neighbors for the first time. The stranger next door was no longer a stranger.

Volunteers can impact the community in ways unknown and unseen.

—ReGina Dobson

When we asked ReGina if Hands on Atlanta has improved her quality of life, she wasn't quite sure. "I don't know if it has improved the quality of my life. I think HOA has added a wonderful and impactful dimension to my life."

ReGina has collected numerous bright memories of her time with Hands on Atlanta, and she intends to gather many more as she continues to volunteer. But—hands down—her biggest reward has been bringing a new, young volunteer onboard. Five years ago, ReGina adopted a seven-year-old girl. She, too, has become an HOA volunteer.

"I hope to instill in her the art of giving to her community and making a difference," ReGina said.

That is one very lucky little girl.

> *Individual commitment to a group effort—that is what makes a team work, a company work, a society work, and a civilization work.*
>
> —Vince Lombardi

What can you do in your own community to help someone in need?

Do you know your neighbor?

Maybe it's time to step out the front door and say hello.

8

Going Global

IN THE LAST CHAPTER, WE TALKED ABOUT WHAT INSPIRES PEOPLE TO volunteer locally. Now, we will zoom out and interview three people who explored the outer ring of their tree—humanity. They ventured beyond family, friends, and community circles. They went global and experienced new locations, unfamiliar languages, and foreign cultures. They also discovered that we are connected. We are all part of the same club. The rings of family, friends, community, and humanity start to blend and become one large, healthy tree of wisdom and light.

These interviews demonstrated to us how exciting it is to reach beyond the comfortableness of our own homes and communities and learn about people from all over the world. We are beautiful in our variety, and going global with volunteer opportunities gives us a chance to experience that beauty firsthand.

It's Simple

Five minutes with Tina Bow will lift your spirits for days. Joy pours out of this remarkable woman. She exudes contentment and happiness.

What is this source of her bliss? Is it success or wealth? Tina Bow has certainly achieved remarkable success in her life, but she will tell you that the source of her happiness is not found there. It lies in the eyes of a child in Somalia receiving his very first toy. It is seen in the humble confidence that exudes from a young man in El Salvador, a former inmate who now has the skills to make an honest living and contribute to his community. It's in the nimble fingers of a woman in Cambodia who has learned to use a sewing machine and is no longer beaten by her husband; her status changed when she became the bread winner of the family. It is in the faces of these people—that is where Tina Bow finds joy.

Tina Bow certainly wasn't born with this exuberance for helping others. The elixir of true happiness eluded Tina for a good part of her life. Tina was born into a military family in Taiwan, but her childhood did not brim over with pleasure. She witnessed the scars of World War II still evident in her country. She watched her parents struggle to provide basic necessities for the family. One of her biggest desires as a child was to own just one toy. Tina dreamed of a life where she wouldn't have to live without, and as she got older, she was determined to make her dream come true.

She was able to go to the university, and in four years Tina received a degree in business administration. After she completed her degree, she became a flight attendant for China Airlines. Her travels with the airline opened up a world of opportunities; Tina's dreams grew larger. She married into a wealthy Taiwanese family that owned a successful textile corporation and began to experience a life of comfort and luxury. Tina thought her fortune was made, but she soon discovered that an opulent lifestyle did not guarantee happiness. The hole in her heart was still there. She did not feel fulfilled.

Eventually, her marriage ended and she immigrated to the United States to start a new path toward her dreams. She thought that maybe what she needed was not just money but a sense of personal achievement. With that goal in mind, Tina started a real estate business in Beverly Hills and became very successful at selling homes to the rich and famous. In a short time she obtained her own wealth and business success. Two of her loftiest goals had been achieved. Was it enough? Not in the least. In fact, when Tina reached the height of her success, she found a new low in her personal life. These times were some of the unhappiest days of her life.

Nevertheless, Tina had a steadfast determination to find joy. She had built a hugely successful business, and she had everything she ever wanted materially. So why was she so unhappy? Maybe it was recognition she needed. Tina's next pursuit was in the category of fame. She launched herself into the political world and hoped that it would lift her public status and consequently boost her feeling of self-worth. This experiment gave her nothing in the way of personal fulfillment. It did quite the opposite. Tina Bow witnessed the greedy and ugly side of human nature through politics, and she was not impressed.

Again, Tina found herself adrift and alone. She had everything, yet she felt as if she owned nothing of value. She regretted not having spent more time with her children, and she had a sense that what she really needed was a new journey of self-awareness. She had to start over in her search for what she craved in life and what role she could play in the world.

The first thing Tina did was downsize. She put most of her belongings in storage bins at the airport and took only one bag on her journey of self-discovery. Tina then traveled the world for a year. She did not stay in the five-star hotels of which she had become accustomed. Instead, she lived quite simply, visiting small villages in Burma, Tibet, Cambodia, and Vietnam. She observed the poverty in those areas as an outsider but connected it emotionally to her own upbringing in the housing projects in Taiwan. She learned on this trip how she could do without a lot of things in her life and still be content. It was the people who were irreplaceable.

When Tina returned from her year-long journey, she trimmed off the excess in her life. She moved out of her five-bedroom mansion and into a one-bedroom condo. Her children were grown, and the extra rooms were unnecessary. Then, Tina returned to education to help her find her way. She started taking classes at a local community college.

The subject of Tina's first seminar was self-development, and it turned out to be a much tougher class than she expected. One of her assignments was to help twenty-five people. Tina's first instinct was to write a check, but that was not an option. She was at a complete loss on how to fulfill this assignment.

Enter Mario Rivera. Tina had hired Mario as a handyman for some of her real estate properties, and she soon found out that Mario was not very handy. In fact, he knew almost nothing about how to fix things. She was outraged and called the contract company that hired him to get an explanation. She started off the conversation by asking exactly why they sent her a handyman who was not even close to being handy. The reply was simple. Mario needed a job. He had a family to support.

That answer gave Tina pause. She understood it at some level. Mario needed to feed his family. She eventually decided let Mario stay on—temporarily—and it wasn't long before Tina saw that Mario was an extremely hard worker, and he learned quickly. But his real value as an employee was yet to be discovered.

Mario was also a pastor who was in the process of building his own church. He was an immigrant from El Salvador and had become very involved in the Latino community in Los Angeles. He made regular trips back and forth to Central and South America to donate slightly used goods.

Once Tina got to know Mario, she realized that he could help her with her school project. She needed to help twenty-five people, and Mario probably knew exactly where to find people in need. Tina approached Mario and explained her assignment. She made it very clear to him that she just needed to help twenty-five people, not twenty-six. She was not out to change the world. Tina just wanted to adequately complete her assignment.

Mario immediately suggested that Tina go with him on a trip to Tijuana, Mexico to deliver goods to people in need. Reluctantly, Tina agreed. The trip was pretty far out of her comfort zone, and when they arrived in Tijuana, she felt as though she had arrived in hell. The poverty was horrifying, especially compared to the extravagant community where she lived in Beverly Hills.

Tina was very hesitant at first. She gingerly handed items out of the beat-up truck she had purchased to make the trip. But then Tina experienced a monumental shift that would change her life forever. She looked into the eyes of the people she was helping. What she saw was indescribable. It lit her from the inside out. Tina experienced true joy for the very first time. One trip to hell inspired a journey of a lifetime. Soon afterward, Tina and Mario cofounded Simply Help.

The following is an excerpt from our talk with Tina Bow in the fall of 2009:

How did that one trip to Tijuana change everything?

I didn't expect it to go this far. I mean, I thought it would only be one week or one trip. Now here we are ten years later. We've taken 130 industrial-sized containers of slightly used items to twenty countries.

We read that you have a connection with the United Nations now.

Yes, Simply Help currently has consultative status with the United Nations. You know, it came about because we have been working in different countries. The United Nations representative for Cambodia saw what we did in that country, and he helped us apply for the position. That's how we got in. I didn't even know we were in until I got the final notice. We have been working in many different countries, and the people in Cambodia encouraged us to apply for it.

How many different countries does Simply Help work in now?

We work in about twenty countries. It's kind of surprising to say that out loud. You don't expect it. All I did was take a first step. Then the whole thing followed. When you climb a mountain, you start with the first step.

How did you come to discover that volunteering was something that was more fulfilling than wealth, fame, or success?

It was an actual feeling. I had been working hard trying to making money, and even still the satisfaction was very short. It didn't last. Then, I went to help with one trip to Mexico. I did a project to help twenty-five people. I think long after I got back home from that trip I still felt it. When I distributed those necessities to the poor neighborhood in Tijuana ten years ago, it was just like heaven and hell where I lived in California compared to Tijuana at that time. So after the trip, after I got back, I felt satisfaction that you don't get in business. One trip was enough.

Tell us about Mario.

Yes, he's my handyman. I asked him to help me. I needed to find a project that would help twenty-five poor people. He said why? I said it was my homework. I went to this spiritual seminar, and they said, well, to move to the next level you need to help twenty-five people. That was my project, to help twenty-five people. So I told Mario, I don't need to help twenty-six. I only want to help twenty-five. Find me a project.

Mario's a pastor, and he took me to Tijuana to help people. I wanted to just give him the money to go without me. He said, no, it's your project, not mine. He's a pastor. He knows. He helped me to take the first step. Usually, the first step is kind of scary. You don't want to do it. You would rather pay the money and have other people do it. But actually doing it is a big step.

What was the difference in your satisfaction level when you took action rather than just sending money to a cause?

You remember the faces of people when you come back, the expression on their faces. When you give to them, whether it is a child or a woman or whoever, their face, their expression is what stays with you. Actually, the first time I was kind of shy and nervous, and I think it had a huge impact on me. A week later I would have images come back to me from the trip. It got me thinking, oh, they don't have blankets; they don't have enough toys; they don't have this or that. Okay, on the next trip I will bring some blankets; I'll bring some toys. So I planned the next trip.

Each trip kind of opened my heart a little more. My life was like a tower. A lot of doors were closed. Each time I saw their faces, I opened one door, then another door, and I saw my life expand.

Do you still feel like you are learning?

Yes. I still open a door with every trip. Every time I participate, I learn something new. I mean, that's why I never stop.

Do the faces of these people haunt you when you return home to California?

Yes, but in kind of a calming and good way. You know, I feel like I want to help other human beings. It may be in a very small way, but it has an impact on their lives.

It sounds like helping others is empowering you in a way that some other endeavors did not.

Yes, and this is a difficult feeling. Usually, people say when you buy your first house you will be satisfied and happy, but that's not what happens. When you have your first house, then you want a bigger house. Then, someone else has a bigger house than you. Human beings compete for these things. We want to keep up appearances. So we never have the feeling that this is "it."

But when you help other people, I think you do get the feeling that this is it. Nothing compares to even the smallest smile from people you help. It is joy.

Do you feel like it was Mario who really helped you find "it" and get this organization going?

Yes. I think when people give money they don't really feel like they want to continue. I mean, sometimes they donate twenty or thirty dollars for the tax break, but the feeling they get from that is temporary. They don't feel really connected to the people they are helping.

So yes, Mario pushed me into personal contact, which was really uncomfortable for me. I had a very small inner circle of friends and family. I didn't want to change that small circle. The charity work suddenly expanded my circle. I no longer belonged to that little, tiny group in Beverly Hills. I belonged to humanity. That was when I realized that my life had been so small and unhappy before.

People have this idea that when they get rich, when they are "it," when they become what they want to be, then they'll give back and help others. But thinking like that just delays your joy. I delayed my happiness for a long time. But now I have joy every day.

What would you like to tell us about Simply Help?

Actually, it has been interesting shipping containers, 130 containers of secondhand items and stock merchandise, all over the world to twenty different countries. In Somalia before the civil war, sometimes as many as 20,000 people would get in line to receive items from one container. People walked for weeks to the location, miles and miles, barefoot.

We are really rich compared to other countries. When they receive something from us, from a complete stranger, they are so happy. They are receiving care and concern. They are getting love from total strangers. It's not about race or religion or political views. We just want to share our lives with those who are unfortunate. It is so good when you can share your life with someone. It is joy—a sense of joy to know they got our message. They know you care about them. Maybe I can't save the world, but right now I can send love to a woman in Africa.

After the first containers went, I looked through pictures of the people who came to get things, all the skinny people in Africa. They were wearing our oversized shirts, because our American shirts, they are big. We're fat, you know. Right? It's kind of funny to look at the photos, especially of the kids. They are so small in those big shirts.

So first we shipped the containers, and then we felt like they couldn't wait for our containers. We had to reduce their poverty. We needed to give them a skill for them to learn to work locally and make money. So we would work with the government or the city to find out what jobs were most needed; things people could do right away that would contribute to the economy.

In some cities they need carpenters; in other cities they need sewing machines or beauty or computer skills. So we started to set up schools to give them a skill. In three months they can be on their own making money. They can support their family. So basically, we started vocational training. Just give us three months, and we will train you to do something. You don't need to beg anymore.

In Cambodia, the girls would sell their bodies in exchange for money. So we had a sewing class in one area and gave them a skill in just two weeks. We taught them how to use a sewing machine. Two weeks later, they could find a job with a manufacturer.

That's how it started, and then some of the moms wanted to have a shop in their homes, so they could support their families and at the same time take care of their children. So we started a tailoring school. The classes came with a sewing machine and five to eight months worth of fabric to get them started in their business. Remember, when our containers were shipped over there, most of the clothes were oversized. They didn't fit the skinny people in Cambodia any more than they fit the skinny people in Africa. Now, these tailors could alter them. They would do custom alterations for people right in the stores.

The clothes we sent them would hang in the store. The customer would come in and say, oh, I like this color. So they would alter the old clothes into a new dress. That's how they started their business.

We started these schools in 2002, and we are still running them today. It has really impacted the communities. Before 2000, the women and girls in Cambodia usually stayed at home. Only the boys got to go to school. The girls had to clean the house and farm the land. Now, there is a change occurring, because women have learned a marketable skill. Now they have a voice. They are making money, so they share in the family's budget, and then they have a say in what goes on in the house. The whole structure has changed. Right now in some areas women have more of a say than the men, because they are now making more money. The entire society is changing in just a couple of years.

I had to give a report to the United Nations last year in a women's meeting. It was called the Status of Women. I talked to them about how the community in Cambodia has changed. The status of women has changed, because now the women make money. The girls can go to school now.

Were these classes free for the students?

Yes, totally free. It basically costs Simply Help about $150 per student. The sewing machine is not electronic. It is a very old style. It only costs about $30 a machine, and then we pay the instructor and also provide fabric. It's not a lot of money, and we found we could train many people relatively inexpensively.

What are your dreams for the future for Simply Help?

I want to do more of the same. What we're doing right now, the vocational schools, I feel like we are giving people a new life. I tell them, give me three months, and we can help you. Some people don't have that much time, so we've done a few classes in two weeks. We can teach them how to use an electronic machine for a manufacturing job in just two weeks. But in three months they can learn a skill. They can stand up by themselves. They can be independent.

I want to continue to put the vocational schools in places where there is poverty. Then, they don't have to wait for containers to arrive. They don't have to wait for help and feel sorry for themselves and cry or whatever. They can have their own power.

I have a school in El Salvador that teaches sewing classes. I recently went to the graduation. Actually, it's a school for inmates—young people, about sixty students from the jail. In the daytime they come over to learn skills. In the nighttime, they go back to the jail.

At the graduation, one of the graduates talked about how he appreciated us giving him a second chance. He now feels like he can create value in this world. He said that he thought he was worthless. He's not worthless anymore. His goal is to be a tailor in his hometown. He saw through our classes that he could make that wish come true when he got out of jail.

I looked at his face. He turned from a criminal into a very humble person. He knows he can create value. He has confidence now. The skills gave him confidence. They change a person's life. Now, he feels like he can do something in life.

So he just kind of touched me. I feel like with very little input they will pick it up and create a new life. They have value when they gain skills. They stand up. They become good citizens instead of criminals in society. That humble young man touched my heart. He showed me that it is worth it.

How is Simply Help funded?

We run on private contributions and volunteers. We don't have grants or corporate donations or anything. People just want to get together and make an impact. It's pretty simple. We do want to make the best out of our dollars, though, because we don't have a lot of money.

How has this affected your quality of life?

I'm busy all the time. I'm in all of these countries! It is a lot of work, but I get a lot of help from all the volunteers.

Do you have any final thoughts you would like to share?

I think when people postpone their lives, waiting for another day when they make money to help people; they are missing a lot of the value in this life. They are missing the joy. When your inner self is joyous and happy, when you have that kind of satisfaction, I think then you become healthy and you feel younger.

Before I was rich, and I hid myself on top of a mountain in a big house. I felt miserable, and I was in real pain. I was afraid of everything and everybody. I was afraid some people wanted to borrow money from me. I definitely wasn't happy. I was scared. I was afraid to live life. My life is much different now.

So does volunteering make you younger?

Yes! I feel much younger today than I did ten years ago.

We just brought some of the young kids to a United Nations meeting in Mexico this year for the NGO (Non-Governmental

Organizations) meeting. One of the boys, about twenty years old, commented on how old everyone was at the meeting. He was right. I think the average age was fifty or sixty. That meeting represented leaders from all over the world.

Now, some of these younger people want to get involved. They listened, and when they came back they were already thinking about ways they could make a difference. So I am trying to choose a couple of younger people for my workshop in the United Nations, so they can express their feelings in an international format. I want to give them a voice, too.

When young people feel like we're listening, then they start to take interest. They start to believe they can do anything, and they don't give up. I want to invite young people to be part of these discussions on world issues. I encourage them to come over and join us. Email us. Come and talk with us. There is a place for you here. Your voice will be heard.

I also want to encourage more people to join Simply Help. If we had more volunteers to help us, we could have a better future. I encourage everyone to just give volunteerism a try. Take that first step. You never know what might happen.

From grudgingly taking part in a college assignment to help twenty-five people to running a non-profit organization that has real impact all over the world, Tina Bow has become a symbol of hope for hundreds of people. She experiences joy every day now. It doesn't come with a designer label or a mansion on the hill. It is delivered in the face-to-face contact she is privileged to experience when she reaches out to help another human being.

Adventures in Preservation

Judith Broeker was working part-time at the Boulder Bookstore when she had an epiphany. One day while she shelved in the travel area—her favorite section of any bookstore—Judith came across a section on volunteer vacations and stopped her work momentarily to browse through it. Suddenly, it hit her.

"This ties everything together!" a voice inside her head started screaming.

Judith loves old buildings; she loves to travel; and she loves photography. On that day working at the Boulder Bookstore, she discovered a way to combine all three—Adventures in Preservation.

Judith has always been intrigued by crumbling architecture. She loves to explore sites with her camera and extract clues about the history of a place. Her passion for studying structures all over the world eventually earned her a master's degree in history with an emphasis on historical preservation. On that quiet day in the Boulder Bookstore, Judith acknowledged her dream. There was a way in which she could translate her passion into meaningful work. She would create volunteer vacations where people from all over the world could come together for a few weeks to work on a preservation project.

Judith immediately began collaborating with her colleague Jamie Donahoe to bring the idea to fruition. They founded Adventures in Preservation in 2001 and set about fulfilling the following mission statement:

Saving the world's architectural heritage by supporting community-driven preservation projects that seek to create economic and environmental sustainability.

Their new organization was global from its inception, but unfortunately, they completed the paperwork right after 9/11. The terrorist attacks had an immediate impact on the willingness of people to travel outside of the country—or even within the country. People hunkered down, and for awhile, Judith was unsure if their idea would ever take hold. They altered their grand plan slightly and started two projects closer to home—one at a grist mill in rural New Jersey and the other at a historic home in Alabama. Luckily, these two projects were extremely successful. Judith and Jamie were inspired and hooked on moving forward with their dream.

Next, Adventures in Preservation got a request from Sicily...then Slovenia...then Ghana...then they were back in the United

States for a few projects. Requests started pouring into the website, and they found it hard to keep up with the need. Nevertheless, they continued moving forward and completed several projects each year.

Interestingly, Judith found that when she went global with Adventures in Preservation, the most important element of success for each project was community.

"Community support means everything," she told us. "Initially, when we started out, we would go to one place for two weeks, and then move to another location. We were excited about every request and wanted to help in as many communities as possible. Now, we are finding that if we go back to a location numerous times over three to five years, we accomplish so much more. Even more importantly, we create ties with the community. That is when we start to have a huge impact."

Judith gave us a great example of the advantage of community support when she described a trip to a small town in Slovenia.

"The town was incredibly cute to start out with," Judith laughed. "So you don't even care what you're doing. Visually it was very cool."

The project involved an old manor house that was built in the 1600s with its own little chapel. The manor was given to the city for a community center, and one of the residents of the city wanted to see if Adventures in Preservation could help them restore the paint scheme in the chapel. Judith contacted a local expert, and with his help, they discovered beautiful angels and doo-dads all over the ceiling on the second story of the chapel. It took two weeks to figure out what the original paint scheme was, and then they had to remove other layers of paint before they could even start the restoration.

The Adventures in Preservation group got about one-fourth of the project completed in the few weeks they were in Slovenia, but that first trip sparked interest. After a few days, people in the community started dropping by to see what they were doing. Then, they held a community meeting about the project, and people from all over the country attended. Over the next two years, the citizens of the town picked up the ball. They formed their own group and finished the entire project. Judith was thrilled to return a few years later and take pictures of the completely restored chapel—accomplished through the enthusiasm and hard work of people in the local community.

There are so many advantages to preservation anywhere in the world. It preserves the heritage and culture of an area; it provides opportunity to boost the economy in an area due to tourism and also employs workers to complete the repair and restoration; and it is a very green thing to do. Making use of existing materials—recycling—rather than tearing down an existing structure and starting from scratch is good for the overall environment. The projects allow communities to be sustainable, both environmentally and economically. Restored buildings can remain an integrated part of the community and become community centers or affordable housing, even while serving as tourist attractions. Buildings are such an important part of a culture. When they are restored, pride in heritage and community receives a huge boost. Seventy-five percent of all travelers include historical site-seeing as part of their vacations, so restoration attracts visitors and helps to develop a sustainable economy as well.

"So why *not* use a valuable resource you have—historic architecture—to make your community appealing?" Judith shrugged her shoulders.

It's a no brainer.

Plus, it's really fun!

Judith's face glowed as she wound through story after story of her experiences over the last nine years. Her idea of heaven on earth is traveling to exotic locations, unearthing the beauty of old structures, and restoring them to their original luster. Adventures in Preservation attracts volunteers worldwide, so there is also an exciting element of random groups of architects, teachers, students, and history buffs coming together to make something new again.

Adventures in Preservation only goes to locations where a local individual or organization generates enough interest to do the groundwork. In other words, they go where they are invited. They have had over one hundred requests in their first nine years.

We asked Judith how Adventures in Preservation has transformed her personally, aside from the fact that she is realizing her dream of combining her love of history, travel, and photography.

"It is huge for me," she grinned. "I'm not much of a joiner, and I found myself getting more isolated. As I got older, I was no longer in school, and I wasn't married, and my daughter was grown up—life just got smaller and smaller."

Judith reversed that trend in a big way.

"As a kid, I just wanted to go everywhere and understand what the world was all about," Judith explained. "Now, I have a chance to do that. It puts everything in a different light when you get your head out of your little, bitty, narrow world. It puts life in a much more positive light for me, because I can help the people I work with save a piece of their history that means so much to them."

Judith found herself asking questions with each project and then discovered the answers in person. Why did the project in Albania continually shift and change? Ah, because these were the survival skills learned living under a harsh dictator for forty years. Yet how do these people remain some of the most resilient, kind, and energetic people she has ever met? She had always been interested in reading about different countries, people, and cultures, but now she gets to actually experience it. It is truly an adventure.

> *Life is either a great adventure or nothing.*
> —Helen Keller

We also had an opportunity to interview a few participants in Adventures in Preservation, and the sense of excitement was universal. Elma Prapaniku's decision to volunteer with Adventures in Preservation came from a desire to travel to the country from which her family immigrated. Her family is Albanian but from Macedonia. The city from which they immigrated, Diber, is actually divided by the border between Macedonia and Albania. She wanted to return to her roots and also experience life from a different perspective. What she took away from the experience was much more than she expected. Not only did Elma learn about architecture—a field she knew little about before Adventures in Preservation—but she also experienced what other volunteers found important and exciting about restoration work. She learned how restoring buildings can rebuild communities, and she learned to value and respect different opinions expressed by volunteers from eight different countries. Elma recently wrote to us about her experience:

> Adventures in Preservation has changed my perception on many things in life. It wasn't only about meeting different people and helping to restore buildings but also about learning to work and function with others, especially with those who were from the host community. It was about working together and accepting the fact that individuals won't always agree with your ideas, no matter how great you may think they are. My experience with Adventures in Preservation has inspired me to participate in the Peace Corps. I want to continue to have opportunities to experience life through the eyes of others and discover what motivates them and how they rise above overwhelming adversity.

Stephen Booker, an architect from Australia, also had an eye-opening experience with Adventures in Preservation. He was nervous about his first trip—two weeks in Slovenia—but the workshop was extremely interesting, and he has since returned twice to Slovenia to visit friends he made during that volunteer vacation.

He described what it was like to immerse himself in a foreign culture.

"Going to a place and knowing little of its background or historical development, its traditions and trades, opened my eyes. I found myself listening intently to the explanations, demonstrations, and information from tour guides at cultural destinations."

Stephen felt like he was doing detective work, finding out why they used certain materials, how tools were developed, and why specific techniques were used in building. He was so taken by Slovenia and the people that he led the next workshop in Slovenia in August of 2010.

Adventures in Preservation has made Stephen more acutely aware of the nuances of different places around the world. Now, when he visits a new place, he focuses on what he does not know or understand, rather than trying to defend the things he does know. It's an incredible opportunity for growth and transformation.

> *Personal transformation can and does have global effects. As we go, so goes the world, for the world is us. The revolution that will save the world is ultimately a personal one.*
>
> —Marianne Williamson

When we asked Judith about some of the highlights of the first nine years of Adventures in Preservation, she launched immediately into a story about their most successful workshop to date. It was the Francis Mill in Waynesville, North Carolina. The project started when a woman contacted Judith and told her about a mill that had been built by her great-great grandfather. It had been in the family and functioning until about 1976, when it was closed and started to fall apart. The building was about to collapse in 2003 when the woman contacted Adventures in Preservation.

The mill was part of the woman's family history, but it was also part of the history of the community. Jamie helped form a non-profit, the Francis Mill Preservation Society, so that they could receive grants pay for the preservation, and the entire community got involved. They found a wood conservationist who worked part-time for the National Parks Service, and under his leadership, Adventures in Preservation stabilized the building in their first workshop. For the next several years, groups from Adventures in Preservation and community members in Waynesville took the project step by step, and within three and a half years, the mill was completely restored. They found that all of the inner workings were still in the mill and raised the funds to get a millwright to come in and set it working again.

Now, the Francis Mill is fully functional, and school groups and tourists visit it regularly to learn about its history and the history of Waynesville, North Carolina. It's a source of pride in the community, not only because the building has been restored, but because people from the community—and from all over the world—came together to complete the project. Together they stepped into humanity and achieved remarkable results.

Judith is the first to admit that not all of the projects have been as outwardly successful as the Francis Mill, but they all exceeded the goal of connecting people and supporting communities. Some of her most wonderful memories have been when things didn't go according to plan. If the group was able to listen to community members and go with the flow no matter what happened, then they invariably had a wonderful and fulfilling time.

It is almost impossible for Judith to come home now. Adventures in Preservation is more than a vacation. It has transformed her life. She talked to us about the difference.

"I come home and go to my other job, where I can go for eight hours without speaking to anyone," she said. "It's easy to isolate. Just turn on your computer and do your work. With Adventures in Preservation, you're a part of the world. There are always people to work with and laugh with, so happy and loving and positive. It's all about experiencing where you are and who you are with. It's not even what we're doing so much. We could be cleaning bathrooms and it would be fun, because we're doing it together as a group of friends."

Now, Judith is sitting in her other job but daydreaming about the next project Adventures in Preservation has lined up. She wonders what it would be like if she could live her life going directly from one project to the next. It's getting harder and harder for her to sit in front of her computer.

"I remember in high school one of our vocabulary words was gregarious. Part of the definition said it was something humans need to survive," Judith recalled. "I thought, wow! Boy, is that the truth.

When you are in high school with friends all around you, who thinks about it? But when you grow up, lack of human connections can be deadly."

When Judith comes to the end of a volunteer vacation with Adventures in Preservation, she never feels like she has been working. It's pure fun.

"I hate to say it, but we are probably getting so much more out of these projects than even the community does. It seems very self-serving."

Judith may think it's self-serving, but the connections she fosters all over the world serve all of us—they strengthen our humanity, our understanding of how we are similar and also our magnificent differences. Adventures in Preservation is a global organization, but its impact is felt locally in each community and in the hearts of every volunteer.

Help a Child

That's how it started for Catherine Franks of the United Kingdom. She helped one child as a volunteer teacher's helper in her own community...then she helped more children in Ghana...and even more in Shanghai...and each experience ignited a passion inside of her to work on behalf of children throughout the world. Catherine's experiences inspired her to found Children's Helpers Worldwide, based in London. It is a global organization with a community focus.

How can you be global and local at the same time? Everyone we interviewed for this chapter understands exactly how that works. In order to make a difference in a foreign location, one must make an extra effort to learn about the community, its people, its culture, and its needs. The object of going global is not to force one's own culture on someone in need. It is to learn, listen, and then lend a hand.

Catherine was eighteen years old and in her gap year—a year off from studies that is often spent traveling abroad. She decided to spend the time as a volunteer for New Life International Orphanage in Ghana, West Africa. She lived in the home of the founder of the orphanage, Ruby Ayivohr, and taught in the orphanage every day.

"Ma Ruby" welcomed Catherine into her family and taught her about the importance of helping others every day. She showed her how one person can make a difference in the life of a child.

Catherine was amazed to see how much happiness bloomed in the faces of children when she just spent a little time playing with them or simply bought them a piece of fruit. She discovered the joy of volunteering through the bright faces of those children in Ghana. Catherine also witnessed the tangible difference Ma Ruby made in the life of every child she helped, and she knew that she wanted to make a difference, too.

The other very important lesson Catherine learned during her gap year in Ghana was that working with local community organizations provided the right kind of help for those in need. Local organizations are part of the community, so they understand much more comprehensively the needs, obstacles, and opportunities in a particular place. Catherine understood that working with local groups would also provide room for development and sustainability. It didn't take Catherine very long after her experience in Ghana to establish Children's Helpers Worldwide, an organization that raises funds for local organizations all over the world that help children. It's global and it's local at the same time.

The event that inspired Catherine to move from volunteer to founder of a fundraising organization happened in Shanghai. Catherine was spending a summer there working in a law internship. In her free time, she arranged to volunteer at a center for children with cerebral palsy. That is where she met another amazing woman who would also become a mentor. Gao Ya Li founded the center because her son was born with cerebral palsy, and she could not find help for him. Her center has now helped hundreds of children in the area.

Catherine felt compelled to help both in Ghana and In Shanghai, but she knew she needed some backup if she was going to make a meaningful difference. Fundraising as an individual was difficult, but fundraising as a global organization would be much more powerful. Children's Helpers Worldwide was born.

After Catherine finished university, she took a second gap year and traveled to a number of different countries to establish links with local organizations that supported children. She found that there were wonderful people all over the world who were taking steps to help children in need in their communities. Many of them simply did not have enough resources to do the work at hand. Children's Helpers Worldwide would become a means to help them raise the funds they needed to continue doing good work. Children's Helpers Worldwide is currently fundraising for children's organizations in Ghana, China, Argentina, Romania, and South Africa. Everyone who works at Children's Helpers Worldwide is a volunteer. No one is paid for their work. All of the money raised goes straight to local projects that help children.

Catherine told us about another exciting project in Romania. She explained to us that in most post-communist countries the word volunteering has a negative connation. But one courageous woman is working to change that. Cristina Birsan established the Atelier Sacelean Association in her hometown of Sacele, Romania. It runs educational programs for underprivileged children in the community and assists a local hospital in giving better care to ill children and babies who are admitted there. Cristina's projects help numerous children living in poverty, particularly those from the large Roma community living on the outskirts of Sacele. Cristina takes on volunteers from abroad and also encourages people within the community to volunteer. She has become yet another strong mentor to Catherine, showing her how to use her resources to do good for others. Cristina is changing old perceptions in Romania, one person at a time, and showing how volunteerism builds communities and helps children.

After volunteering with Cristina, Catherine was even more determined to support her work and increase her fundraising efforts around the world. She refers willing volunteers to the Atelier Sacelean Association and the New Life International Orphanage and raises funds for the organizations.

Catherine told us that lending a hand to people in need around the world has put her own problems into perspective. It has allowed her to focus on the things that really matter. She gave us a stunning example:

> I was volunteering at a home for adults and children with disabilities in Argentina, and it was a beautiful, sunny day. One of the staff members at the center said I could take a woman who lived at the home out for a short walk around the grounds. This woman has cerebral palsy and is blind and deaf. She cannot walk by herself. If you come close to her, she will grab onto you and hug you for support. So I took her out, and we walked around the grounds enjoying the warm sunshine. I was very nervous that particular morning, because I was about to get the results for my law degree. After I finished working at the home that morning, I would have to go to the Internet café to find out how I had done. As I walked around, making sure this woman could get some fresh air, I realized that if I failed those tests, it would not be so important. Other people obviously had much bigger problems in life. As it happens, I didn't fail, but if I had, I could still continue to do care work. My results would not have kept me from doing that.

In following her passion for helping children around the world, Catherine has met a number of inspirational adults who have guided her along the way and inspired her to continue with her work. We have already mentioned Ma Ruby, Gao Ya Li, and Cristina Birsan. There are many more.

David Kwesi Acquah was once a street child in Ghana. He has now started his own orphanage and school—Sankofa. Anne Siroky was at one time the number-one volleyball player in South Africa. She has started the Future Factory, which runs sports programs and feeds hungry children in Cape Town. Rita Benjamin, also of Cape Town, dreamed of starting a crèche for some of the poorest children in the city. She left her job to make her dream a reality. Jan Calos temporarily moved from the United States to Romania to start a children's home called Casa Mea. And Cecilia Gonzalez Biatturi is a primary school teacher in Argentina who works to raise awareness for children's rights in her municipality.

Catherine has learned from all of these powerful individuals. She has learned that if you have a dream or believe in a cause, it is possible to achieve results. Catherine's dream is helping children worldwide, and she is achieving it every day.

When we asked Catherine Franks if her volunteer activities have improved her quality of life, she said, "They have actually changed the path of my life! Instead of going on a gap year to volunteer abroad for awhile and then coming home and forgetting all about it, my experience with the children in Ghana led me to starting Children's Helpers Worldwide."

Tina Bow, Judith Broeker, and Catherine Franks are strong cases for the premise of this book. They had the courage to step out of themselves and into humanity when they went global with their volunteer efforts. As a result, they were transformed. These women are powerful examples of how one person can make a difference in this world.

What are your dreams?

What would you like to change in this world?

Do you believe you have the power to make it happen?

Do you have the desire to alter your present path, even slightly?

9

STEPPING OUT OF YOUR COMFORT ZONE

WE HAVE NOW COVERED ALL OF THE RINGS OF OUR TREE: SELF, FAMILY, friends, community, and humanity. We are starting to see how the circles blend when we become fully engaged in the idea of *MORE Than me*. A stranger becomes a friend when two people work together on a project. A brother and sister join forces and volunteer in a foreign land. The tree of life grows stronger. Its branches become lush and green from the nourishment all of the rings provide.

In this chapter, we will take a look at what some may call *extreme volunteerism*. Maybe someday it will be a reality TV show, but until then, we've got this book and our imaginations.

There is a small, daring group of volunteers who are brave enough to step into uncomfortable situations when lending a hand to those in need. They are willing to say—what the heck—and jump off that cliff into the unknown.

The bold individuals in this chapter will tell us why they do it. They will teach us about the exhilaration they experience when they take a risk and choose volunteer opportunities that allow them to stretch beyond their comfort zone.

> *And the day came when the risk to remain tight in a bud was more painful than the risk it took to blossom.*
> —Anaïs Nin

After the birth of their second child, Mary Kritenbrink and her husband made a decision that she would become a stay-at-home mom. She had no idea how their decision would transform her life. Mary found that the transition from the workplace to the home gave her a personal opportunity to blossom. She considers motherhood her most important role, but becoming a stay-at-home mom also offered Mary an opportunity to step out of her comfort zone. Suddenly, she had the time to do more, be more, and help more.

As Mary reflected back on her life for our interview, she remembered times when she volunteered, but she really didn't become committed to volunteerism until about seven years prior to when we spoke with her—about the time she became a stay-at-home mom. Mary remembered that her dad would often volunteer to help neighbors with odd jobs or help complete various projects at church. Her mother also sent casseroles and baked goods to church for funerals or fundraisers. Mary followed their lead and helped neighbors with yard work and volunteered to be a lay reader in church. It would be fair to say she learned by example, and she grew up in a culture of volunteerism.

However, there was a turning point in Mary's life in 2003 when she had the time to start volunteering regularly with a couple of groups: Interfaith Hospitality Network of Greater Denver and Advocates for Children.

"I don't think I fully appreciated the joy of volunteering until I began doing that," Mary told us.

Mary took a giant step out of her comfort zone when she committed to these projects. Her new volunteer work opened her eyes to the darker side of life.

"We all watch the media reports of homeless people and abused and neglected children," Mary said. "But that's all it ever becomes to most of us...a news report."

When Mary got involved with Interfaith Hospitality Network of Greater Denver and then Advocates for Children, her transformation started in the mind. Mary found that she held a number of judgmental views that were very often wrong. She had a false image of homeless people, and her direct work with the families helped to change her views. Her biggest discovery was that any one of us could find ourselves in dire need of aid.

"We all make choices every day that direct us to where we are in the present," Mary explained. "Some decisions are good; while others we know are wrong from the start; still others are made with the best of intentions but turn out poorly. I realized that financial disaster can strike any one of us at any time, due to economic or health issues."

How did Mary come to this realization? Her transformation occurred through face-to-face contact with adults and children in need. Mary went from being one step removed to being on a first-name basis with many homeless individuals who were struggling to survive in the Denver area, and she learned from each one of their personal stories.

Interfaith Hospitality Network is, as its tagline states, a community response to homeless families. It's a national organization that manifests itself locally in partnerships between diverse communities of faith. IHN provides 90-day emergency shelter, meals, and supportive services to families experiencing homelessness.

IHN of Greater Denver operates under a model of hospitality not humiliation. Volunteer organizations serve as hosts, and they treat the families as guests. Mary became involved with IHN by bringing the opportunity to her church—St. Andrew United Methodist in Highlands Ranch, Colorado.

There were many challenges to overcome in bringing this opportunity to her church. The first challenge Mary faced was to convince her fellow members that this was not a shelter program. St. Andrew would not become a homeless shelter. Other concerns were for the safety of program guests, the logistics of where they would stay within the church, the safety of the church property, and how they would consistently come up with the large number of volunteers it would take to pull the project off long term. Mary did her homework and presented her findings to the church; then St. Andrew stepped up to the challenge. A large number of people in this church community agreed to step with Mary outside of their comfort zones. St. Andrew joyfully became part of the network of IHN churches in greater Denver.

Since partnering with IHN, Mary and the volunteers at St. Andrew have endured snowstorms, illnesses, emergency room visits, missing parents, missing dinners, transportation issues, and other minor problems. But everything was handled by caring volunteers who found out that nothing compares to the smiles on the faces of families as they sit down together for dinner or cuddle on a couch to watch a movie. They leave the volunteer job satisfied that they helped bring some sense of safety and hope to families.

St. Andrew now regularly hosts families through IHN for a week at a time, and it takes an army of volunteers to provide the guests with comfortable living quarters in the church, meals, friendship, assistance with laundry and other essentials, and shuttle services to and from the IHN day site, where the guests work with counselors to find employment and permanent housing. It is a very personal way to give families a hand up, not a hand out.

Mary has learned a lot from her involvement in this organization, and her leadership in bringing IHN to St. Andrew has set off transformations in numerous other volunteers.

"I have seen that people are genuinely good and want to do what's best for them and their children," Mary said. "When given the opportunity to have a fresh start, help with basic life skills that they may lack, and a little assistance, they can become successful again and provide for their family."

When Mary became involved with Advocates for Children, her understanding of those in need in her own community deepened. Mary was shaken to her core by what she learned when she began her training as a CASA. The grim world of child abuse and neglect became very real.

A CASA is a Court Appointed Special Advocate—a trained volunteer from the community who speaks on behalf of children in the courtroom. Most of the children that CASA volunteers help are victims of abuse and neglect. The overall goal of a CASA is to carefully research the background of a child and their current needs to help the court make a sound decision about the child's future. CASAs are appointed to each case by a judge. This is not a job for wimps.

Mary took another brave step out of her comfort zone and completed her training as a CASA, and now she volunteers regularly as an advocate for children. She learned that the news reports only reveal a small fraction of most child abuse or neglect stories. In fact, they often downplay the growing cases of abuse and neglect in our communities. Mary also learned one painful and undeniable truth: the child is always the victim. No child asks to be abused; no child asks to be neglected.

As a mother, Mary fully understands that children (especially teenagers) can sometimes push a parent to the limit, but when that parent crosses the line from discipline to abuse, or when the parent chooses addiction over caring for their child, someone needs to step in and protect that child. Mary has become one of those people, and her life has changed as a result.

Courts can punish parents, order services to teach proper anger management and parenting skills, and provide counseling for victims of domestic violence or drug abuse. However, the child's needs are sometimes lost beneath the needs of the parent. CASAs make sure that the children are not lost. They become the child's voice in court. As a CASA, Mary has helped bring valuable information into the courtroom. She has provided proof that a child will be hurt again if action isn't taken. Mary has also provided relief for foster parents and helped siblings stay in contact when they have been separated by the foster-care system. Most importantly, Mary listens to the kids. She becomes a caring, consistent, and trustworthy adult in their life—sometimes the first adult they have ever been able to trust. The children in Mary's care learn immediately that she is interested in their wellbeing. She is their advocate, and they are not alone.

Mary made a decision to become a stay-at-home mom, and that decision gave her an opportunity to grow in an area she didn't expect. Her perception of the homeless has completely changed, and she has developed a passion for helping children and families. She didn't know she had the perfect qualities within her to be of service to these important groups of people.

She told us about her passion at the end of the interview when we asked her if she had any advice for potential volunteers.

Every one of us has a passion within us that we find gives us great joy or gives us great anger. Figure out what that passion is and find a way to use it within your community. An example is my passion for at-risk kids. Kids in homeless situations or kids who are the victim of abuse and neglect are in the category of the highest at-risk kids in our community. Through my work with IHN and CASA, I can reach out to these kids and their families. I can help them find success, security, and happiness in their lives.

Hundreds of lives have blossomed because of Mary Kritenbrink's choice to step out of her comfort zone. And Mary will be the first one to tell you that her life has bloomed, too. Her ability to make personal connections with people in need has dramatically changed her from the inside out. It is also giving her children an example of a life well lived—a model to emulate. Stay-at-home moms don't just stay at home. They are a force for change and love and hope.

A Single Idea

"It takes only a single idea, a single action to move the world."

That is the motto of Spanda Inc. and its founder Dr. DeAnn Fitzgerald. We discovered the limitless power of this simple motto when we interviewed Dr. Fitzgerald.

Dr. DeAnn Fitzgerald has incredible focus. Maybe that's why she is an excellent optometrist. She has a straightforward and joyful approach to life that has led her directly into some amazing situations. She's not the type of volunteer who responds to requests for aid—she sees an opportunity, goes for it, and encourages others to follow. She is a leader among volunteers—one of the ones who lights the fires and leads the charge.

DeAnn Fitzgerald's enthusiasm for life and the opportunities it holds every day is enticing. Her interview left us with butterflies of excitement and a churning feeling deep inside to do more. She inspires everyone around her to get into motion. To her, it's not complicated. It only takes one single action to get the ball rolling.

DeAnn Fitzgerald grew up in Centerville, a small town in southern Iowa that boasts about six thousand people, mostly descendents of immigrants who came to the area to work in coalmines. She was very fortunate that both of her parents had college educations. Her mother was a nurse, and her dad was a pharmacist.

DeAnn's grandparents farmed in northern Iowa. That was also a gift, because it allowed DeAnn to spend the summers of her youth helping out on their farm. She loved caring for the animals, and that led to a lifelong pursuit of caring for living creatures, great and small.

Valuable mentors showed up in strategic positions throughout DeAnn's young life, and their wisdom shaped her into a person who is deeply involved in a greater humanity today. One woman in particular—Dr. Marilyn Heinke—was quite influential in DeAnn's decision to become an optometrist. DeAnn met Dr. Heinke on a career day at school. Dr. Heinke was an optometrist and also a very unique woman. She was a trailblazer, the only woman in her class in optometry school. Dr. Heinke was also a widow and a mother of four. This woman had overcome tremendous hurdles in her life, and she wanted to pass on her passion for medicine. She offered DeAnn a summer job, and DeAnn eagerly accepted. Dr. Heinke had two practices, one in Wisconsin and one in Iowa, and DeAnn quickly became her chauffer when she discovered that Dr. Heinke enjoyed reading while driving between the two locations. Not only was the summer safer for all drivers on the roads between Wisconsin and Iowa, but it was also a turning point for DeAnn. She had applied to pharmacy school and to law school and had been accepted to both, but a conversation with Dr. Heinke helped her make an important decision.

How did Dr. Heinke talk you into becoming an optometrist?

Dr. Heinke asked me what I thought of optometry. I said, well, it is very fascinating, but I will probably go to pharmacy school. She told me to ask my dad how he likes his job. I said, well, I already know—he doesn't really like it all that well. Then she said every day I get up, I love what I do. My job is a hobby. Every day I have this hobby I get to do. Her words stuck with me.

DeAnn paid attention to her mentor and she blazed her own trail, becoming one of only seven women in her class to graduate from optometry school. She picked up the ball when Dr. Heinke passed it off to her. Today, over 52 percent of optometrists are women.

Obviously, DeAnn Fitzgerald is a bright and driven woman. But how does volunteerism fit into her history?

Has volunteerism always been part of your life?

My first thought when I saw that question was, gosh, I don't know if I was a very good volunteer growing up. I guess I did different things with my folks. I remember doing things for church, and we also volunteered to paint our school building when I was in the third or fourth grade.

But there was a trigger point for me in volunteering when I got to Pacific University. I was in my first year of undergraduate, and I told the softball coach that I would love to do a pitching clinic. We advertised it as a free clinic. Young women were invited to come out and see what we had to offer. It was the 1980s, and softball wasn't that big yet, so we didn't expect a huge turnout. Well, over four hundred young women between the ages of six and fourteen years old showed up. It was a fabulous camp! We had a great time, and from that day forward, Pacific University offers the camp every year.

Even as a freshman in college, DeAnn was lighting fires. She didn't respond to a request from the softball coach. She went to the coach with her own idea—a single idea. That was all it took to put things in motion.

Fast forward to 2006. DeAnn was now Dr. Fitzgerald. She had been practicing optometry for about sixteen years and opened her own practice in 2004. She went to hear a missionary speak about

Kenya and was very moved by her story. Dr. Fitzgerald continued to correspond with the missionary via email.

In one conversation, DeAnn told the missionary woman about a race she was training for called the Pig Man. It's a half-mile swim, fifteen-mile bike ride, and a three-mile run. The woman's reaction was interesting. She wrote, *If you want adventure, why don't you come over to Kenya and bounce around in a Jeep?*

It didn't take long for DeAnn to light another fire. She wrote back, *The only way I'll come is if I can bring eye care.*

That conversation launched a whirlwind of preparation. DeAnn passed on her excitement to her staff, and they started collecting supplies and used glasses. Pretty soon her patients caught the spark, and they got involved, too. Between staff, patients, friends, and family members, DeAnn raised nearly $25,000 in her very first fundraiser. She has a unique knack for encouraging people to show up and offer their support.

Eight months later, a team of four took their first trip to Kenya: Dr. Fitzgerald and Dr. Ellen Miller, optometrists; and Roy Brandt and Laurie Beaurivage, opticians. They had twenty-seven bags and boxes of eyeglasses and equipment and $25,000.

Why all that cash?

They were told that they were going to have to buy their way into the country.

Three days before the trip, DeAnn made another bold move:

> I decided that I wasn't going to buy my way into the country. First of all, I didn't know if I would go to jail for bribery. I didn't want to do that. Plus, I just thought it was wrong. So I told everybody on the team, I said, you know what? If we get up there, and we can't get into the country, we are not going to buy our way in. We're just going to take our bags and call it a vacation. They were like, WHAT?!

Dr. Fitzgerald was true to her word. When they got to customs, they were stopped.

"What is all this worth?" the customs officer growled.

"In the United States it's not worth anything," DeAnn replied calmly.

"Oh, come now!"

Dr. Fitzgerald went at it with the customs officer for over two and a half hours. All the while she was giving the worried missionary on the other side of the barricade a smile and a thumbs-up.

"Is there anyone else I can talk to?" DeAnn asked finally.

"What? No! I am it! It is 11:30 at night!" The customs officer scoffed and rubbed his eyes.

"Okay," DeAnn said, not wearing down in the slightest. "Is there anything we can do? Because, you know, we came here to help."

It was like the hair on the customs officer's arms stood on end. He stared at her for a long moment, and then he spoke.

"I know your heart is with our Kenyan people. Take your stuff and go. Now!"

Seconds later the team of four was running through the airport with their things, just in case the customs officer changed his mind.

They arrived at their destination—an orphanage in Kipkaren—tired and a little apprehensive, but they got right to work. They were ushered into a dining hall where they started to set up their equipment for the examinations. That's where they hit the next hitch in their plan. They forgot to bring the stand for the phoropter (the gadget you look through when the optometrist asks you which one is better, one or two).

Dr. Fitzgerald quickly took control of the situation. She was shown to a plumbing room where she started to use various items to build a makeshift stand. Once it was ready, they hauled the heavy stand into position.

As they finished setting up, a gentleman approached them and pointed to some writing at the base of the stand, "Do you know what this is?"

Obviously none of them had a clue.

"Well, right now it's our phoropter stand," Dr. Fitzgerald grinned at the man.

"That's where we get bovine semen from," the man smiled back.

They quickly covered the writing with a blanket so none of their patients would be alarmed when they saw it.

Their start was a little shaky, but that small team of four people saw over six hundred patients on their first trip. At one point, Dr. Fitzgerald stepped away to take a breather, and Roy walked over and sat down next to her for a moment.

"So Doc, how are you feeling?" he asked.

"Roy, I am so far out of my comfort zone, it just doesn't matter."

Why would four people from Iowa go to a place halfway across the world to do this?

Actually, DeAnn Fitzgerald wrestled with that very question. Before they even left the United States, she was wondering about the wisdom of what she was doing.

> I had to really think about why we were going over there. There was no running water, no electricity, and very little food, and we were bringing them eye glasses? They can't eat a pair of glasses. I asked several of my mentors if this was the right thing. Is this what I should be doing?

DeAnn's concerns were completely removed at the end of the first day. That's when they met Esther. They saw well over sixty-eight children that first day, but Esther stood out. Her eyesight was very poor, so she needed a strong prescription. When they fit her with a pair of glasses, she was elated.

The next day, Esther's mother came back to talk to Dr. Fitzgerald.

"You saw Esther yesterday," she said.

"Oh, yes," DeAnn recalled, nodding her head. "How does she like her glasses?"

"They are wonderful," the mother could not stop smiling. "She can see her father now at the end of the lane. You know, Esther is the brightest of all my children, and she wants to become a doctor."

That would have been enough right there to make the entire trip worthwhile, but there is more to this story. Esther was, indeed, very bright. She was a straight-A student, and that should have earned her a scholarship to the University of Kenya. But because of the political unrest in 2008, her credentials were somehow lost, and Esther was denied entrance. All of her hard work didn't pay off in the end.

Wait—it gets better.

Dr. Fitzgerald took action again. She had a single idea, and she got together a few friends to make it happen. Esther is now a freshman at Mount Mercy College in Cedar Rapids, Iowa—the same town where Dr. Fitzgerald has her optometry practice. This little girl in the middle of nowhere, in a home with no running water and no electricity, is now a college student in the United States. Her dream is to become a pediatrician and go back home and care for the people in her village.

Another gift came from the inaugural trip in 2006: Julius. Julius is a bright and willing member of the village. DeAnn and her colleagues trained him on how to use the optometry equipment. Now Julius continues to treat people in the village and surrounding areas year around. When he has questions about a patient and is unsure what to do, he communicates with Dr. Fitzgerald via the Internet to get her advice. That's another thing the team of four left behind—a satellite dish.

In 2006, the weary team of four left their equipment and reading glasses behind in the care of Julius, and as they were getting ready to leave, the village chief came to talk to Dr. Fitzgerald.

"You are leaving?" he asked with a frown.

"Yes, we need to go home now," Dr. Fitzgerald replied.

"When will you be back?"

Dee Ann could hear her team behind her taking one giant step away from her.

"I will be back in a year," DeAnn Fitzgerald said looking directly into the chief's eyes.

"Let's shake on it," he suggested.

As the two new friends shook hands, DeAnn said, "My word is all I have, and it's good. I'll see you in a year."

DeAnn Fitzgerald didn't go back on her word.

After that first trip, Spanda Inc. was official, and DeAnn Fitzgerald's life will never be the same. Spanda means movement. The mission of Spanda Inc. is to combine optometry with other healthcare specialties to improve the lives of all individuals—regardless of age or personal situations—throughout the world. DeAnn and her colleagues proved that a single idea, a single action can move the world.

Did any of your team return with you the next year?

Well, that's an interesting question. Roy Brandt, one of the opticians, can take a pretzel and turn it into the most awesome pair of glasses. He was the one on that first trip who kept saying oh, Doc, they are going to ask you back. What are you going to do? He kept saying I don't think I can come back. Of course, he hasn't been able to put his hand down since. He has been on almost every subsequent trip with me.

What did you do with the $25,000?

When we got back home, we started talking about it, and we decided that we would take that money and build a clinic in Kipkaren. Half of it is dedicated to optometry, and the other half is dedicated to medical/dental.

When we went back in 2007, we were in for a surprise. I heard the clinic was moving along well, but I didn't know how far they had gotten. There were five of us this time—three in optometry; Michele Burnes, a physician's assistant; and Sharon Dieter, who is an

ER nurse. And we had another twenty-seven boxes of supplies. I guess twenty-seven is our lucky number.

We got over there just as they finished building the clinic, so we had a golden opportunity to be there for the opening. The celebration was so cool! We had warm pop in those small glass bottles from the old days, and they planted one of the most precious trees of Kenya in our honor. It was fabulous.

As soon as the opening festivities were complete, the team of five started seeing patients. The word had gotten out that they would be there, and people came from all of the surrounding areas.

One man got up at four o'clock in the morning. He had ironed his pants the day before, and he was on the road walking to his mother's hut long before the sun came up. He arrived at his eighty-year-old mother's home an hour later, and the two of them took a bus, a bicycle taxi, and walked for over three hours to get to the clinic.

They were very nervous when they arrived and saw the huge line of people waiting, but they got a number and hoped for the best. The man's mother had not been able to see for a long time. She had very dense cataracts.

At about one o'clock in the afternoon, Dr. Fitzgerald examined the old woman and fitted her with a pair of reading glasses. The only thing this woman wanted was to read her Bible again. The clinic represented a tiny bit of hope for her.

At about three o'clock in the afternoon, one of the staff saw her sitting outside and approached the elderly woman. They asked her how she was doing and if she had a good experience in the clinic. She looked up at the staff person and tapped her glasses.

"This is God," she said.

The woman's son called the director of the clinic late that night to thank them again for everything they had done. He had just dropped off his mother at her hut, and he had another hour to go to get to his own home, but he had to say thank you one more time for the gift his mother received. They had no running water, no electricity, and not much food, but they had a cell phone to make that call!

Another gentleman who stands out from that trip was a twenty-four year old man named Simon. When Dr. Fitzgerald saw him, he was very sad. He was a teacher, but he could barely see the blackboard in front of him. The prescription he needed was so strong that Dr. Fitzgerald could not make it in Kenya. She had to take it back in the States and then send the glasses through a missionary group in hopes that he would get them.

Dr. Fitzgerald had no idea what happened to Simon, until she caught up with him on their latest trip in 2009. She thought she saw Simon across the courtyard and walked up to him tentatively.

"Are you Simon?" DeAnn Fitzgerald asked.

"Yes, I am," he smiled broadly.

"You are wearing your glasses!"

"Yes, I am," he replied. "You made a difference in my life. When I was a teacher and I couldn't see, I thought about not teaching anymore. How do you teach if you cannot see? But I got these glasses, and now I can read and see! Now, I am the headmaster of my school."

DeAnn looked at him grinning from ear to ear, and she knew that what they were doing was important. Maybe you can't eat a pair of glasses, but the gift of sight is not something to be taken for granted.

DeAnn had just come back from their third trip in late 2009 when we interviewed her. This time they took an eye team, a medical team, a dental team, and a water team. That's right, a water team. There were wells around the clinic, but most of them were not viable—they tested very high for bacteria. There is only one good well, and it is by the children's home.

Spanda Inc. partnered with another group to see if they could work together to dig a new well. As of May 2010, the well was being dug, with the Kipkaren villagers shouting, "Maji ni Uhai!" Water is life!

Why is the water team so important to add to what you are doing?

Everyone in the world wants the same thing. We want a roof over our heads, nourishment on the table, and clothes on our backs. Those are the basics, and clean drinking water is part of those basics. One billion people in the world do not have clean drinking water; 42 percent of those people reside in Kenya.

We took over filters and chlorinators for the villagers to use while we did the necessary research for digging a well. What was really neat was we gave one chlorinator to a woman named Betty. She has been diagnosed with HIV, and she is doing well with treatment, but clean water is essential to her survival. She was one of the first people to get a chlorinator. We found out on our last trip that Betty is using the chlorinator, and she is also helping six other families by distributing water to them. It's that ripple effect that really sets things in motion.

A gentleman by the name of William got the second chlorinator. He is so clever! He contacted the Kenyan government, because he wants to get permission to make chlorinated water in bulk and distribute it to people who need it.

Sometimes I hear uninformed people say things like, well, they probably like living that way. But when you see what just two people are doing with the chlorinators, we know that they absolutely do not want to live that way. They want to improve their conditions and help everyone else around them. They have such a different model in Kenya. I mean, sometimes our model is to hold things close. Their model is to set things free. They don't have a lot, but what they have, they share.

How long do you stay when you take these trips to Kenya?

We go for a very short period of time. This year, we were there from October 7 through October 17. We go for such a short time because, while we are there to help, we are also draining their very precious resources when we visit. We have to be extremely careful about that. Even though we take most of our own stuff, we are still using their water and various other incidental things. We have actually changed how they do mission work there. Mission groups used to go for two to five weeks. Now, they go for a few days, and it works out much better for the village.

What are your dreams for the future of Spanda Inc.?
Our first dream is to get clean water to Kipkaren. Then, we will continue to work to increase the services the clinic offers.

When I was over there this last time, I went up to the northern part of Kenya to a place called Korr. I met with an amazing couple, Lynn and Nick Swanepoel. They have been missionaries in the northern part of Korr for thirty-two years, and they have been working very closely with the Rendilles, which is a tribe in that region.

Nick and Lynn are unbelievable people. The Rendilles had no written language, and Nick has been able to give them a written language. He has translated stories, numerous books, about 82 percent of the New Testament, and 32 percent of the Old Testament into their language. It is awesome that he gave them their own language to read, instead of forcing them to learn a new one.

Right now, they are in the middle of a horrendous drought in Korr. They desperately need a well. I asked Lynn what it would take for us to find out if they have water nearby. She said a water survey costs $2,000. I said okay; let's see what we can do. She kind of looked at me like, are you serious?

We are learning that there is a model that works in this particular environment. First, set up communications; second, dig a well; and third, set up a health clinic. We reversed the order of the well and the clinic in Kipkaren, and we learned that it would have been better to dig the well first. Lynn and Nick in Korr have step one in place already, and we are helping them with step two, digging a well. Step three for them will be building a clinic.

She took one trip to Korr in October of 2009, and already DeAnn has a plan. Anyone who knows Dr. DeAnn Fitzgerald knows she's absolutely serious about lending a hand to those in need. No doubt she'll raise the money for that water survey and work with the Swanepoels and the Rendille tribe to dig a well.

DeAnn Fitzgerald is most definitely in motion in Kenya, but she is also getting things moving in the United States. She recently started a clinic in Cedar Rapids, Iowa, and the overall goal is very similar—setting those in need in motion.

Tell us about your clinic in Cedar Rapids.

I have two clinics in Cedar Rapids. One clinic is Dr. Fitzgerald and Associates. We do basic eye care: eye exams, glasses, contact lenses, that kind of stuff. Then, we have a second clinic called CR Vision in Motion. It was a brainstorm that came out of looking at children and adults who are challenged, whether it is from a traumatic brain injury, a stroke, a learning disability, low vision, or whatever their challenge may be, but vision is a primary concern. We help them, no matter what their means, to be able to live safely in their homes. It is empowering their future, so that they can stay in their homes and live a better quality of life.

My philosophy and the philosophy of the clinic is that if you get them in motion, we can help them attain those goals more quickly. When you get people in motion, you change their state of being. It's not just a philosophy; it is backed up by scientific research. When you are in motion, your body releases a chemical called BDNF (Brain-Derived Neurotrophic Factor), and it is fertilizer for the brain.

We also work with young people, a lot of kids with ADD/ADHD, autism, and Asperger's. When we get them in motion, we speed up their ability to succeed in reaching their goals.

Now, if there was anyone you could pick for your team, wouldn't it be Dr. DeAnn Fitzgerald? She is a winner and a fearless leader. Dr. Fitzgerald encourages everyone around her to get into motion and accomplish great things.

There are hundreds of examples of how DeAnn Fitzgerald positively affects others. But how has helping others affected her? Her answer was short and to the point.

How has volunteerism affected your quality of life?
It has allowed me to solidify what I believe: living is giving. There is absolutely no way you can be depressed if you are giving to someone else.

That says it all. Dr. DeAnn Fitzgerald is living an amazingly rewarding life simply by giving. She gives her ideas, her time, her expertise, and her love to people far away from home and people in her own backyard. How could she possibly be depressed?

Just a Hammer and Nails (and a few blisters)

Moving back into the family circle for a moment, we interviewed Kelly's cousins John and Janice Wiitala, who have been very involved in Habitat for Humanity. This huge and highly visible organization is an ecumenical Christian ministry founded on the conviction that every man, woman, and child should have a decent, safe, and affordable place to live. Habitat for Humanity builds with (not just for) people in need, regardless of race or religion. As of April 2010, Habitat for Humanity had built over 350,000 houses around the world, providing more than 1.75 million people in 3,000 communities with safe, decent, affordable shelter.

Janice lives in Chicago and John lives in Houston, so it took a little strategic planning for them to find a building project together. One year they decided to take a brother-sister bonding trip outside of their comfort zone when they participated in a Habitat for Humanity blitz build in Korea. We corresponded with Janice via email to learn more about their experience. The following is an excerpt In Janice's own words from their incredible journey:

> I always respected the organization. But really, I got involved with Habitat for Humanity when John asked. He had been involved in a Houston build the prior year and was organizing a group to go to Korea for one of their international blitz builds. While there were a number of people interested in

going early on, the group whittled down to just the two of us closer to deadline. John asked me if I still wanted to go.

I really did it to spend time with my brother. It's rare as an adult to get one-on-one time. I didn't want to miss the opportunity. I knew it would be a great volunteer experience, but I was a little selfish in my motivation.

It was great to spend time with him on the Habitat projects. In Korea we shared a dorm room, slept on mats, and spent 24/7 together. Now that John and his wife, Joy, have a daughter, his vacation time revolves around family, as it should. I'm glad we took time out for that trip. He told me it would be the best vacation I would ever take, and he was right.

In Korea it was over 100 degrees during the day. We'd come home each night dirty and sweaty from the job site. First thing was clean up. I still remember how good it felt to be clean and in air conditioning. Then we'd head down to dinner and talk with other volunteers (people from Korea, Africa, Japan, the Philippines, and all over the U.S.).

I was in pain every night—but a good pain. Since I was low skill, they gave me a hammer. I hammered frames, I hammered roofing, I hammered siding. They would point at it, and I would hammer. The first day John looked at me and said, "You can't hammer like that all day." He taught me how to swing a hammer—in true big-brother form. I was tap-tapping by swinging my wrist instead of leveraging my arm. Even though he corrected me, I had a blister the size of a silver dollar and a swollen wrist that first night. I got a bit of a rhythm later on.

We registered late. Us, late? Shocking, I know. So when we got to the site, they hadn't assigned us a house. There were forty homes to be built. The first night we met a great family from Arizona, the Crowleys. They had been on multiple builds together. Mimi (the mom) said, "Aren't you cute, how you're so cute," when she found out we were brother and sister on the trip together. They adopted us for the duration of the project and brought us over to join their house.

Since the Crowleys had been on multiple builds, they were working on one of the more prestigious houses right next to the "Jimmy Carter House." President Carter is actually a crafted woodworker, and he and Rosalynn are very committed to the cause. Since we were also working on a special house, President Carter joined our house dedication. John was standing right next to him during the prayer where we join hands. Cool, right? That wasn't our first encounter with Jimmy and Rosalynn.

One night we were late to dinner. Us, late? I know, shocking! The dining hall was pretty full, but surprisingly there were a couple tables in the middle of the room that were wide open. We sat down. Come to find out, the tables were reserved for Jimmy and Rosalynn Carter. Oops. We noticed the secret service. I guess they realized we were harmless, so they allowed us to stay. Rosalynn sat a table over and introduced herself. She's so gracious. The international blitz build used to be JCWP—The Jimmy Carter Work Project. It's now the Jimmy and Rosalynn Carter Work Project.

I should mention that John ended up standing next to Jimmy during our house dedication because we were finishing up something inside and slid out the door at the last minute. Technically, we weren't late, but we really weren't on time for the dedication. Lesson learned: being late is okay.

After the trip to Korea, we also went to Anniston, Alabama on a Habitat blitz build. We intentionally signed up with the Crowleys. I mentioned Mimi Crowley. During the Anniston build, we also got to know Bob Senior and Bob Junior. They are pretty experienced builders. (I know, Bob the Builder.)

A coworker of mine brought his family, and one of John's friends came, as well. My coworker Dan is a model volunteer. He makes me want to be a better citizen. He probably goes home and volunteers an additional forty hours each month for Habitat, his church, his local fire department... Anyway, he's a very experienced volunteer builder and leads a group each summer on a local Habitat build. Between Dan, my brother, the Crowleys, and others, we had a pretty skilled team.

In Habitat, the leaders are selected because they are skilled workers. And on the build site, the leaders/skilled workers tend to work rather than lead. So you'll often have low-skilled workers waiting for someone to tell them what to do, because no one is really leading them. I was fortunate on the Korea build. I was there with my brother. John is skilled, so I was often his apprentice. Good thing he couldn't fire me. Other unskilled people would spend a lot of time waiting and wandering.

Alabama was different. Dan, my coworker, was one of the house leaders. He would walk around the house and find people without a task, teach them how to do something, and come back and check on them. He asked how people were doing, and he made them feel confident that they could learn how to rewire a room or build rafters. Of course, he knew it would be faster and easier to do the task himself, but instead he took a little more time to teach others. Our house was one of the first ones done—we even landscaped. I overheard someone else referring to our house as "The Better Homes and Gardens House."

It was a great lesson in leadership and coaching. It takes a little more time to coach someone, rather than do it yourself, but in the long run, you end up being more efficient and you have someone trained for next time. All around, the team feels a greater sense of shared achievement.

A side benefit of Habitat volunteering is learning about home construction, drywall, wiring, etc. I'm less afraid to take my sink drain apart or wire a new light now. I think everyone who owns a home should work on a Habitat build.

I love the Habitat model. They offer a hand up rather than a hand out. Recipients must meet core requirements to qualify, and they must agree to fulfill a minimum sweat equity requirement. For the head of household, it's two hundred hours. Everyone over the age of sixteen who will live in the house enters this shared partnership with Habitat.

When we built in Korea, there were family members working along with us. I remember one woman in particular. She was a nurse and had two children. This was to be her home. She and her husband had already completed their requisite sweat equity hours, but she was there with us. She drove us nuts sweeping up repeatedly. A construction site needs order, but dust free is a bit unrealistic. It struck me about the third day that this was her home, and it was important to her to keep her home clean.

So many times when we volunteer, we don't see the direct impact on the individual. During the house dedication, she explained that it is Korean custom to bow as a sign of respect, and the depth of the bow is related to the level of respect or gratitude. As she shared this, she brought her arms around and kneeled to the floor and touched her forehead to the ground as low as she could possibly bow. It still makes me teary when I think about it—a simple expression of gratitude. We all cried. Even John was tearing up.

I learned a lot about the differences in our cultures. The last night of building, we stayed late. Note: I didn't say we *were* late; we *stayed* late. John was determined to finish the trim work, so we stayed. There were five of us: John, me, the house leader, the house interpreter, and another volunteer from Korea. When we finally finished, we were among the last to leave the site. We had missed dinner, so the house leader took us out to a local diner. I don't know what I was expecting, but this casual restaurant served us in traditional Korean style—about twenty small dishes on the table served family style. I thought that the traditional style was reserved for special occasions or our equivalent of Sunday night dinners. Evidently, it was an everyday thing.

During that dinner, the house leader, Ki Noh, talked about his family and Korean business. Our interpreter, Jin-Buh, a PR professional for Korean's equivalent of eBay by day, talked about the stigma of being a single twenty-five-year-old woman in Korea. The other volunteer, Moon-Kuen, was studying architecture and wanted to design music venues. It seems like we opened ourselves up a bit more in that type of situation. I had just met them, but there was such an honest dialogue. It takes awhile to build that kind of trust in other circumstances. But I guess the experience of volunteering brought us together more quickly.

After reading this email from Janice, Eric and I were—for once—speechless. We were in awe. We had the impulse to run out and grab our own hammers! Janice and John had the courage to step out of their comfort zones. They traveled far away from home to help people they knew nothing about before the trip. The joy and satisfaction they received in return is unmistakable—the unique experiences, gained understanding of different cultures, new and lasting friendships, and of course, the strengthening of their own family bond. Once they experienced Habitat for Humanity once, they both became repeat offenders—they continue to volunteer with Habitat for Humanity whenever they get a chance.

We asked Janice if Habitat for Humanity was her first transformational volunteer experience, and we found out that it is just one of a multitude of journeys into humanity she has taken. She described the first volunteer experience that really transformed her. It happened when she was in high school:

> I think my first transformational volunteer experience was when I was involved in a school-based program aimed at

> resolving peer challenges. I was selected for the group, and at the time I felt honored. In hindsight, I realize that they designed the program to pull in students with diverse experiences and backgrounds just to get us talking to each other—not so much an honor as a gift. There was a student who had limited upper mobility, was confined to a wheel chair, and could only communicate by pointing at words on a board. I remember sitting and "talking" with him about his concerns. It was illuminating for me. He worried about his mom taking care of him and what he was going to do after high school. He was smart and thoughtful and kind. Prior to that conversation, I had judged him. Because he was physically limited, I had viewed him as mentally limited, as well. I was shallow and I was wrong. That was an important lesson: to be open-minded and not make assumptions about people.

Volunteerism has shaped Janice's life in other ways, as well. She is heavily involved in two professional fraternities that have not only given her an opportunity to serve her community, but they have also given her a venue to grow professionally and personally. She told us about a series of events that took her once again outside of her comfort zone:

> Being involved in my professional fraternity, Theta Tau Engineering Fraternity and Educational Foundation, has definitely been transformative. Fraternities often are positioned as Animal House type entities. However, the intent of most of these organizations is leadership development, personal development, and service. Professional fraternities have the added benefit of dedication to a particular course of study.
>
> In my early experience, I was asked to speak with a handful of students in front of the State of Iowa Board of Regents. We were asking them to consider funding on their

docket for an expansion for the college of engineering. I prepared my speech, but somehow got it in my head that it should be memorized. I was awful. I'm sure it was painful to watch as I stumbled through my message. It was not my finest hour.

Months later, I was asked to speak at a chapter initiation dinner. I decided not to memorize this time, but still, I was struggling. I looked up in the middle of the speech and saw a friend. He was sitting on the edge of his chair, smiling, nodding, as if I was clear and insightful. I know I wasn't, but that moment left a lasting impression. Taking risks are essential for growth. The people I was speaking to were dear friends, and I love them. If I failed in front of them or with them, they would pick me up, tell me how not to fail again, and love me anyway.

In the years since, I've spoken in front of numerous Theta Tau audiences, and this has benefitted me professionally. I speak in front of executive audiences and have facilitated team and board of director retreats. Public speaking is a core business skill. I shared that lesson at Theta Tau's biennial leadership academy. The point is—this is a safe place to take risks. It's a safe place to fail. We encourage each other to take risks.

I'm on the leader side now, and I see young, eager students ("aren't they cute, how they're so cute"). I will meet them at their first national meeting, bright eyed, nervous to introduce themselves to the group. And then flash forward a couple years—they are leading sessions in front of hundreds of students, confident and poised. Engineers tend to be more introverted, and the transformation is amazing to witness.

I have also had the great benefit of working for HFMA, a personal membership association for leaders in healthcare finance. We are graced with thousands of volunteers. Our member base is primarily executive level. Even so, members find the time to give back to healthcare and to each other. I see firsthand how my colleagues in this organization take time out to share ideas and experiences with others. They also network and establish friendships. It is not uncommon for volunteers to plan family vacations with their counterparts. These friendships form the basis for professional networks; these networks advance individuals in their jobs and help them find new roles. Most importantly, the knowledge gained helps healthcare organizations make better use of their resources so that they can continue to provide great care to their communities.

Janice and John...and Dr. Fitzgerald...and Mary Kritenbrink are not afraid to step out of their comfort zones anymore. In fact, they go out of the safe zone on purpose—and often. They know about the rewards on the other side. They know what it feels like to grow and transform, and they want more of that. The connections with humanity they have gained—the understanding and appreciation of people around them—are enormous. One cannot achieve that kind of transformation without action.

Are you a person who is willing to step across the line and experience a brief sense of discomfort in order to gain experiences you can only imagine at this moment? Give it a try. Find out what lies beyond the comfort zone. The journey will be worth it.

10

CREATING A LEGACY

THROUGHOUT THE FORTY-PLUS INTERVIEWS WE CONDUCTED, THE WORD legacy continued to pop up—like a beach ball persistently rising from under the water and bursting through the surface of stories we collected. We finally decided to stop ignoring it and swim after it. We started with a simple definition to focus in on how legacy relates to volunteerism.

According to *Merriam-Webster*, a legacy is a gift or bequest from an ancestor or predecessor. Traditionally, a legacy is something valuable, such as money or property. We're not the first two people to recognize that legacy may also refer to intangible things—such as knowledge or wisdom—that are learned and passed from one generation to the next.

When we looked back through the first eight chapters of this book, we realized we had already seen evidence of legacies of volunteerism—even through our own family stories. We have personally experienced what a gift it is to grow up within a legacy of giving.

In this chapter, we will focus on three interviews that solidified for us the value of creating a legacy of volunteerism. It is interesting to note that not all legacies are passed down from parent to child. In fact, the first story we will share illustrates the beautiful legacy a daughter left to her mother.

Pint-Size Inspiration

At age four, Alexandra Flynn Scott went to her mother in their home in Pennsylvania and voiced one simple wish.

"I want to have a lemonade stand."

Many parents have heard similar requests voiced by pint-size entrepreneurs all over the country, but this one was different—Alex had cancer.

Alex's goal was not to make enough money to buy a bike or a doll or a video game. She had a much bigger plan in mind—to raise funds to help doctors find cures for all childhood cancers. She knew it might be too late for her, but she wanted to be part of an effort that made a difference in the lives of other children.

Liz Scott gazed at her little girl in disbelief. When her daughter needed a miracle of her own, her thoughts were not on herself. She was thinking about other kids.

Alex Scott did get that lemonade stand. Her parents helped her make her wish come true. Liz stood close by and watched her daughter work in the stand on that very first day. Alex's smile was bright with hope and a true sense of accomplishment.

When Liz put her daughter to bed later that night, Alex told her mom a little secret.

"This was the best day of my life."

At that moment, Alex gave her mother a priceless gift—a legacy.

"It was an amazing feeling to see my daughter, who was fighting a deadly disease, be authentically happy and accomplished," Liz recounted. "Volunteerism was a true gift for her, and she passed that gift on to me. She inspired me to reach out and make a difference, too. I think it gave my daughter happiness unlike anything else."

The precious legacy that Alex gave her mother appeared prominently throughout our interview with Liz Scott:

Has volunteerism always been part of your life?

Yes, I think volunteerism has always been a part of my life. However, within the last ten years, it has become so much more a part of my everyday life. Of course, I myself have volunteered and continue to do so through lemonade stands. But more than anything, it is the volunteers that help carry on my daughter's legacy of hope that I am thankful for. Alex's Lemonade Stand Foundation for

Childhood Cancer honestly could not exist without the thousands of volunteers who hold lemonade stands every year. To this day, nearly half of our funds come from these front-yard lemonade stands held by volunteers. They are allowing us to fund research at leading hospitals and institutions, as well as help nurses improve the quality of life and care for childhood cancer patients and their families, assist families who face the need to travel for their child's cancer treatment, and so much more. These volunteers are truly making a difference in my life, but I think more importantly, they are making a difference in the lives of children fighting the disease. They are an integral part of finding the cure.

When did you first discover the joy of volunteering?

I think I first discovered the joy of volunteering when my daughter Alex held one of her very first lemonade stands to fight childhood cancer. It was something that she had wanted to do for quite some time, and when she finally had her stand, I understood why it was so important. The lemonade stand gave Alex a purpose of sorts, an outlet to turn something negative into something positive.

This one may be obvious, but we'll ask it anyway. Was there a specific person who encouraged you to volunteer?

Absolutely! It was daughter Alex. At the age of four, Alex voiced a simple wish—she wanted to hold a lemonade stand to raise funds to help doctors find a cure for all childhood cancers, including her own.

Alex taught me so much about life, including doing good for others. Though Alex was raising funds that would likely not be able to save her life, she saw the bigger picture—that if she started this volunteer movement, she could make the lives of other children suffering from cancer better.

Sometimes it makes me sad to think that Alex was not able to reap the benefits of what she started, but I know she wouldn't think that way. She would be proud of the work that has been done...but I think she'd want more too. She was such an inspiring individual, and I know that I carry on my own volunteerism in her honor.

What volunteer projects over the years have really inspired you?

I have seen so many amazing volunteer projects over the years, but I think what has inspired me the most is the kids, much like Alex, who have an innate sense of how they are making a difference. It is so amazing to watch kids volunteer, because you know that this is really what they want to be doing, and that they want to help people. I think that as adults, sometimes we lose sight of how much good we can do by simply holding a lemonade stand or spending a few hours at a food bank. But I think kids have a different view. Alex knew what was possible, and I have seen so many kids since then—both those who are fighting cancer and those who just want to help—know that they are part of the change.

Tell us about Alex.

Gosh, there are so many things to say about Alex that I don't know where to begin.

Alex was the second of four children, and the only girl. She was special from the moment she was born. She was born prematurely, and they warned us that she might be small, but of course, she came into the world screaming and healthy.

Unfortunately, as the first year of Alex's life went by, I noticed that something just wasn't right. Instead of eating cake on her first birthday, Alex was in the hospital undergoing surgery for neuroblastoma, a form of childhood cancer.

Something happened within the next few months that really proved who Alex was. There was a complication during the surgery, and doctors told us that she would never walk again. Without any feeling in her legs, Alex taught herself how to walk, overcoming one of the first—but not the last—obstacles in her life. Alex was determined to live her life to the fullest, to overcome any barriers, and to help others. I cannot express in words how proud I am of her and how she continues to inspire me each and every day.

Alex was an incredible human being. I take my cues from her to this day. My life is better because Alex was in it, and though, of course, I would rather have her here with me, she has left me with a gift, her foundation, which allows me to keep a part of her with me always.

Did Alex surprise you when she came up with her idea of having a lemonade stand to fight cancer?

I am not sure if Alex surprised me so much with the idea for the lemonade stand to help other children with cancer, but her determination and dedication were certainly surprising. Initially, we thought that Alex would hold one stand, raise some money for her hospital, and that would be the end of it. That certainly wasn't the case. Alex raised $2,000 on the very first day of her first stand! But the day hadn't even ended when she started talking about the next stand.

What is your dream for the future of Alex's Lemonade Stand for Childhood Cancer?

I think my dream is simple: I want the foundation bearing Alex's name to improve the lives of children and their families facing cancer. Of course, the ultimate dream is to find cures for all childhood cancers, and I think that we'll get there one day.

In the meantime, it is so important to find ways to improve children's lives now. I know that there are better, less harsh treatments to be found. I also know that there are simple ways to improve quality of life.

So for me it's simple. I want the foundation to make the lives of children with cancer better, easier, and brighter.

Has lending a hand to someone in need changed your life?

I think the most amazing part of volunteering has been seeing other people become involved. There are so many people that we met at Alex's first lemonade stands who are still involved to this day. They are more than friends; they are family.

The Miller family comes to mind. They first became involved with ALSF in 2005, led by fifteen-year-old Riley Miller. She holds her stand in memory of her two younger brothers who lost their lives to childhood cancer, Reid and Randon Miller. The Millers started fundraising after losing their first son Reid, and prior to one of the initial stands, Randon lost his battle as well. In their memory, the Millers and their friends and family host community-wide Alex's Lemonade Stands every year. The stories are amazing of how people get involved and how they are inspired to mobilize their friends and family, as well.

They have all helped to change my life, and they changed Alex's life, too. They allowed her to achieve her dream of raising $1 million in her lifetime. It's funny how something as simple as holding lemonade stands to help other kids with cancer has really been so rewarding to me personally, and to my family.

If someone was considering getting involved in a volunteer project but was hesitant, what would you tell them?

I would simply tell them to give it a try. The great thing about volunteerism is that it doesn't take a large amount of time to make a difference. You can spend just a few hours building someone a home, working at a food bank, or of course holding a lemonade stand. If you don't feel accomplished at the end of the day, you can try something else.

Have volunteer activities improved your quality of life?

Absolutely, 100 percent. Not only have volunteer activities improved my quality of life, but they have changed my life. Losing my daughter was probably the hardest thing that I have ever had to go through in life. Through my own volunteer experiences and the continuing support from volunteers across the country, I have been given the gift of continuing Alex's legacy.

Every single volunteer who holds a lemonade stand or an event in the foundation's name is a part of the difference we are making in the childhood cancer world. My life is better because of volunteer activities. My life has a purpose. And this allows me to always be connected to my daughter.

Alex lost her life to cancer in 2004 at the age of eight, but her dream continues to grow every day. Alex's Lemonade Stand received national attention shortly after she got started. Soon Volvo offered to become a sponsor of Alex's Lemonade Stand. The organization helped Alex raise over $1 million to fight childhood cancer in her lifetime. Now other kids and adults have taken up where Alex left off, and they continue to raise millions of dollars to fight childhood cancer.

Never underestimate the power of one little four-year-old girl with a very big heart and a very bright soul.

Tiggers, Too

Alex left a golden legacy for her mother. Now, we will flip the coin and get to know a mother who is building a precious legacy for her daughters.

Christine Jones is a single mom who successfully balances a law career with raising two active young daughters. We wondered about what a scheduling nightmare it must be for Chris to juggle her own commitments with soccer games, new puppies, school activities, riding lessons, and whatever else her daughters enjoy; but Chris smiles like a Cheshire cat in the middle of it all. She exudes joy and contentment—the eye in the middle of a storm of activity. And did we mention she does black-and-white photography on the side?

Chris's Centennial, Colorado home was vibrant with action when we interviewed her in December of 2009. For dessert, Hunter and Hayden, her two daughters, picked a piece of candy from a gingerbread house in the center of the kitchen table, and then they dashed off to find new opportunities for play. In the meantime, two adorable black and brown puppies slipped and slid around the kitchen floor at Chris's feet, begging to go outside. Suddenly, Chris gave the word, and the whirlwind of girls and puppies vanished within about two seconds. Hunter and Hayden escaped to the basement playroom and the puppies to the backyard. In sudden quietness, we found ourselves alone in her living room conducting the interview.

Chris started out by telling us a little about her past. She grew up on the East Coast in Greenwich, Connecticut.

"My parents were essentially products of the early sixties," Chris smiled. "When I was very young, my dad had long hair, and many of our family friends were hippies."

We also found out that Chris's parents were very cognizant of the power of volunteering. Chris's mother helped run the Connecticut branch of the Fresh Air Fund, which is an organization that provides free summer activities in the country for New York City children from disadvantaged communities. Several inner-city children lived with them every summer, and her parents continued to communicate with the children after their visits. Chris's mother also volunteered part-time as a tutor in the schools.

The legacy of volunteering reaches even further back. Chris mentioned that her grandparents—grandmothers in particular—were very active in their communities. Her paternal grandmother volunteered at the Smithsonian, and the maternal one was politically active—marching with Martin Luther King and lending her passion to various causes. Chris's family tree is ripe with the fruit of open-minded people who have continually been compelled to get involved in their communities and help wherever they can.

In high school, Chris became a competitive swimmer, and that led to another opportunity for volunteering. She used her skills as a swimmer to help at a rehabilitation facility for individuals with severe physical disabilities.

"I worked in the pool primarily with physically challenged children. Some of their disabilities stemmed from accidents; others suffered from spina bifida or other significant birth conditions. Most were confined to a wheelchair…but it's amazing what people can do in water that they can't do on land." Chris's face glowed as she recalled this experience from her young adulthood.

The rehab center volunteer experience led to many years as a volunteer for the Special Olympics once Chris completed college, and she remembers those years as some of her most rewarding volunteer experiences ever.

"You know, the thing that I loved most about volunteering with the Special Olympics was the exuberance of the children!" Her signature grin reappeared. "You'll have six children swimming in six lanes, and the one who comes in last is just as happy as the one who comes in first."

When Chris was a young lawyer, she moved to Washington, D.C., and there she had yet another opportunity to serve others through D.C. Cares.

"That organization was incredibly well run," Chris recalled. "It was wonderful, because D.C. is such a big city, and, through D.C. Cares, working adults have the opportunity to volunteer in so many different areas and in ways that fit their individual schedules. As a young lawyer, I didn't have a lot of free time, so I helped out in the soup kitchens in the morning. I would wake up at five o'clock, walk to a church right downtown near the White House, and serve there before I went to work."

It's obvious that volunteering has always been part of Chris's life, and she has taken advantage of a wide variety of opportunities to focus less on herself and more on where help is needed. However, she told us that there was a time when she limited her volunteering. It was shortly after she moved to Colorado, about fifteen years prior to our interview. The change of environment and added responsibility of one, and then two, daughters caused her to back off a little on her volunteer commitments, but she continued to lend a hand when she had the opportunity.

As Chris's daughters grew, she had an increased sense of the need to refocus their lives. She knew that her children had many opportunities that other children did not have, and she wanted to find a way to show them how to be empathetic and helpful to others without feeling better than. It's not an easy lesson to teach a child who has never gone hungry, a child who has been loved and cared for by a strong parent who makes her feel safe and valued. Chris wanted to create a legacy of compassion for her daughters, and she wanted to do it through actions rather than words.

An average night on the couch in front of the TV ended up giving Chris her epiphany. Chris recounts the evening that changed her life:

> It was just one of those average nights; the children were in bed and I was flipping through the channels. There was nothing on. For some reason I stopped on a news magazine program that was running a segment on an individual named Randy Pausch, of whom I knew nothing about. Within a few minutes, I was glued to the TV and sobbing by the end of the hour. It was probably one of the defining moments of my life. I saw a young man who was dying from a horrendous illness. He was giving this last lecture as a professor at Carnegie-Mellon—and he was happy! He didn't look back at his life with regret, even though he had two small children and a wife that he was leaving.
>
> Randy Pausch delivered his last lecture at Carnegie-Mellon, but he really wrote the lecture for his children more than anyone. It's a handbook on how to live a great life—a legacy for his children. I realized then that I wanted my daughters to have a handbook, too. How could I show them?
>
> After I watched that show, I pulled up The Last Lecture on You Tube and watched the whole thing. A couple days later, I decided to form the Colorado Tiggers.

Chris had already been thinking about creating a legacy of giving for her daughters; then she saw the TV show that solidified her thoughts; and finally, she took action. That last step is the most important one.

The first thing Chris did was to look for volunteer organizations that would be open to small children. Unfortunately, her daughters were too young to take part in most volunteer opportunities. But Chris knew that the younger she could start creating her own handbook for her daughters, the better chance they would have of growing into accepting and caring adults. It was an important legacy, and she was not willing to postpone the idea.

One particular aspect of Randy Pausch's last lecture really resonated with Chris. He mentioned that it's important to go through life as a Tigger, not an Eeyore. Be a child. Dream big. Be happy. Help others. Chris could not have agreed more. Within two days of watching the TV show, she created her own volunteer organization: the Colorado Tiggers.

The mission of the Colorado Tiggers is for parents and young children to volunteer their efforts and time at least once a month to a worthy project and, in the process of doing so, improve this world and help their children to become compassionate, understanding, and giving people. In a sense, Christine and her daughters—Hunter and Hayden—are creating a legacy together.

There is no age limit for the Colorado Tiggers. In fact, Chris giggled when she admitted that their youngest member was only a few months old. They have families with newborns, and those newborns come along on their projects. The babies may not be particularly helpful, but they certainly are not excluded.

> *Never lose the childlike wonder. It's just too important.*
> *It's what drives us. Help others.*
> —Randy Pausch

Chris immediately emailed a number of her friends who had children. She invited them to come together on a certain date to talk about forming a parent-child volunteer group. To her surprise, about thirty-five adults and children showed up for the first meeting. They voted unanimously to start Colorado Tiggers, and then the children sat with the adults and worked together on what they wanted to accomplish and how. This was not a project where the parents dictated to the children what they would do. Everyone had a vote, and everyone got a chance to have a hands-on volunteer experience. At the first meeting, they came up with twelve different volunteer activities, one for each month, and families could decide which ones they wanted to attend. Colorado Tiggers was born.

We were very intrigued by the concept of a parent-child volunteer group and asked Chris exactly how the organization works. The following is her explanation:

> We have a planning meeting once a year around January or February. During that meeting, we come up with ideas for volunteer activities the group would like to do. As soon as we have twelve good ideas for the year, we assign one family to each month, and that family figures out how to make it happen and on what date.
>
> So for instance, let's just say in May we want to volunteer for a race where we hand out water to the runners. One of the families works out the details, and then an email goes out to everyone in the group. We don't want to make this too difficult for families, because it shouldn't be a hardship. If a family wants to participate in that particular volunteer activity, that's great! On the other hand, they don't have to feel compelled to take part in every activity.

When we're connected to others, we become better people.
—Randy Pausch

The Colorado Tiggers have come up with some amazing activities in their few short years of existence. They have picked up trash in parks; decorated food delivery bags for Project Heart; delivered baked goods to local firehouses on 9/11; held huge garage sales to benefit the Kunsberg School at Jewish Medical Center (an onsite day school for chronically ill children); and collected books for the Reach Out and Read program. These are just a few examples of their deep and ever-growing list of activities.

Chris is very clear about one thing—variety is good. "I don't want the children to see it as service that only involves helping people that have certain economic needs. I want them to also see that this is about the environment; it's about animals; it's about community. Helping has such a broad definition. I don't think we should be limited in the way we think about assisting other people or other things."

And the children do not just follow their parents' lead. When they collected books for Reach Out and Read, every child in the group went into his or her own room and picked out a few books that they were willing to donate. The children also do chores around the house and then use the money they earn to buy school supplies for children in need or donate to another project during the year. So it's not just moms and dads buying items and donating them on behalf of the family. The children are actively participating, too.

Is it working?

Chris has certainly noticed a difference in Hunter and Hayden. Nothing big—but she sees a series of little changes that are very exciting. The girls were only seven and five years old when we conducted the interview, but Chris was pleased. She could already see them acting in more considerate ways and seeking out opportunities to help in school and at home. She reported that ever since they cleaned up the trash in the park, both girls have been diligent about wanting to throw away trash whenever they see it. It's not exactly the most sanitary new routine, but it still makes Chris smile when one of them goes out of her way to put a plastic bottle in the trash. She draws the line at cigarette butts, though, if they're not willing to use a shovel or some rubber gloves!

"I think it's not only because of me and the Tiggers, though," Chris added. "I watch school systems now, and they are much better than they were in the past about having children get involved in giving projects. I think the community at large is doing a better job, too. There is a lot going on that fosters generosity and compassion in children."

Chris went on to add a global perspective:

The Colorado Tiggers also engage in international projects. Personally, I like the idea of volunteering both domestically and internationally. We are increasingly becoming a global society, and we need to think more along those lines. As countries become less insular, it's important for our children to embrace different cultures and, in doing so, work to create to a better world for everyone.

I had a friend who was one of the astronauts aboard the Space Shuttle Columbia when it exploded. In an email he sent to family and friends on one of the final days of the mission, he observed that, when he looked down at Earth from space, it was hard to imagine why anybody fought. The earth was so beautiful. He wrote that had he been born in space, he would have wanted to visit the beautiful Earth even more than he had ever yearned to visit space. It's a wonderful world.

And it's really true. When you think about it that way, it's just one world. I think our children are going to experience that more and more. I really hope they do.

Finally, we asked Chris if volunteering has changed her personally and if she believes that volunteerism has the power to transform the giver as much or more than the person on the receiving end of aid. Here's her response:

I think that volunteering helps me to stay grounded. It puts things in perspective for me. I'm not the center of the universe. So whether it's working with the Colorado Tiggers or working with hospice (Chris takes black-and-white photos for hospice patients) or helping out at my daughters' schools, it removes me from all those daily chores of living that I think are so important at the time. It puts me in a different place; a place where I can get outside of myself, quiet my mind, and think about what is really valuable in life.

The more volunteering I do, the better person I become. In some ways it takes up a lot of your time to volunteer, and yet, because of the perspective you gain from it, you end up devoting a lot more time to your family and friends. You realize that the things in life are not quite as important as the people in your life.

I want my children to grow up and be good people. I want my daughters to go out in the world as accepting, tolerant, and understanding young women. I want them to include others and help when there's a need.

I believe that this generation of children is going to be genuinely happier and more selfless than previous generations because of the giving and understanding that they are experiencing now in their lives.

Christine is turning her hope into a reality. She is creating a legacy for Hunter and Hayden and showing them through her own actions how to live a great life. Chris is creating a very precious handbook, and the Colorado Tiggers is an integral part of that handbook. Her girls will carry its lessons with them and change future generations. It's that simple, and it's that profound.

Gotta Dance

Stacy Van Dyke has always been an artistic soul. One might say it's in her blood. An accomplished performer with a sultry alto voice and a captivating presence, Stacy is not a typical diva. Her warm personality draws people in, and her easy and frequent peals of laughter create an immediate comfort zone around her. Stacy enjoys life—every minute of it.

Where does this inner glow come from? Is it simply the flame of innate talent? We believe there's more to it than that. Stacy's connection with humanity fuels her joy. She grew up within a legacy of giving. Her father is an active volunteer, and she has taken the legacy he gave her and used it to discover her own passion for volunteering—particularly in the arts.

Stacy calls Phoenix, Arizona home, but she utilizes her creative talents to build a legacy of giving all over the country and the world. Dance in particular is pure joy to Stacy. She revels in the experience of the dance, and she lends much of her time to cultivating and promoting the talent of young dancers.

> *The truest expression of a people is in its dance and in its music. Bodies never lie.*
> —Agnes de Mille

Stacy's involvement in non-profit organizations feeds her passion for life and her desire to reach out to others and lend a hand. Her broad smile and open, honest sense of humor are assets to any volunteer effort, but Stacy is really in her element when she is able to use her experience in the performing arts and talent to encourage young artists from around the world. One of her favorite opportunities to create a legacy in the arts is her participation in an event called Celebration of Dance.

Celebration of Dance is Arizona's contribution to National Dance Week—and what an incredible contribution! The purpose of National Dance Week is to bring nationwide visibility to the dance-arts, and this event takes that motto quite seriously. Celebration of Dance invites nearly thirty dance companies and solo artists to display their creative works in an amazing concert that has included over 200 dancers in a single performance. All dance styles are enthusiastically embraced, and the result is a blockbuster night of entertainment.

This is where Stacy is in her element—cultivating young talent and celebrating life—building a legacy of appreciation for the arts. She has been an enthusiastic volunteer for over ten years.

The following is an excerpt from our interview with Stacy:

When did you first discover the joy of volunteering?

About ten years ago, my choreographer friend Dee Dee Wood (choreographer for Mary Poppins, Chitty Chitty Bang Bang, and Sound of Music, to name just a few gems on her resume) asked me to go to a concert called Celebration of Dance, which celebrates National Dance Week. I was blown away by the talent and passion of those young choreographers and dancers. The next year I offered whatever help I could give—which included being a judge for the auditions and doing local radio and TV talk shows with Dee Dee to promote the concert.

Tell us more about why you chose to get involved with Celebration of Dance.

At a time when being a young person seems especially challenging, it is so inspirational to see these dedicated, hardworking people display their talent and creativity. It seems to me that when they are working so hard to reach their goals, there's no time for abusing drugs or alcohol or acting in self-destructive ways. Seeing and feeling their passion for what they do is breathtaking!

I live vicariously through the dancers. I have taken many dance classes and have had dancing parts in musical comedies—but a dancer I'm not. I have always appreciated dance. When I watch them on stage, I am physically helping them…moving when they move. Hopefully no one around me notices!

What other types of volunteer activities have you been involved in over the years?

Every Christmas in Los Angeles, my dad, my son Ryan, and I work at the Midnight Mission, which is a rehab facility that gets the down and out back on their feet and helps them function in society. I've also helped at Halo Animal Rescue, a local no-kill animal shelter.

Was your dad the main person who inspired you to volunteer?

My dad is and always has been a huge inspiration to me. He started working with the Midnight Mission many years ago, and he has helped raise $5 million of the total $17 million needed for them to build a brand new facility. He has definitely taught me the importance of giving back, of being part of something bigger than myself.

I truly believe that I receive far more than I give when I take part in a volunteer activity. Celebration of Dance and other organizations would continue on just fine without me, but when I volunteer with them, I feel like I'm contributing to the whole of society and in some small way helping to make it better. Giving these young people a bit of support and an opportunity to express themselves and their creativity fills me with an altruistic joy. It helps me get out of myself and selfish pursuits for awhile and fills me with gratitude. It shows me exactly how precious life is at that exact moment.

Stacy's unique gift as an artist has given her an opportunity to create a legacy that honors the beauty and inspiration of dance every year. She also continues to build the family legacy that was passed on to her from her father—one that she in turn passes on to her son, Ryan, when the three of them volunteer together at the Midnight Mission. Ryan has inherited the artistic talents that run so strongly in his family tree. He has recently launched an exciting career of his own as a songwriter and musician. But talent isn't the only thing Ryan inherited. His family has bestowed the gift of giving within him by actively involving him in the Midnight Mission and encouraging him to find his own passion for volunteerism.

This beautiful circle of giving strengthens by example. Stacy enthusiastically encourages her son's career and dedicates her time and talents to Celebration of Dance and other volunteer organizations that feed her soul. Stacy is a shining star who is willing to use her light to nurture others and lift them into the spotlight.

By the way, you may have heard of Stacy's inspirational dad. His name is Dick Van Dyke.

11

Hobbies Help

WRAP YOUR MIND AROUND THE POSSIBILITIES IF YOU CAN: THE OPPORTUNITIES for giving your time and talents to others are staggering. You will have difficulty narrowing down your options. One very good place to start is with your hobbies. Begin your search with activities that bring you personal joy, and find out if there are volunteer organizations built around those activities. You will be surprised to discover that you can help others simply by sharing your hobbies and leisure time activities.

Are you a skier or snowboarder? The National Sports Center for the Disabled needs volunteers to spend some time on the slopes with individuals with disabilities. What about fishing? There's a wonderful organization called Casting for Recovery, where volunteers teach women recovering from breast cancer how to fly fish.

In this chapter, we will interview two inspiring individuals who let their hobbies help them help someone else. They strengthened the circle of humanity simply by participating in something they thoroughly enjoy. The first interview is with a woman many of you may recognize.

A Warm Hug

It is not hard to find a Debbie Macomber book. This New York Times best-selling author is prolific and extremely popular. Her books take up complete sections in most bookstores. They also hold prominent places on private bookshelves across the country and the world.

Debbie Macomber's tales are well-known for their down-to-earth style, terrific storylines, and uplifting nature, and her fans are loyal and numerous. She is also solidly planted in the non-fiction genres of cookbooks and knitting guides, which makes Debbie Macomber a powerhouse in the book industry.

We had a chance to correspond with Debbie Macomber about volunteering, and we found out that this extremely successful writer has a heart that is equally inspiring. She is a dedicated volunteer with a number of organizations, and she is quite candid about how her volunteerism has intertwined with her writing to transform her life.

We did not have an opportunity to meet Debbie Macomber face to face, but it was amazing how her responses came back to us like rays of pure sunshine…and a warm hug.

Debbie Macomber is a great storyteller. Case closed. She's one of the best. In a single page this woman can suck you right into one of her beautiful tales, and pretty soon you feel like you've known the characters for years. You might swear she is writing about your best friend, your aunt, your mother, or the guy who owns the restaurant down the street. The tagline on Debbie Macomber's website says:

Wherever you are, Debbie takes you home…

They're not kidding. Throw in a homemade blanket and a cup of hot chocolate, and you're there.

Another great thing about Debbie's books is they incorporate many aspects of her real life. That's probably why they ring true to so many of her fans. One theme that makes a frequent appearance is lending a hand to those in need.

We found out when we interviewed Debbie Macomber that her books very accurately reflect the woman behind the stories. Debbie Macomber is an upbeat, grounded woman who has a very healthy volunteer resume to go with her accomplishments as an author. Her life is a warm, thick blanket of experiences and connections with people she admits she would never have had an opportunity to meet if she didn't step out of herself and into humanity on a regular basis.

Debbie told us very honestly that she was not prepared for the unexpected gifts that came her way as a result of her volunteer experiences. One woman in particular had a huge impact on Debbie's life—but we'll get to that story in a moment.

In the midst of knee replacement surgery and a book tour, Debbie Macomber still found the time to respond to our interview questions. She is a remarkable person, and she must have many reserves of energy hidden away somewhere, because her accomplishments are astounding. We are honored that she took the time to correspond with us about two things that are near and dear to her heart—writing and volunteering.

Here is a bit of our correspondence:

Has volunteerism always been part of your life?

I've been a volunteer for almost as long as I can remember. I was raised in a farming community, and from the time I was a teenager, I worked with the children of migrant farm workers. While a high school senior, I was also a candy striper at our local hospital. Later, after I was married and Wayne and I started our family, I traded childcare with a friend so we could each work one day a week for a local charity. (Mine was a legal aid program.) I watched her children on Wednesdays, and she looked after mine on Fridays.

Because I firmly believe in giving of ourselves, I have continued volunteer work in different ways throughout my life. When our children were raised and on their own, I became involved in a mentoring program, and that involvement later grew into becoming national ambassador for Big Sisters/Little Sisters.

Currently, I'm on the board of directors of four different organizations:

- **Point Hope**: a charity organized by radio host Delilah. Point Hope supports a refugee camp in Ghana.
- **Guideposts**: helps keep the message of Norman Vincent Peale's The Power of Positive Thinking alive.
- **Warm Up America!** This is a knitting charity—a chance for me to combine my passion for knitting and volunteer work.

- **Cast On To Your Dreams**: an organization that is still in its infancy. It hopes to teach children at risk how to knit…and later children in hospitals, too.

We read about your charity work with Warm Up America. Did they contact you, or did you contact them first?

Actually, Warm Up America found me, and I'm so glad they did. I'm a perfect fit for their board of directors. Not only am I passionate about knitting, I'm equally fervent about reaching out and helping others. To me knitting is a wonderful way to show another person we care.

When you knit for Warm Up America, you make seven-by-nine inch rectangles, and a number of these are pieced together to create a blanket. Now, most knitting projects require a swatch to check gauge. By making this swatch seven-by-nine inches, knitters are doing double duty. Not only is this a great way to check gauge, it can also be used as part of a blanket for someone in need of TLC!

Does your work with various charities affect your writing in any way?

I believe that everything that happens in my life turns up in a book at some point or in some way. That's just how a writer's brain works; we incorporate our own experiences into stories. That's what makes our books real.

Actually, the character of Alix in the Blossom Street series is based on a high school girl I mentored several years ago. One of my current passions is helping foster children…and you'll notice a couple of foster children (like Casey in Summer on Blossom Street) have made appearances in my recent books, as well. Plus, I have woven references to charity knitting throughout this series of books.

If someone was considering getting involved in volunteerism, what advice would you give them?

First, I'd suggest that you examine your own passions, and then find an organization that aligns with them. When we're passionate about something, we're able to inspire and encourage others.

My second bit of advice is just do it. Don't wait for the perfect opportunity. Don't wait until all the stars are aligned and your life is in perfect order—just do it. I can guarantee you won't be sorry.

Third, I'd suggest involving as many members of your family as possible. Nothing builds family togetherness more than working toward a common goal, especially when that goal is to improve the life of others.

Toward the end of our questions, we asked Debbie Macomber if she had any personal stories about volunteering that she would like to share, and she told us about one young woman who had a striking impact on her life.

Debbie contacted a local high school a few years ago and said that she would like to do some volunteer work by mentoring a young person who was interested in becoming a writer. They sent her Serena.

Serena was an eighteen-year-old single mother who was living on her own with her baby and surviving on welfare and the money she could make on weekends as a topless dancer. She also told Debbie when they first met that she was a practicing witch.

Debbie met with Serena on a weekly basis and encouraged her writing. She even eventually gave her a job. The two women soon became friends as well as writing colleagues. One of their best moments was when they sold a short story they had written together.

When Serena graduated from high school, her life took an unfortunate turn. She moved to Seattle and started topless dancing again to make ends meet. Eventually, Serena became homeless, and her son was taken from her and placed in foster care.

Debbie did not abandon her friend in this dark time. She and her husband, Wayne, invited Serena to move in with them. Serena lived with them for a summer while she got back on her feet. After that summer, she joined the Army, where she learned extremely valuable lessons in responsibility, structure, and purpose.

Here is the conclusion of the story in Debbie's own words:

> I started out volunteering to mentor a young writer and ended up with so much more. Serena enriched our lives and opened our eyes to the plight of a young, single mother without the foundation and support of a loving family.
>
> Volunteering helps me look outside myself. It has made me aware of the needs of others. It's far too easy to get wrapped up in self and to judge others. Being a volunteer has expanded my horizons, giving me insight and perspective. I gave of myself, yet I was the one who received.

Debbie Macomber continues to give of herself through her volunteer work almost daily. Where she finds the time, we'll never know! She is a shining example of how lending a hand can enrich one's life and strengthen connections to the larger humanity that we are all a part of. Our world is warmer and brighter because Debbie Macomber is actively involved in it.

Green Thumbs

> *When we have an ample harvest, we should be giving this food away.*
>
> —Gary Oppenheimer

Gary Oppenheimer is well acquainted with the concept of serendipity. He thinks it played a huge role in a project he's spending most of his time on these days.

"I accidently, serendipitously stumbled on a problem and inadvertently discovered a solution, and by total happenstance I found some great people."

That is how Gary describes the birth of AmpleHarvest.org, a non-profit organization that helps food pantries and gardeners with extra produce to find each other.

But let's go back to the beginning of the story. It's important to see where this idea came from and exactly how serendipity played a role in turning it into a reality.

Gary Oppenheimer lives in the township of West Milford, New Jersey. This beautiful town—as large as Brooklyn, yet with only 28 thousand people—rests in the tranquil western part of Passaic County, about fifty miles from New York City. The entire area is dotted with nearly forty lakes and boasts quiet country roads and scenic valleys. It's a good place for things to grow. After all, New Jersey is the Garden State.

It was in the Garden State that Gary Oppenheimer really started to hone his skills as a gardener. He and his wife own a large piece of property in northern New Jersey. It is a gorgeous stretch of land deep in the woods. About six years ago, Gary carved out several sections of it to create his own gardens. He soon found out that he liked to grow things.

Gary, who became a Rutgers Master Gardener in 2002 (and followed that with a Rutgers Environmental Steward certification a few years later), doesn't think small. After putting in a third-acre fruit orchard with eighteen trees, he created two food gardens, one of which was a six-hundred-square-foot vegetable and herb garden. He also taps several maple trees every February to make maple syrup. Keeping the deer, bears, and other animals out of the garden is the biggest challenge, but the payoff is worth it. He has found that he loves planting, tending… and then waiting.

Soon, the tomatoes start coming, and then the cucumbers, and next it's the squash. All of a sudden, Gary had so much produce that he had to give much of it away to friends and neighbors. His wife finally put her foot down and said, "No more of that stuff is coming into this house."

There are only so many tomatoes and squash a family can eat; there are only so many cucumbers one can give to his friends before they stop calling him a friend.

Here was the dilemma: Gary had a very green thumb. His garden was thriving; the plants continued to produce; but nobody he knew wanted any more of the fruits and vegetables he was growing. He couldn't stand the thought of all of that nutritious food going to waste.

So Gary came up with a solution. He knew of a battered women's shelter in West Milford, and he gave them a call. He told them he had some extra food from his garden—a lot of extra food—and he asked if they would like it. They said they would love it! Gary packed up forty pounds of produce and took it right over to the shelter. A very nice lady answered the door, and Gary will never forget what she said.

"As I was leaving, she said, and these words stuck with me; she said, 'oh boy, now we can have some fresh produce to eat,'" Gary recounted. "It struck me as an odd thing to hear. I remember walking away thinking, boy, are you always eating canned carrots and beans or something? Little did I know, that is exactly what they were eating."

In the summer of 2008, Gary ran into the same problem. His garden didn't produce quite as much as it did the year before, but it was still an ample harvest, and he had at least twenty pounds of produce he couldn't give away to family and friends. So he went right back to the same battered women's shelter with a full bag of stuff. The same nice lady answered the door, and she made the same comment when he left.

This pattern planted a seed in Gary's brain that would soon start to grow.

The next serendipitous event happened in October of 2008. David and Wendy Watson-Hallowell run a non-profit organization in town called Sustainable West Milford. It is a sustainability organization that Gary says has turned the town upside down. The Watson-Hallowells support a number of great projects to contribute to the sustainability of the township and surrounding areas. One of those projects is a community garden.

The woman who was running the community garden in 2008 was about to leave to move on to other endeavors, and the Watson-Hallowells knew that Gary was a master gardener who was into environmental stuff. They badgered him for months to take over the garden.

"I thought I have my biking; I have my business; I have my own fourteen acres in the woods. Do I need this?" Gary laughed. "But what did I say? I said yes, I'll do it. Fine."

So Gary agreed to run the garden, but he wasn't going to work there. The people in the garden did the work, and he managed it. What he learned from reading comments collected in prior years was that as the growing season went into full swing, people left more and more food in the community garden to rot. They got bored with gardening; they went on vacation; or they just got overwhelmed.

Gary also started to hear people in the garden commenting on the wasted food. It was a garden of thirty plots, about a third of an acre, so there were many green thumbs out there throughout the growing season.

Finally, Gary decided to pull a group of people together from the garden, and he told them that it really bothered him to see all that wasted food. They agreed that it was a bad thing and something should be done. That meeting was the first time the words ample harvest came out of Gary's mouth.

"You know," he said to the group of gardeners. "When we have an ample harvest, we should be giving this food away."

The group decided to form a committee to find a way to get all of the extra produce to food banks in the area. Gary's first task as part of the committee was to go on Google and find out where the nearest food pantries were located. He was in for a bit of a surprise. Google said the nearest food pantry was in Morristown, New Jersey, twenty-five miles away.

Now, West Milford is not a tiny town. Gary was certain there were a number of food pantries much closer, but he had no idea how to find them. As he started asking, Gary found out that there were food pantries all over West Milford and in surrounding towns, but nobody knew about them. He realized at that point that the only reason he knew about the battered women's shelter where he donated his own produce was because they owned a thrift shop in town. If he had been a member of one of the churches in West Milford, he probably would have known if it had a food pantry, but Gary is Jewish. His synagogue didn't have a food pantry. By the time Gary finished his homework, he found out there were six food pantries among the twenty-four churches in town.

Why didn't anybody know about them?

Then, it all came together. Gary was relaxing at home on night, and he had an epiphany. He thought about the food he couldn't give away; the pantries he couldn't find; and the fact that 49 million people in the United States are hungry; and it all just came together into one brilliant thought. Gary got up the next morning, immediately got on the Internet, and found out that the AmpleHarvest.org Internet domain name was available. He grabbed it, and that was the first nine dollars he spent to form this new organization. Incredibly, those nine dollars represent 10 percent of what Gary Oppenheimer has spent on the entire project so far.

Gary goes on to describe his epiphany in more detail:

> Now, 49 million people are a lot of people, but what does it really mean? I was trying to visualize it. I crunched some numbers, and here is what I came up with:
>
>> If you took Alaska, Arkansas, Connecticut, Delaware, Hawaii, Iowa, Idaho, Kansas, Kentucky, Main, Missouri, Montana, North Dakota, Nebraska, New Hampshire, New Mexico, Nevada, Oklahoma, Oregon, Rhode Island, South Dakota, Vermont, West Virginia and added them up all together, you still would not quite be at the number of people who are hungry in this country. That is twenty-three out of fifty states. Or put another way, we have more people in this country who are hungry than the entire population of Canada. Simultaneously with my idea for AmpleHarvest.org, I realized that I could make a difference, and I could help other people make a difference.
>>
>> The National Gardening Association had a study they put out in 2009 that said 43 million people in American grow

fruit, vegetables, and herbs. We have 43 million people who grow food and 49 million people who are hungry.

Is it a coincidence that those numbers are so close?

Gary sat down that morning and started brainstorming what AmpleHarvest.org would look like. He made an outline of the website, and then through another series of serendipitous events, he found the perfect website designer, a woman from Missouri interested in doing the job free of charge. It turned out that she herself was a former food pantry client. When Gary spoke with her by phone the first time, they immediately connected. He looked at samples of her work and found them to be absolutely stunning, so she became the next member of the team. Next, Gary talked to a man in northern New Jersey, and he agreed to join the team in building the website. Then there were three. Gary did the outline, the other two did the web design and structure, and Gary wrote all of the content.

As an example of the dedication of this small team, Gary tells another story:

> My goal was to have the website ready for testing on April 15 to go live on May 15. Those were the dates in my head. I had to get it out early enough so that there would be enough pantries online by the time gardeners started making donations in mid-summer.
>
> Around April 15, Maureen's [the female member of the web team] mother became very ill, and a few days later, she passed away. My first thought, other than feeling terrible for her, was that the project was going to fall behind schedule. I was subsequently stunned to learn that in the intervening week between her mother's passing and the funeral, Maureen had continued to work on the project. I would have never asked anybody to do that. I was shocked by the dedication she had for this.
>
> So instead of coming out on May 15, we rolled out on May 18.

Gary and his small team of website gurus got another shock when they launched the website. It immediately started grabbing attention. Even The Huffington Post picked it up. Google liked the project, too, and soon Gary was able to secure a $10,000 Google grant for free advertising—$10,000 every month...indefinitely.

Next, Gary started reaching out to faith organizations around the country, not because there is anything particularly religious about AmpleHarvest.org, but because most food pantries are in houses of worship. Many of those organizations pushed information about AmpleHarvest.org out to their members, and the project snowballed.

"This was one of those things where all of the atoms in the universe converged at the right moment, in the right place, and at the right time to make something brand new," Gary said. "Any number of things at any point could have happened, and it would not be what it is today. It's almost like it was in the stars, if you will."

The entire last year has been one giant ball of serendipity, as far as Gary is concerned.

> I am not one to believe in higher powers moving things around. That's not me. Although, if I were one of those people, I certainly could have pointed and said this is a great example of a miracle. If I unwound the story and did it again, it would probably turn out dramatically different. I didn't come into any of this with a grand plan on how it was going to happen. I am still largely in the mode of, you know, I feel like the conductor of a large orchestra, but I don't really know how to play any of the instruments. I can move the pieces around and look at the beautiful music, but if you gave me a musical instrument, I wouldn't know what to do with it. I'm not out in front leading the charge. I'm following the crowd so I can lead them, if that makes sense.

He must be doing something right, because AmpleHarvest.org already has 1,430 (as of February 2010) pantries registered on the site. The organization even has its own iPhone app! They received a micro-grant from the Good People Fund to develop it, and it became available in January 2010. Just type in Ample Harvest in the app store, and you will find this little gem of a free app. It can tell you immediately where the closest food pantries are to where you are standing. If you click on any of the pins marking the spot of a pantry, you will get a lot of information on location, contacts, hours, and even items that the food pantry could really use at that particular time.

The premise of AmpleHarvest.org is to get the food out of people's backyards and into food pantries. It is a directory to connect gardeners with food pantries all over the country. Gary's goal is to have at least 10,000 pantries registered on the site. Then he will feel like he is starting to see good saturation across the country. Every day more pantries are registering, and recently the USDA endorsed AmpleHarvest.org. Gary is clearly rocketing toward that goal.

So what causes a guy in West Milford, New Jersey to take on a project like this? Why was he compelled to connect with humanity in this way?

We found out that giving food to people who are hungry has been a meaningful act for Gary throughout most of his life. He has a habit, when there is extra food from a restaurant meal, of asking the restaurant for a "doggie bag." Then, on the way home, his favorite thing to do is drop the bag of warm food next to a sleeping homeless person who will wake up to an unexpected warm meal without having to suffer the shame of begging for it.

When he was a high school student visiting friends in White Plains, New York, he often ran across down-and-out individuals asking for a quarter or a dollar. Instead, he took them into the nearest deli and bought them a tuna sandwich.

Reaching out to the hungry has been a part of Gary's life for a long time. It is a very real and simple way that he continually steps out of himself and into humanity. Gary may not have experienced what it is like to go hungry himself, but he has heard about it from his mother-in-law. She spent five years in Russia escaping the Nazis...and starving. She described how her typical daily meal was a loaf of bread the size of a softball that was half made of sawdust. The image of all of those people starving in Russia stuck in Gary's mind. Now, he has found a way in which he can help stop hunger here in the United States, and it seems to feed his own soul.

Gary was never asked as a child to participate in volunteer activities, but he was surrounded by examples of volunteerism. His mother and father and his grandparents were all connected with the community in some way. His mother volunteered with the Yonkers Fair Housing Committee, an organization that helped African-American families find fair housing in the 1960s. His grandfather escaped the Nazis and moved to New York with his family. He kept their small community synagogue in the Bronx alive and functioning throughout its existence. This was a very demanding volunteer position that Gary's wife, speaking from her own personal experience, equates with "doing time." It was not an easy job. Gary didn't learn until his father died in 1995 that he had been a Big Brother to an inner-city child for a number of years. The young boy had emotional issues and did not open up with many people in his neighborhood, but he completely engaged with Gary's dad. "He opened up with this little Jewish man who was nothing like him," Gary told us.

So volunteerism has never been anything special or unique in Gary's life. It is just a part of him. It's what he does; it's what his parents did; and it's what their parents did. In fact, Gary is proud to have recently found out that his daughter is involved in a volunteer project in college where she works with inner-city kids. Volunteerism is part of the DNA of his entire family. It's who they are and what they do. He talks about a Jewish proverb that he often heard growing up.

> One of the things I grew up with is a Jewish expression that sounds like it comes from The Lion King. It doesn't. It is called Tikkun olam and it literally translates to "repairing the world," or as I put it, leaving the place a little better than you found it. That has been an important thing for me all my life.

> You know, whatever you do in your life, make sure that when you leave, the place is a bit better than it was when you started.
>
> Now, that doesn't apply to all aspects of my life. My wife would be the first to tell you I don't pick up after myself. So it doesn't apply to everything. But in terms of doing something for society, it's good.

When we asked Gary if volunteering has changed his life, he replied honestly that it hasn't. It is hard to think of something being transforming if it has always been a part of you, and lending a hand to someone in need has been part of Gary's life since he was a small child running a carnival in his backyard for Muscular Dystrophy. He has always reached out to help those in need. So the answer is no. Volunteering has not changed his life; it is his life, or a very important part of it.

Then, we asked Gary if volunteerism has improved his quality of life, and we got a much different answer.

> Yes! I feel great about what I'm doing. I've always sort of carved my own trail through the forest. I was not one to follow others. My friend Dave sums up life really well. He says you should have fun, do good, and make money—in that order. That is what I've done. I would encourage people to find something they can support, whether it's stopping hunger, supporting a political candidate, working on environmental issues, or something as simple as stopping an old tree from being cut down. Find something you can identify with and then connect to it, become a part of it.

It is that connection to something bigger than you—a relationship with community—that Gary finds so satisfying. He told another story about corn in Pennsylvania to illustrate his point.

Gary is an avid bicyclist, and his daughter (who is now a sophomore in college) was the number one female cyclist in New

Jersey and seventeenth in the country when she was in the eleventh grade. One year when Gary took his daughter to a race in the middle-of-nowhere, Pennsylvania, he struck up a conversation with a local corn farmer.

The farmer explained the unique way they grow corn in Pennsylvania that connects the farmers with the community. There is sweet corn that people eat, and then there is feed corn that animals eat. The real money is in feed corn, which is harvested corn, stalk, leaves, and all and fed to livestock. What the farmers decided to do was plant a four-foot perimeter of sweet corn around their feed cornfields.

At harvest time, the farmers invite everyone in the community to come by and pick as much sweet corn as they want before they harvest the entire field and sell it for feed. It costs the farmers nothing extra to let the people in their community pick the sweet corn, and they can still harvest the entire field, stalks and all, for the feed corn.

Why would they do that?

Gary asks, "Why not?"

They are creating a connection to something outside of themselves. They are strengthening their bond with people in their community. They're giving back some of their ample harvest.

Gary Oppenheimer lives by that rule, too, and for him, life is very good.

"You don't have to be rich to be wealthy," he said with a chuckle. "Anyone can buy a packet of seeds for two dollars at the local hardware store and create wealth with a little bit of dirt, sunlight, and water. It doesn't take much. I've got to tell you, you do feel good after you do it. Even if nobody knows you are doing it, and nobody should know. You shouldn't be doing it for the glory. You should be doing it because it's the right thing to do...but it does feel really good."

Debbie Macomber and Gary Oppenheimer have been lifelong volunteers in a variety of arenas, but they have also shined the light on one area: hobbies. They shared their hobbies with others as part of their volunteerism. They opened up to the circle of humanity and contributed the gifts they have to offer. Stepping out of oneself and into humanity does not need to be difficult or scary. It can be as joyous as participating in your favorite pastime. What do you really take pleasure in doing? How can you use it to connect with those around you and make the lives of others just a little bit better?

12

You've Got Skills

WHAT DO YOU DO FOR A LIVING?

Are you passionate about your career?

We hope so. You chose it, right?

You most likely found you had an aptitude in a certain area, and then schooling, training, and employment followed. If you are lucky enough to be working in a fulfilling job today, it can lead you to a rewarding volunteer experience.

Not all volunteer activities are unskilled. You may have expertise in your professional life that could be very useful to volunteer organizations. Are you passionate about what you do from 9 to 5? Maybe you can channel the skills you already have to help others.

There are numerous organizations out there looking for professionals in IT, marketing, human resources, law, and other areas to help them. Do you have skills that might take a nonprofit organization to the next level?

We interviewed two people who put their professional skills to work. They offered their expertise pro bono and found that what they received in return was priceless.

Tap into a Good Thing

Sometimes connecting with others and contributing to the greater good is a surprise; it's not what one sets out to do. In fact, sometimes it happens in spite of a person's best efforts to do something else entirely. Is that synchronicity? Is it fate?

Mark Rice doesn't believe in any of that.

Mark started his adventures in volunteerism ten years before our interview by helping at a shelter for homeless women, mostly doing landscaping. He ended up as the Program Manager of the Los Angeles branch of the Taproot Foundation. Certain people might call that fate. Mark Rice doesn't believe in it. He thinks the idea of a master plan is silly.

Nevertheless, Mark's journey from point A to point B is intriguing. Even this East-Coast-turned-West-Coast skeptic, who has spent thirty years in advertising and marketing, is starting to develop empathy. When pressed, he might even admit to feeling more fulfilled in his current job than he ever has in life. Of course, he was faking it a bit at first.

Maybe, just maybe, Mark has tapped into a good thing.

We could tell Mark Rice was not going to be a typical interview right from the very start. For a person who works in the nonprofit sector, he's a little rough around the edges. His answers are short and clipped; he's not shy about sharing his opinions; and he has no problem letting you know exactly what he thinks. So how did this guy end up in the touchy-feely world of nonprofits? That's what we wanted to know.

The first question we asked Mark was whether or not volunteerism has always been part of his life. The answer was a resounding no; Mark's first and only experience as a volunteer, before he started working with the Taproot Foundation, started over ten years ago.

The company Mark was working for at the time decided to send a group to help one weekend in the garden at a local women's shelter. Mark agreed to go along.

"I had just moved from New York, where I had an acre and a half of property, to Los Angeles, where I had none," Mark recalled.

Evidently, getting outside and working with his hands was exactly what he needed to offset his cramped accommodations.

"So I just asked if they would mind if I came back and continued to do landscaping work for them."

Ten years later, Mark has completely transformed the grounds around this homeless shelter for abused women and kids. He has bought thousands of dollars worth of plants and flowers, and spent many of his off hours carefully planting, watering, and weeding. It has been good to spend time away from the screaming city, getting his hands dirty and watching a small patch of land change into something quite beautiful.

At first, Mark had little contact with the women and children in the shelter, but eventually it was the kids who pierced his tough exterior.

"One Halloween, I decided to give the kids there an opportunity to experience pumpkin carving. I brought my two daughters and about thirty pumpkins, and we did arts and crafts with the kids. They would draw pictures of what they wanted us to carve, and we would carve the pumpkins and hollow them out. It was great."

There was a slight glimmer in the tone of his voice, but Mark quickly masked it.

"That's how it started," he continued, clearing his throat. "It really started when I worked with the kids directly. To be perfectly honest, I had little interest in the women in the shelter at first. They were all very young, and a few of the mothers had as many as six kids. The kids were the ones who were suffering from all that. You know, the kids always called me Mr. Mark; I loved that."

Again, softness buffed the edges of his voice.

"I think I was really about the only positive male influence that those kids had in their lives. So it was very powerful."

Powerful? That was a pretty strong word coming from this tough guy.

"I have great pictures, if you ever want them," he offered. "About a year ago I took a bunch of pictures at Halloween of the kids in their outfits. I'm a pretty good photographer." Then, Mark's voice lost a little of its intensity. "I was looking at the pictures, and I saw how sad they were...so I decided to do a little bit more. That's when I started to do some tutoring with the kids two or three afternoons a week."

Mark Rice was hooked. He made a connection to something bigger than himself, and there was no going back.

"Right in the middle of that, I had an opportunity to do some pro-bono work with the Taproot Foundation," Mark continued. "I said what the heck. I'll give it a go."

One wonders if he would have taken the opportunity with the Taproot Foundation if he hadn't first volunteered at the women's shelter. But don't call it volunteerism! Mark does not like that word.

"I would call it less volunteerism, more landscaping and helping out," Mark corrected.

He then went on to tell us a little about the Taproot Foundation, and we soon realized why it is such a great fit for a man like Mark Rice.

First of all, they don't use the word volunteer at the Taproot Foundation. They are pro-bono consultants. There is a big difference.

Ever since it was organized in 2001, the Taproot Foundation has strived to leverage top talent in the areas of strategic HR, strategy management, marketing, and IT to support the greatest needs of communities around the country. They are currently working in six major cities (San Francisco, New York, Chicago, DC, Seattle, and Los Angeles), and they specifically choose large cities because they yield a plethora of talented individuals from top organizations.

So how can these business gurus help people in need?

You would be surprised.

The Taproot Foundation makes sure that nonprofit organizations have access to something they don't very often get to experience: top-notch professional services that will help them achieve their missions. Pro-bono consultants help deserving nonprofit groups in critically important areas where they lack the experience or the time. They are not messing around here. In fact, the Taproot Foundation is the largest nonprofit consulting firm in the country, and they are just as picky about choosing their pro-bono consultants as they are about choosing the organizations they will help. There is a rigorous application process on both sides.

To give us an example of what they do, Mark told us about his first experience as a pro-bono consultant with the Taproot Foundation.

"It was a website project for a homeless women's shelter in downtown L.A. I was asked to take the website development project on, and I identified six Taproot pro-bono consultants to join the team: a web developer, a photographer, a graphic designer, a copywriter, a project manager, and a marketing manager."

Mark oversaw the entire project, from the discovery process (including interviewing the staff, members of the board of directors, volunteers, and several homeless women who frequented the shelter), to the website design, implementation, and client training.

What Mark and his team realized early on in this project was that they needed to give the women in the shelter an opportunity to share their views on the website. These women did have access to the web through caseworkers and shelters, and they had something to contribute. He made sure that on each website page the women who utilized the shelter services had a voice.

How did Mark and his team know to do this? Again, it was through personal connections. They met the women at the shelter; they had lunch with them; they learned about their life stories; and suddenly these women were not nameless faces. They were real.

"When we got our team together for this project, we had our first lunch at the women's shelter," Mark told us. "We all split up and ate at different tables to get to know the women. At first, I was a little bit anxious and nervous, but they couldn't have been nicer. In the middle of the lunch, the client got up and introduced each one of us. There were about 110 homeless women who were eating lunch there—every one of them stood up and cheered. They cheered for us! That was a powerful moment for me."

There's that word again—powerful.

Mark finished the project about two months before our interview with him in 2009, and the pride in his voice was unmistakable. If you would like to check out the site, go to www.dwcweb.org.

Shortly after this experience, Mark had an opportunity to become a full-time employee of the Taproot Foundation. He jumped at it.

Of course, he doesn't really tell it that way....

"I didn't get the job at Disney."

Mark knew that the open position at the Taproot Foundation matched his skills very well. On the other hand, he had applied for a job at Disney that was an upscale move and offered a lot of money and global opportunities.

"To be honest, I would have taken the Disney job," Mark said unapologetically. "But I didn't get that job. Instead, I was able to get the job at the Taproot Foundation. In hindsight, it's the best thing that has ever happened to me. I love this particular work, because it matches my skill set perfectly and allows me to make a meaningful difference for so many deserving nonprofits. That is very hard to find. If I did believe in fate, I would think, yes, definitely the stars were aligned. But I don't believe in fate."

Now, Mark oversees forty-eight different pro-bono projects with five experienced professionals on each team. They create websites, key messaging, annual reports, and provide strategic and HR guidance. He now has an opportunity to make a huge difference in many different organizations through the service grants that the Taproot Foundation awards.

So what are these service grants?

Service grants are people—extraordinary people. They are the teams of five business professionals who have been carefully screened by Taproot. In fact, Taproot only accepts one out of every five people who apply for a pro-bono position to make sure they provide nonprofits with highly qualified experts. These teams work with organizations and help transform them. If an organization went out and hired a team of experts of this caliber, it would probably cost $50,000 to $60,000. The Taproot Foundation does it for free. Mark is overseeing forty-eight pro-bono teams working in L.A. right now; the Taproot Foundation as a whole has done over 1,200 service grants across the country. That is what the organization is all about. It brings the power of pro bono to nonprofits.

Mark Rice believes what he is doing is a step beyond volunteerism—and not just because he is now making a modest salary.

"People at the Taproot Foundation aren't just helping, like I was helping with the landscaping, or like someone picks up trash on the beach. Anybody can do that. We are taking people's real skills and applying those skills in a well-organized way to make a quantum difference in an organization. It's very fulfilling."

There is another very important aspect of the Taproot Foundation that Mark Rice understands: it doesn't just help the nonprofit. The Taproot Foundation has over 350 active pro-bono consultants in L.A. and 3,000 across the U.S. It brings professionals into the world of nonprofits, a place they may have never visited before and know very little about. These pro-bono workers become more engaged in their communities, and they see how they can use their professional skills to work together with others and make a huge difference.

Mark gets it. He knows that there is power in face-to-face contact, and there is power in leveraging your own personal skills for a greater good.

"I just talked to our founder, Aaron Hurst, a genuine visionary. We were discussing how we can better deliver a brand message for Taproot; a message that will inspire people and for-profit corporations to join in the pro-bono movement. We discussed a concept that we will call pro-bono moments." Mark's voice ratcheted up a notch in intensity. "We are going to reach out to all our consultants and look for that moment when it really hit them—the power of what we can accomplish as a pro-bono team."

Yes, Mark knows exactly what he's doing. He didn't arrive at this job or this place in his overall journey intentionally, but he admits that he loves it now that he's here. He is fulfilled—maybe even inspired. We asked him if the Taproot Foundation has changed his life.

"Well, I'm broke," he laughed. "My salary went down dramatically. I used to have a large corner office, and now I share an interior office. So from one perspective, it has been a challenge." Then there was a short silence. "But I love making a difference. I am in a very special position to hear amazing stories from the consultants, but I also hear from the people in the nonprofits who are getting the benefits. What Taproot does is truly powerful.

"I am currently working with one of our consultants who lives in a very upscale neighborhood in Southern California. She is involved in a project for an organization called NDLON, National Day Laborer Organizing Network. They offer services to Hispanics who are day laborers, who stand on the side of the road and wait for trucks to come by. What this organization does is help day laborers and immigrants by providing English lessons, visa guidance, and advocating for job reform. It is a wonderful organization.

"So this pro-bono consultant was interested, but she had concerns, because many of the people that NDLON helps are illegal immigrants. I said, well, why don't you just give it a go?

"She has been on the project for two months; she has visited three or four of the shelters and done a number of interviews; and she has been completely transformed. This woman is now telling all her friends how the Hispanics have been treated unfairly, how hard they work, and how they are just not getting ahead. She is imploring her friends to do something to help. She has been transformed from, I would say, having issues with illegal immigration to understanding and treating the people there like...like people."

Next, Mark told us about another organization Taproot is working with called The Unusual Suspects. They work with kids who are in juvenile delinquent homes and prisons, and they help them put on plays. Yes, plays! The goal is to mentor these kids and prepare them to adjust to the world when they are released. They do this very creatively through theatre work.

Mark recently received a letter from a pro-bono professional who has been working with the organization for three months. She has become so enthusiastic about the work the organization does that she spends two or three days each month at Chino Prison working with the kids. The clients at The Unusual Suspects have been so pleased with her involvement that they have invited her to be on the board of directors of the organization. Mark couldn't help but laugh with delight in retelling the story.

"I sent her back an email saying did you ever think you would be writing a sentence like 'I am spending this Sunday at the Chino Prison with a theatre group'?"

Mark thrives on the positive energy that pours out of each one of his experiences at the Taproot Foundation—and he gets to live in that energy all day long. He does not miss the world of marketing and advertising one bit—with the exception of the nice office.

"I feel much better about myself," Mark admitted toward the end of our interview. "I'm very happy about what I do."

While his quality of life has dramatically declined from a material perspective, Mark makes one last very important point.

"When you are an HR director at a major corporation, or a strategic planner, a copywriter, a graphic designer, or an IT guy, the business world often takes advantage of your skills. Here at the Taproot Foundation, YOU are taking advantage of your skills. You can actually use your skills to help nonprofits and truly make a difference.

"There are so many people out there who can make a huge impact on the world, and they are not even aware that they can do it. Our challenge is to 'tap' into those people and show them the way."

Focusing on Charities

Trishna Shah also found that her professional skills could inspire change when she and a group of friends founded an organization called CharityFocus. This organization has a slight twist on the usual non-profit mission statement: instead of capitalizing on external impact, they focus on internal transformation. Projects are means for volunteers to experience personal growth. That inward change then results in meaningful outward impact on the community.

Nevertheless, CharityFocus and the Taproot Foundation share one very important starting point—leveraging professional skills to help others—and they have both been highly successful in achieving their goals.

> *I shall pass through this world but once. Any good therefore that I can do or any kindness that I can show to any human being, let me do it now. Let me not defer or neglect it, for I shall not pass this way again.*
>
> —Mahatma Gandhi

Trishna Shah grew up with a strong foundation in volunteerism.

"I've volunteered ever since I was a kid," Trishna told us in an email early in 2010. "My father was a huge source of inspiration to me as a child. He was always helping others, whether it was a neighbor, friend, colleague, or family member. He taught me the joy of giving early on in my life by living his own life in this way."

She remembers one volunteer project that inspired her to do more:

> One project was a huge source of inspiration for me later in life. When I was fifteen, I wanted to organize a Christmas activity that would capture people's imaginations and get them involved in giving—and also help someone in need during the holidays. So I ran a campaign to collect toys and children's books in the weeks leading up to Christmas. We collected hundreds of books and toys, then I got twenty or thirty volunteers together at my house, and we wrapped everything beautifully. We took all the gifts to a shelter where I had prearranged with a local orphanage to host a Christmas party for the kids. We had a lovely time with them playing loads of games. Toward the end of the party, we gave each child one of the gift bundles we had prepared. They were so thrilled!
>
> This experience touched me in many ways: the event moved me personally; it totally melted my heart to be able to help such vulnerable children; I was also excited to be able to create an opportunity for my friends to get involved. They were equally moved that day.

Volunteering has really helped me to practice selflessness, which over time has created a shift in my outlook and encouraged me to focus on giving.

Trishna also told us about a vivid memory of another volunteer experience that had a huge impact on her in high school. She was about sixteen years old and taking a summer course at a local university. One of the assignments in the course was to commit a random act of kindness and then write a paper about the experience.

She teamed up with a friend, and they made one hundred sack lunches—peanut butter and jelly sandwiches and a piece of fruit—and set off to deliver them to homeless people all over town. They had a great time driving around handing out the lunches in brown paper bags, but they still had quite a few sack lunches left a few hours later.

That's when Trishna remembered a homeless shelter nearby where she had once volunteered. They arrived at the shelter just as lunch was served, and the coordinators of the shelter were happy to let Trishna and her friend set up a table at the front of the line to give away their lunch packs. They had an opportunity there to talk to many homeless people as they waited in line.

Trishna remembered being shocked to hear about the struggle for food and shelter that the people she met dealt with daily. She was happy to provide even a small amount of support and humbled to witness the relief ripple across their faces when they took a meal that would get them through one more day. Trishna's experience humanized the term homelessness and helped her understand its harsh realities. She understood that she couldn't solve all of the problems of the homeless people she met, but she could offer a glimmer of hope and a bit of relief simply by handing them a sack lunch and sharing a moment of connection with them.

Trishna's experiences through young adulthood were a springboard for future actions. They allowed her to think outside of the box when a college friend called her up one night with a new idea. Trishna was a junior in business administration at University of

California, Berkeley, and her friend Viral mentioned that his older brother Nipun wanted to start a nonprofit that created opportunities for volunteers to build free websites for nonprofits. A couple of months later, she was watching a PowerPoint presentation at Nipun's parents' home in Santa Clara.

Trishna couldn't wait to team up with the group of young individuals who were passionate about helping others. She didn't need a PowerPoint presentation to convince her to join the team.

"After much deliberation about organization models—I had to try to put my business major to good use—we arrived at the conclusion that we'd all just get stuck in and see how we got on," Trishna remembered. "Several projects later, CharityFocus evolved into what it is today."

And what an evolution! CharityFocus is indeed unique, from conception to maturity. The founders altered their focus and changed their lives. We'll let Trishna explain it in her own words:

> CharityFocus is quite different from other web-based nonprofits doing good work. It is built on strong and unique values focused on three core principles: remaining completely volunteer-run; never asking for outside contributions; and enabling people to experience internal transformation through small acts of service, rather than focusing outward on creating large external impact to try to change the world.
>
> These principles are core to everything we do and have enabled us to keep CharityFocus pure in its intentions. The values resonate with people from so many different walks of life and draw them into the organization—from professionals to students to CEOs to monks!

Monks? Well, maybe that makes sense. The volunteers at CharityFocus continually ask how they can learn to give more selflessly and grow in generosity. Their approach is practical and brilliant in its simplicity.

"Our mission is not to end homelessness, dissolve poverty, or bridge the digital divide in the nonprofit sector," Trishna said. "We aren't trying to become a nonprofit You Tube. Instead, we strive to create avenues and opportunities to inspire people to be the change. We provide individuals with a practical way to create an internal shift in perspective from scarcity to abundance, from transaction to trust, from isolation to community."

Trishna's friend Nipun likes to compare CharityFocus to a soccer team. Every single member of the team is important, and each contributes in his or her own unique ways. There is no hierarchy or division between administrators and volunteers, as the entire organization is volunteer-run. They do not focus on achieving any specific, external goals. Instead, the volunteers focus on creating opportunities to cultivate inner goodness, selflessness, and generosity. Their goals are pure, non-controversial, and not affiliated with any particular faith-based organization, so they appeal to just about anyone.

We thought that sounded great, but in the back of our overachieving minds we wondered if they ever accomplished anything with no obvious leaders and no clear goals. Does just going with the flow actually work in the real world?

Trishna smashed our skepticism with an overview of the reach and measurable outputs of CharityFocus as of mid-2010. The ecosystem of CharityFocus projects is made up of 19 web portals that collectively attract 6.5 million unique visitors and send out 55 million inspiring newsletters without any advertising each year. Furthermore, they have over 325,000 subscribers from 193 countries with over 15,000 registered as volunteers.

Trishna also shared a story of the evolution of one of their early projects, which demonstrates the value that CharityFocus creates.

> One story I remember vividly is about a website project I worked on in the early days for an organization called Tooth Mobile. We put together a volunteer team of three

professionals to help this nonprofit develop its first-ever website back in 1999 in order to enable more people to find out about the incredible work they were doing to provide mobile dental care to people in need who couldn't afford it or access it any other way.

I still remember walking into their offices in San Jose with my fellow volunteers to meet with one of their founders, Mike Reza, and talk about what they did so that we could build a suitable website for them. At the time, Mike had absolutely no experience whatsoever with the web. He had no idea where to start but was thrilled at the thought of being able to have a website for the Tooth Mobile. We spent a few hours with him to learn all about his story, what the organization does, and how they change lives. In turn, we provided him with loads of ideas on what the website could include, how it could be structured, and what it might look like.

Our team left the meeting super inspired by Mike's stories and really excited about the opportunity to help Tooth Mobile get on the web. Over the next couple of weeks, we went back and forth and developed a really beautiful website for the organization. After we launched the site, we had another meeting with Mike to wrap things up and hand over the site to him. I will never forget how ecstatic Mike was when we presented the final site to him. He just couldn't believe how wonderful it all was—and that it was completely free! He had received help with absolutely no strings attached from a designer who worked for Netscape, an engineer who worked for Cisco, and a UC Berkeley business school student.

At the end of our meeting, he gave each of us a hug and invited us to visit him at his home so that he could thank us for all the help we provided. The whole project was such an amazing experience for the three of us. It felt wonderful to offer our time and skills with no expectation of receiving anything in return.

Trishna was true to her word. Their motives were pure. They didn't go into the project with a specific goal. They went in with open hearts, listened to Mike's story, and dug in and started to help. Now the story of the Tooth Mobile is spreading like wildfire across the Internet, and the organization in turn is reaching more people in need. If that's not an incredible achievement, what is?

Next, we asked Trishna if her work with CharityFocus has changed the quality of her life. Her initial reaction to the question was that everything she has done with CharityFocus hardly qualifies as work. Here is the rest of her answer:

> My "work" with CharityFocus involves being the change and transforming myself through service. It has thoroughly impacted my life. CharityFocus gives me the opportunity to practice being selfless in a very grounded, practical, and real way. I'm grateful for that. It enables me to cultivate generosity, which ultimately makes me a happier person. As so many others have said, in helping others we are truly helping ourselves. I feel like I am always learning about myself through the variety of projects I've participated in with CharityFocus. I have had a chance to slowly experience this inner shift toward becoming a more compassionate human being.

Finally, we asked Trishna…if someone was considering volunteering, but a little hesitant, if she had any advice to get them off the fence. Her response was interesting, especially coming from a founding team member of a volunteer organization:

> In so many ways, it's not about whether or not you get involved with a volunteer organization. It's all about doing selfless things for others—even if it's simply in your everyday life. When you practice acts of kindness and acts of service in a very conscious and deliberate way, over time you will

experience a shift in your outlook. You will start wanting to help others and seeking out opportunities to do so every day.

So if you are hesitant about formally volunteering with an organization, don't sweat it. Start by consciously doing acts of kindness in your own day-to-day life, and you will start to notice an inner transformation that begins to take place. Volunteering formally can sometimes help to provide a structure or vehicle through which you can do this, but it's by no means the only way to experience this inner transformation.

Don't sweat it. Just start reaching out a hand to others. You have skills to help someone in need—whether it's a degree in marketing, business, IT, or the ability to make a mean peanut butter and jelly sandwich. You have the ability to help right now. You don't even need a formal organization to get started. What can you do today…right at this moment? Start with a single, random act of kindness and see where it leads you.

13
Answer the Call

THERE ARE MANY PEOPLE IN THE WORLD WHO KNOW THE JOY OF volunteering simply because they were willing to answer the call. They might not have spent much time pondering all of the possibilities, thinking about their aptitudes, or searching their souls for what ignited their passions. Someone asked for help, and they simply responded.

Have you ever answered the call? What's it like to be the one to take action? What do responders get out of stepping up when the anonymous crowd says, "Gee, somebody ought to do something about this."

To find out, we talked to three people who answered the call.

He Got By with a Little Help from His Friend

George Coon thinks of volunteering as a learned lifestyle. Both he and his wife, Ruth, came from families that were active in their church and community. Assisting others is what they have always done and what they always will do. (In that respect, they sound a lot like our parents.) It's hard for George to think of volunteering as a transformational experience, because it has always been part of his life. But George does love one thing about volunteering—he always gets to meet new people and make new friends. Some of George and Ruth's closest friendships have been formed through volunteer activities.

He told us about one volunteer who had a profound impact on both of them:

> Probably the most significant person to encourage our volunteering was a St. Andrew church member, Don

Schlup. In the early 1990's, we joined a Mexico work team that painted and repaired a Methodist church building in farming country near Mexico City.

Near the end of this project, our team leader had a massive heart attack and died. Don Schlup took over the handling of the team during this crisis and became the driving force for four more Mexico work teams in future years.

With Don's encouragement, Ruth and I participated in three of those teams, and we became very good friends. I might add that adult work teams were not a usual thing in those days. Don put together the entire project. We learned many organizational guidelines from those trips, and the church staff picked up the work team system and made it into the corporate project model that currently exists.

Each friend represents a world in us, a world possibly not born until they arrive.

—Anaïs Nin

George and Ruth Coon have built numerous great friendships by answering the call. George admits that he doesn't always equate the word volunteering with joy, but he almost always walks away with some new and interesting friendships. If the cross country ski group needs a leader one year, he steps up; if a teen center is short of volunteers, George is there; if their child's high school needs someone to run the concession stand, George and Ruth will do it; when the Girl Scout troop needs an area coordinator, Ruth picks up the task (for eleven years).

"Things need to get done," George told us. "And some people are willing to get involved. Surprisingly to me, most people are not willing to get involved."

When we met George Coon, he was pushing a blood drive for Bonfils Blood Center between church services at St. Andrew. He jokes about how he was roped into this volunteer effort, but the story is another example of George answering the call and coming to the aid of a friend in need. In his own words:

It started with my good friend Vernon Norman. Vernon worked for the government, and (as I understand it) spent quite a bit of time at locations that had been used for atomic bomb testing. It is suspected that this radioactive exposure may have led to his tendency toward the occurrence of cancer in his body.

Vernon had been the church coordinator of blood drives with Bonfils Blood Center. Vernon also occasionally asked me to transport him to and from the hospital where he was treated with a chemotherapy cocktail. Things were becoming difficult for him, and on one of these trips, Vernon asked if I would cover the St. Andrew blood drive. I said of course, and I'm still doing it four times a year.

To be completely honest, George often finds this volunteer job annoying. The threat of Mad Cow Disease has cut down on his potential donors, and sometimes people growl at him on the phone when he calls at an inconvenient time, but he's not about to take back a promise to a friend. Although, a few years ago, George did try to pass the job on to someone else in the church.

"When I asked about finding someone else to do this job, they said, 'Oh, no, this is a lifetime commitment.' I guess I either have to die or move out of town," George smiled ruefully. "So what are the positives of this particular volunteer job? No committee meetings."

As much as George jokes about the downside of volunteering, he enjoys talking about the friendships he has made through volunteering and the friendships he has honored through his volunteer efforts. George and Ruth's lives are shaped by their constant practice of reaching out to those in need, by saying yes when they get the call.

"When someone is in need and I think I might have qualifications to help, I'm very likely to step forward as a volunteer."

How lucky we are that George and Ruth answer the call.

May I never get too busy in my own affairs that I fail to respond to the needs of others with kindness and compassion.

—Thomas Jefferson

What is Your "Sole" Worth?

Apparently not much.

That's what a former stand-up comic, present day minister found out one day in a downtown Denver park.

But we're jumping ahead in the story.

Meet Jerry Herships, the funniest pastor we've ever known, and also one of the most inspiring. We knew right away that we wanted to interview him for this book, because he is doing some really exciting things around Denver and with our church. We don't think St. Andrew had any idea what they were in for when they hired this guy!

In May of 2010, we were sitting in the 9:15 service at St. Andrew, and The Rev (that would be Jerry) got up and gave a perfect synopsis of what this book is all about. We wanted to jump out of our seats and holler, "That's IT! That's what we're talking about!"

We didn't do that.

Instead, we quietly picked up a printed copy of his sermon (grinning like Cheshire cats) right after service. We have included a few quotes from it throughout this section.

Jerry answered the call a few years ago when he completely changed professions. He listened to a small voice within, and eventually the comedian found himself at Iliff School of Theology in Denver.

By the time Jerry was officially ordained in 2009, he was a man on a mission. Jerry developed a new concept for worship called After Hours: More Love, More Laughs, Less Judgment. The group meets at a satellite location in Denver that is within a few blocks of bars, tattoo parlors, and free clinics—the ideal location for this urban missionary.

After Hours is a "come as you are" approach to worship. It feels a lot more like walking into your local pub or restaurant than walking into church. It takes place at five o'clock on Sunday nights, and instead of sitting in neat rows, the attendees gather around circular tables covered in big sheets of white paper with crayons as part of the centerpiece. The music doesn't come from a hymn book. Instead, you might hear the band play Pink Floyd's Comfortably Numb or some other popular tune. And the best part is during the service when everyone makes peanut butter and jelly sandwiches!

That's right, PB&J, rock music, coloring on the tables, and God.

What the heck is this guy trying to do?

Oh, and the sermon is more of a discussion group.

After Hours is church for people who don't do church.

So why did Jerry completely turn his life upside down, go back to school to become a preacher, and then start a church service that's nothing like church? By the way, Jerry's wife Laura should get some serious brownie points for backing him all the way. It was obvious in our interview that Laura is a major support and source of inspiration for Jerry—as is their son, Hudson.

When we sat down with Jerry at a Starbucks for about an hour, we found out where he's coming from and where he's going with all this.

> *There are people that consume church. I did, for years. I went and took and took and took. And I remained...stuck. It was fun and I made lots of friends. I saw cool shows and heard amazing things. But the truth was...I was stuck. I never felt anything close to a transformation. Nothing changed for me until I learned English. Yep, English was what brought me around. I had to learn that "church" was not a noun, it was a verb.*
>
> —Rev. Jerry Herships

Jerry is turning church into a verb. Every After Hours service is a volunteer activity. Those PB&J sandwiches go to El Centro, a day labor site in Denver. Jerry also teamed up with his friend Ryan, who is a pastor on the campus at the University of Denver. Ryan started making sandwiches with college kids, too, because he found that they were tired of having religion shoved down their throats. They were much more willing to make sandwiches for homeless people than listen to a long, boring sermon, so Ryan focused on the sandwiches. He throws in a little scripture reading and some other stuff, but the college students are there to make about 100 sandwiches every week. It's their first chance to volunteer as adults in the world and they're, well, they're eating it up.

So now Ryan and Jerry take sack lunches to homeless people in Civic Center Park in downtown Denver, and they also drop off sandwiches at El Centro, and it has been a pretty cool deal. It's not just two guys hauling sandwiches, either. The college kids and the people from After Hours take time out of their schedules to do it, too.

"I swear, when someone has that first face-to-face interaction with anybody that has had to live on the streets for any length of time, it's pretty transforming," Jerry told us when he recalled what it's like to go with groups of people to deliver sack lunches. "It's amazing to me how much people are willing to engage in the kindness of volunteering, as long as they don't have to buy into the dogma of orthodox religion. They just love the fact that we're doing stuff with Denver Urban Ministries; we're doing stuff with the homeless; we're doing stuff with migrant workers. To them that's the real deal. There's no BS involved there. There's something very pure about it."

Jerry estimates that about 40 percent of the people who come to After Hours have never been to church before. That's the group he wants to reach. We asked him about how people react to his slightly radical concept of worship.

"They're like, so...you make sandwiches during the service? Okay, we've got to see it just for the freak factor alone," Jerry imitated the skepticism he witnesses just about every Sunday night. "I've got to see how that looks. You know, Jesus and peanut butter are not quite, um, o-kay."

Jerry's pretty convinced most people show up once just because they want to win a bet. But they stay because something very real is going on. It's that church as a verb thing.

"I grew up Catholic, and I was an altar boy and did that whole deal," Jerry said. "I left that when I moved out to Los Angeles. I didn't have a beef with religion. It just wasn't, what's the term everybody uses? Relevant."

Jerry stopped going to church when he moved to L.A., but he never lost his spiritual side. His roommate Steve was Jewish, and both of them volunteered for quite some time taking hot chocolate and peanut butter and jelly sandwiches to the homeless. Jerry asked Steve one night why he did it. Steve looked at Jerry like he had two heads, "Because it's the right thing to do."

It was pretty simple.

A few years later, Jerry and Laura got married and then moved to Florida where Jerry was a night club manager. Laura grew up Methodist, and so they started attending St. Luke's United Methodist Church in Orlando where they really connected with the pastor, Bill Barnes. It was Bill who asked Jerry one day if he ever thought about going into the ministry.

"I had never thought about it," Jerry laughed. "But having worked in night clubs and been a bartender and all that, I thought if I did it, I would probably do it differently."

Jerry was pretty sure back then that you couldn't do church differently. He just assumed you had to do it the way everybody else did it.

"How do you blend the bartender with the priest's robe? You know, I didn't see how that was going to work."

Eventually, the Herships family moved to Denver and started attending St. Andrew, and Jerry started taking classes at Iliff School of Theology. His idea for After Hours was still brewing, and he shared his thoughts with Harvey Martz, the senior pastor, and Cindy Bates, the senior associate pastor.

"They knew my background, and I was feeling very much like one of these things is not like the other. But they said, hey, give it a shot."

That's all Jerry needed to hear.

"I knew a lot of really good people when I was a bartender," Jerry explained. "You know, people who worked in food and beverage. I was going to church, and they were always saying we don't go. So I asked them, do you have a beef with church? They said no, but we get home from work at 3:30 in the morning. Church is at like 9:30. They had a really good point."

That's how Jerry came up with the idea of an evening service. Then, he and Laura just started ripping off everything from the food and beverage world that they could use—comfortable tables, a band, drawing with crayons at the tables. They knew they couldn't call it Joe's Pub Church, so they eventually came up with After Hours, and it stuck. Making sandwiches started out as a side thing, but it turned into a centerpiece of the service because people felt like they were making a difference every, single week.

"There's something very clean about, I make a sandwich today, and tomorrow somebody eats," Jerry told us. "People started writing notes on the paper bags. You know, we're praying for you; I'm sorry things are tough right now; good luck; I hope you find work today."

Jerry didn't even know about the notes until Laura told him people were taking the crayons from the tables and writing on the bags. It was a straight line of service. They wrote the message one day, and they knew someone would receive it the next.

"People thought that was pretty cool."

Jerry wanted to increase the number of those straight-line connections.

> We don't take stuff to be transformed; we give stuff to be transformed. Now, it might just be a coincidence that the people I see being transformed are people that are reaching out into the world. It could very well just be a coincidence. But I doubt it.

—Rev. Jerry Herships

Next stop, Civic Center Park.

Jerry was at a prayer breakfast downtown, and he asked one of the pastors a simple question.

"Are any of the churches going down to the park and actually, I don't know, feeding people?"

The pastor didn't think so.

"I said, well, that's stupid. I mean, we're not New York City, but Denver isn't a tiny town," Jerry said. "And I was like, hey, I'm ordained now. I can do communion anywhere."

Jerry always had this vision of doing communion in the park. He decided to make that vision a reality. So he just did it. He went down to the park one afternoon and set up a card table, a cup of juice, some bread, and a ton of sandwiches. Guys came up and looked at him kind of funny. Jerry asked them if they wanted a sandwich, and they said sure.

It wasn't exactly the beautiful moment Jerry envisioned, but it was a start.

"I was picturing like all these people standing around for communion, but the guys were like, thanks, brother. I asked them if they wanted to stick around to have communion. It's going to be a great service. You don't want to miss this. But they were like, nope. I'm good. They took the sandwiches, and they were gone."

Jerry then described what happened next:

There was one guy who walked up to me and said, "What's in the cup?" I told him it was grape juice. He said, "What are you going to do with it?" You know, at St. Andrew we pour the leftover juice on the ground after communion. This guy said, "Do you mind if I take it?" I said no. So I've got this chalice, and he's got his water bottle, and for a moment it was like all my heavy Catholic orthodoxy came crashing back. I thought can I do this? Is this okay? God, are you cool with this?

But then I thought, man, this embodies the whole idea of communion. It's pretty heavy stuff when you get to pour juice into a homeless guy's water bottle because he doesn't have anything to drink. I gave away the bread, too. It wasn't just symbolic. It actually was the bread of life on that day. That dude had nothing else to eat. This was it.

The first experience of communion in the park really shook Jerry up—in a great way. He went back to After Hours, shared his story, and they regrouped and really started coloring outside the lines.

> *I think it was when I started to listen to that call of the homeless that things began to change for me. There was a transformation. Church became a verb. It wasn't something I consumed weekly. It was something I DID. Church is at its best when we go out and do.*
>
> —Rev. Jerry Herships

They knew that socks were like gold in the homeless community. People's feet get cold, and they get wet, and they never dry. So a group from After Hours went to Wal-Mart and got packages of ten pairs of socks for ten dollars and started giving them out with the sack lunches. There was no real strategic planning; the After Hours group just went with the idea. So now they were giving away sandwiches, socks, and a little communion on the side.

"Almost every person takes communion when they come by the card table now," Jerry smiled. "I just started saying, hey, you want communion before you go? They were like, sure. It's not a big, formal thing. There's enough spirituality that it's cool, but we're not shoving it down anybody's throat. And by the same token, the real deal is, you know, help a brother out. I mean, they've got nothing."

So now every Tuesday at noon, somebody is feeding the homeless in the park. Sometimes it's Ryan and his group of DU college students, and other times it's Jerry and the group from After Hours. They set up their card table at 14th and Broadway, right across the street from the Denver Public Library. Stop by and lend a hand if the spirit moves you.

Jerry has heard some incredible stories from the people he's met in the park. One guy who flew his sign a few blocks away told Jerry that a lot of people who drive by tell him to "get a job." He had a job six months ago…and a car… and an apartment. People didn't even know his story. It's just so easy to drive past.

That guy disappeared for months, and Jerry had no idea what happened to him. Then, in August of 2010, he showed up again wearing a big grin. He walked right up to Jerry and said, "I got a job. I'm off the street. We have an apartment. Life is great."

Another guy asked for two sandwiches instead of one when he came up to the card table.

"I said sure. Like I would tell him, sorry, only one act of kindness per person."

Turns out the guy wasn't being greedy. When Jerry put his card table in the trunk of his car a few minutes later, he saw the man walking hand in hand with his wife, each of them eating a sandwich.

There is another man Jerry has become friends with named Cecil. About three weeks before our interview, Cecil came by the card table for a sandwich. Jerry asked him how he was doing, and Cecil said, "Great! Me and my wife have got a place now that's right behind a pawn shop. I set up a tarp, so we stay nice and dry. And there's a Seven-Eleven next door, so there are security cameras. It's a sweet setup! You know, some people out here are really in bad shape."

Jerry sat there and thought, remind me never again to complain. My biggest problem this week was they were out of fries at McDonald's. What do you mean you're out of fries?! How can you be out of fries? This guy's doing great because he has a tarp behind a pawn shop.

And it was Cecil's 53rd birthday that day. Jerry gave him half the communion loaf and everyone sang happy birthday.

A few weeks after the communion in the park deal got going, Jerry really checked himself when he was complaining to Laura that he couldn't find a pair of shoes he wanted to wear.

"I thought, dude, you have shoes you can lose," Jerry shook his head. "The fact that you can't find them speaks volumes."

So Rev. Jerry became the "sole" man. He took ten pairs of shoes out of his closet and brought them down to the park.

Unfortunately, Jerry was in for a humbling experience.

He thought the shoes would be gone in a matter of minutes, but when it got down to the last three pair, he couldn't give them away.

"It is humbling when you try to give a homeless guy a pair of your own shoes, and he's like, nah. I'm good. Those just don't work for me."

Jerry had to pack the three pairs of shoes back into his bag to try to give away another day.

On the flip side, a few weeks later Jerry was in the park and he happened to be the only person down there that day. A guy walked up, and he was wearing Jerry's shoes.

"I-I don't even know what to call the feeling it gave me to see him wearing shoes that were once lost in my closet," Jerry stuttered. "It was really strange. It did make me realize how stupid my problems are."

Methodism has had a slogan for a number of years:

Open Hearts, Open Minds, Open Doors

It's a great slogan, but Jerry wants to take it one step further. He's glad that the doors are open, but he wants to see more people walking out of them and into a world that's hurting.

> *See, the irony is that for so long I thought that we went out into the world to help THEM; whoever the "them" was. That's wonderful and it is great to help others but really, it is when we help "them" that we feel the change. We thought it was for them, but it is really ourselves that we are helping. Transformation happens when we put them first. And when we do that, we get*

closer and closer to finding out what it is that God has in store for us.

—Rev. Jerry Herships

September 2010 was the one-year anniversary of the project in Civic Center Park—50 lunches a week; 50 pairs of socks a week; cases and cases of water; and a whole lot of communion.

Jerry's vision of After Hours is really taking shape and making a difference, too. People come to After Hours for the volunteer activities now—probably even more than for the sermons—and that's just fine with him.

"I think Jesus would think this is cool. A teacher of mine once said, Jerry, I can do church in a Jiffy Lube. Truth be told, my ideal gig would be to have church in night clubs. When I worked there, I started my shift at 7pm. There's plenty of time to do a service before then—and there's a stage, full lighting, why can't it be there?"

The theme that's rising to the top again is face-to-face interaction. People crave community, whether they're sharing a sandwich or passing on a message of hope. Jerry's dream for After Hours is that it will continue to be a vehicle for people to step outside of the doors and reach out to others.

"I'm not worried about getting people to come in. I think we should be more worried about going through the doors and into the community," Jerry smiled. "The question for the church for years has been how we get more people to come to church. Maybe the question needs to be how we get the people in church to go out into the world. If we can do that, God only knows what kind of transformation we will have."

Don't Forget Your Second Wind

Some people will do anything for love. In Jeff Lamontagne's case, that meant holding up a diseased, blackened, human lung while his high school girlfriend gave an American Lung Association presentation to middle school kids. Hopefully, the two of them saved many lives by discouraging children from smoking. Jeff felt that his contributions helped, and getting outside of his daily concerns made him feel like he made a difference. It was his first volunteer experience.

Jeff has come a long way since then to head another organization that saves lives: the Second Wind Fund. The Second Wind Fund helps teens get connected to specialized, licensed mental health providers who teach them coping skills and that their problems need not lead to suicide. Once connected, the fund pays for the life-giving counseling that the youth receive.

How did he get here?

Jeff had no idea his law career would be interrupted when a rash of teen suicides hit Green Mountain High School. Part of having a volunteer spirit is recognizing inspiration when it hits and answering the call when it comes.

"Somebody needs to do something," his friend Scott Fletcher said.

Jeff listened. He was working as an environmental lawyer at the time.

Flash forward to a recent, warm Colorado September day. A flock of white doves circle over the Jefferson County Fairgrounds. They zigzag back and forth in the Indian-summer sky between the hills and above the cities of Lakewood and Golden. Frantically flapping wings give the appearance of sparkles of silver, like fireworks in the daytime sky. The release of doves marks the beginning of the 8th annual fundraising walk/run/ride benefitting the Second Wind Fund of Metro Denver. Each bird represents a beloved child lost to suicide; the flock symbolizes hope for a generation of youth, too many of whom tragically believe that ending their own life is their only solution to their problems.

Below the rapidly receding doves, a flock of people—four hundred to be exact—circle the fairgrounds with purpose. They are the volunteers that make this great event happen for the thousands of runners, walkers, and bikers eager to get on the three-mile course. The race participants can be considered volunteers, too. All in attendance have given up their time and money to help the Second Wind Fund.

Watching over the flocks of doves in the air and the humans on the ground is Jeff Lamontagne, director of the Second Wind Fund. Pride wells up within him as he realizes how far this event has come in its eight short years of existence. What was supposed to just be a one-time gesture of goodwill, with sixty-six participants and eight volunteers in 2002, has grown into an annual event with over four hundred volunteers and over three thousand participants.

What inspires these four hundred souls? Jeff likens them, in the best sense, to an ant colony, everyone selflessly moving in all different directions to accomplish a larger task. What makes them report for duty at six o'clock in the morning on the day of this event each year to do mundane things like peel vegetables, pick up trash, and direct traffic? Jeff thinks it is because they all know their hard work counts for something; they enjoy being part of a team that makes a difference. Helping prevent teen suicide is a cause righteous enough for these enthusiastic people to come back year after year and "work like crazy," he says.

That enthusiasm drives Jeff, as well. It helps explain how he went from being an unpaid volunteer to taking a paid director position with the Second Wind Fund. He answered his friend Scott's challenge and has made it his life's pursuit.

Jeff's goals for the Second Wind Fund are lofty: go national! He thinks the model that works so well in metro Denver can function in other cities, too. In fact, they have already seen the model serve kids in other Colorado communities. Soon, he hopes funding will be in line to take his important mission across the country.

What makes the Second Wind Fund work? Jeff believes that the success the Second Wind Fund experiences is due in large part to the fact that staff, volunteers, and supporters alike place the common good of the organization and kids above their own personal agendas, experiences, and prejudices. The result: in just a few short years after its inception, the Second Wind Fund is one of Colorado's largest providers of mental health services to youth.

When a teen needs help, a call is placed to the Second Wind Fund. The youth is then matched quickly with a nearby counselor, who provides services at half their normal rate—services paid for by the Second Wind Fund. The cost to the teen is nothing, for up to 20 sessions as frequently as they need. Jeff estimates that nearly 1,900 kids have been helped in this way.

"It's outlandish how well it works," Jeff says.

Outlandish selflessness, generous giving, more-than-me thinking—call it what you want. The world needs more of it. Over one thousand teenagers in Colorado owe their lives to this program.

You've been keeping to yourself these days,

Cause you're thinking everything's gone wrong.

Sometimes you just want to lay down and die,

But that emotion can be so strong.

But hold on 'till that old second wind comes along.
—Billy Joel

Many people over the years have influenced Jeff in his road to volunteerism. His wife certainly did by offering her own volunteering spirit as an example. Her continuing support makes his involvement with the Second Wind Fund possible. We have found this often to be the case: behind every dedicated volunteer stands an equally dedicated and supportive spouse. Jeff started out at the Second Wind Fund as a volunteer himself; and then it got too big. The hours were crushing. He had his wife's support.

Jeff credits Scott Fletcher, the Second Wind Fund co-founder, as the person to which the organization owes its existence. Scott had the temerity to make the outlandish statement, "Somebody ought to do something about this." He backed up his statement by volunteering countless hours and sitting on the Board of Directors ever since.

But most of all, Jeff credits the Second Wind of Metro Denver army of volunteers as his biggest source of influence and inspiration. A cast of thousands, they come to him asking what they can do to support a cause that inspires them. The Second Wind Fund no longer recruits volunteers. They arrive at Jeff's (Second Wind Fund's?) doorstep in droves, eager and willing to serve.

In a way, we are glad Jeff Lamontagne was among our first interviews for this book. He gave us ideas that changed the course of our project. He also started a pattern that continued throughout the interviews: each person we spoke with changed our perspective on what it means to volunteer and why it's so important to do something for another person.

Our interview nearly done, Jeff offered up his own personal theory on why selfless acts are so important to humanity and why he feels the Second Wind Fund volunteers are so effective.

Jeff believes that people follow a three-step evolution to selflessness in their lives. The first step, when we are born, is selfish: we look to our own needs for warmth, food, and comfort. The second step happens when we get older and start identifying with our family, group, or nation. We learn to place our group above ourselves, but that's not the final step according to Jeff. The third step occurs when a person starts identifying with everybody and placing the greater good of humanity above themselves and their own group. From me, to us…to everybody.

How much concern do we have for the greater good of humanity, and what are we really doing about it? Jeff asks himself that question often and admittedly finds himself lacking. But for the most part, he feels he and his team spend more time in that third place—when working on Second Wind Fund's work—than average people in average situations, and that is what makes the Second Wind Fund the vital organization it is.

Giving people the nudge to take that third step is one of the main purposes of this book. Step outside of yourself and into humanity.

Jeff provided us with another pivotal moment in this project when we asked him the question, "How has your experience with the Second Wind Fund transformed you?" He paused, unable to speak for a very long heartbeat.

"Entirely...this is the hardest..." He paused again; clearly he was emotionally affected by the question and didn't know how to proceed. That speechless moment spoke volumes to us about how the power of doing something for someone else can change you for the better. When he gathered himself, his eloquent answer caused a glow within us for days. We feel that glow after hearing each and every story and want others to feel it, too.

In Jeff's own words:

> It's really hard to say, and almost impossible to overstate. I don't even know where to start...
>
> I've said sometimes that it has restored my faith in the human spirit, because—not that it was ever lost entirely—but you know when Scott and I talked about doing something because there were four suicides next door, the church came out and supported it. That was gratifying, because it's such a scary, difficult issue.
>
> I think what really started changing me was not that the church got on board, because churches are kind of like that. But after we decided to expand it, part of me felt like this was a lost cause. It was clear to me early on that we needed widespread public support, not just from people who had lost their kids to suicide.
>
> Every day on my way to work I would stop and knock on the door of a business. Or on my lunch hour I would call a church and see if they wanted to join us. And sure, we got rejections, but we got enough people saying, "Yes, we'll help. We knew one of those kids," or "Yes, I lost someone to suicide," or "I know! I used to have suicidal thoughts." We started getting some momentum. And then, the more we were able to go out and talk about it, the more people just joined in.

Every day I think to myself, what's more amazing? Is it more amazing that someone makes it through the most painful experience a person can imagine, losing a kid to suicide? I would really challenge you to think of anything more painful. I'm really not sure that there is. It's hard to imagine, and yet they come out. Most people want to sweep it under the carpet or forget about it or just run away. But our volunteers come out and live it all the time when they work for us. That's amazing.

Or is it more amazing that here is this dark, difficult, mysterious issue and people who have never experienced it say, "I get it! Let's do something." Does that surprise me? Not really.

We have had around ten thousand people give money to our organization, and six to seven hundred people have volunteered over the years. It is amazing. People are so selfless!

I mean, sometimes it's the amount of money that people give that shocks me. You know, checks that I could never write myself for kids that they are never going to meet. They give a ton of money and volunteer effort.

We have around one hundred volunteers who have donated one hundred hours or more of their time in the last few years. That's a lot. For some of those people, that represents a significant sacrifice, a significant impact on their lives—on their personal lives—just to make room to volunteer for this organization.

Our meetings with staff and volunteers are so productive in this organization; people always get back to the issue at hand. If people come in with ego or personal agendas, they don't find it very welcoming. The conversation always goes back to what's best for the organization and how we are going to help more kids...It's just the culture.

And so here we have hundreds of people who all put aside their personal egos and agendas to make something happen around something like suicide, a subject that is almost unfathomable, and most people don't even want to think about.

So whatever else happens in my life, I'm blessed to have been a part of this, much less to have led it. I wake up and say I can't believe I'm doing this. But really, the bigger thing isn't the surprise; it's the amazement at what people are really capable of when a culture is set, a culture around helping other people.

It's a little strange saying this, because it all started because some kids died. On the other hand, I think we've saved a lot more lives. I just feel incredibly fortunate and blessed and so...how did I get to do this? There are so many good people, and there are so many smart people in this world. I don't think that very many have the opportunity to start something that is totally new, that no one else is doing. That's what we're doing today. Really, no one else is doing this. And to save lives, much less young lives, and to have the opportunity to lead a group of people that care about what they're doing in some cases more than themselves.

I am just...I am just grateful. Whether it is being grateful to God, or to circumstances, or whatever, I just feel like it transformed my life. I have lived a good life already just by what has happened in the last seven years with this organization. I mean, I hope to have more success, but even if I failed at everything else I ever tried...I would be okay.

How much time to you spend in that last ring of humanity?

If someone were in need of your help today, would you answer the call?

14

Empowering Opportunities

Several people that we interviewed cited empowerment as a gift they give when they volunteer. Whether they are helping a person die with dignity through hospice work, teaching an immigrant to read English, or volunteering in a soup kitchen, they get a huge rush out of helping someone who is helpless move into a place where they feel capable—strong and secure...and hopeful.

Once again, when a person connects on this level, they end up receiving exactly what they give. They may offer empowerment, but it boomerangs right back and gives the giver a jolt of power in return. The circles strengthen each time we reach out to help one another.

> *Be of service. Whether you make yourself available to a friend or co-worker, or you make time every month to do volunteer work, there is nothing that harvests more of a feeling of empowerment than being of service to someone in need.*
>
> —Gillian Anderson

The following three stories exemplify the strong circle of empowerment and the miracles that occur when we step inside it.

Lace Up Your Sneakers

"I don't know. That's a hard question." Dottie Mann grinned and cocked her head to one side.

We were sitting with Dottie at a Panera Bread Cafe and had just asked her when she first started volunteering. We thought that was such a straightforward question when we started this project.

Turns out, it's a hard one for people to answer when volunteerism has always been an integral part of their life.

"The first thing I remember doing on my own might have been in middle school. I participated in the March of Dimes Walkathon. I just thought that was really cool. I don't know why I did it. I know I did it with a friend." Dottie smiled at the memory. "That's the first event I remember participating in that wasn't church."

When we followed up on the question, Dottie revealed that her family was very involved in taking care of their extended church family, and that was probably what planted the seed of a lifetime of service. Dottie's family delivered food for funeral receptions, participated in youth group projects, and got involved in just about everything that came along at church. Dottie could hardly wait to get into high school, so she would be old enough to participate in one of the youth group trips to Haiti. Unfortunately, by the time she reached the right age, travel into Haiti had stopped and so did the youth trips. She felt a little cheated.

Dottie certainly made up for her loss as an adult. From the moment Dottie and her husband John first met, they attended church together. Church and service work were a big part of John's family history, too. Soon, the young couple became involved with youth ministry, and it has been a big part of their lives ever since.

When we interviewed Dottie in the fall of 2009, she and John had been married twenty years, and they had been leaders of youth ministry together for about twenty-three years. It is such a huge part of their lives that they find it hard to imagine life without it. They have lived in Cincinnati, Pennsylvania, and Denver and attended churches of all shapes and sizes. The one constant is their involvement in youth ministry. If you met Dottie and John, you would know immediately why this vivacious couple is good for young people—and vice versa. They're a couple of spark plugs.

As an adult leader of youth ministries, Dottie finally got to go on that mission trip she'd been waiting to take since she was a child. Her first trip was one that she herself organized. Dottie took eleven teenagers to a Native American reservation near the Four Corners. That was the first of a "bazillion" youth mission trips for Dottie.

"The youth are so easy to work with," Dottie told us. "They never say no."

Dottie also got involved with Urban Peak after they moved to Denver. It's a shelter for homeless teenagers, so it was right up her alley. Dottie and her family still spend every Christmas at Urban Peak. John has been their Santa Claus on Christmas Day for twelve years and running.

So Dottie and John have found their niche. They love working with youth. Dottie explained it perfectly:

> I think along the way you find things that don't work for you. I found out that I really don't ever want to go on a mission trip with adults. Really, no thank you. And most adults tell me they would rather pull out their thumbnails than spend a week with a bunch of teenagers and sleep on a hard floor with mosquito nets. I'm like, hey, I'm all over that. To me, that's my idea of vacation. That is as much fun as lying on the beach for a week with umbrellas in your drinks.
>
> So I think you have to figure out what it is that moves you. There were some things along the way that moved me—things I never imagined would. Frankly, there are things I really wish didn't move me, because now I'm doing them, and they aren't easy.

Life takes surprising turns, and grace shows up in completely unexpected places.

Dottie was the youth director at St. Luke's United Methodist Church in Highlands Ranch. She was flying by the seat of her pants running the youth program, but she loved it. Her co-director was studying at Iliff School of Theology at the time, and Dottie learned a lot from her. They were running the program and actually doing a very good job.

Then on April 20, 1999, two high school seniors walked into Columbine High School, killed twelve students, a teacher, and injured twenty-one students. This tragedy—the deadliest for an American high school—sent the entire country into a panic. Dottie was at ground zero with her youth group students.

"I had kids who were hurting," Dottie almost whispered. "God, they were hurting. They asked if they had to forgive them. Where was God? And then there was a fight, because somebody saw God there and somebody didn't. It wasn't a real fight, because there was no energy to do that. But I was sitting there thinking I'm in way over my head here. I have no idea what to do."

Dottie knew enough to just let the kids talk. She knew enough to not strong arm them into believing one thing or another.

"That's when I said, wow," Dottie brightened a little. "I need some theology training, because I don't know how to do this."

Dottie remains very good friends with a lot of the kids who were in the youth group during that very difficult time. They still call her in good times and in bad, so she thinks she must have done okay in helping them process such an unfathomable event.

"I learned a lot from the youth at that time," Dottie told us. "They were able to ask questions that adults were afraid to ask. Adults sometimes have embedded belief systems that make us think we're not allowed to question certain things. That's when theology becomes harmful, when we can't let go of some beliefs. But the kids, if it doesn't work them, they move on and find something else. They're not afraid."

The Columbine tragedy sent Dottie to Iliff to study theology. Two years later, when she was in the midst of pastoral classes, a friend was diagnosed with ovarian cancer. She deteriorated so quickly that family and friends were reeling, completely unsure of what to do for this woman who was so dear to them. They were paralyzed in their feelings of powerlessness.

Dottie stopped to visit her friend at home one day and found out that she had been taken to Porter Hospital. She was in really bad shape. Dottie told us about what happened next:

Her husband told me not to come. So I sat in my car on the street and cried. I called my minister and said I don't know what to do. He asked what my heart was telling me. I said my heart is telling me I need to be there. Actually, my heart is telling me I need to be there for him. He said then go. He said what's the worst that can happen? I said he could throw me out. He said can you live with that? I said, yes. So I went in.

That was Saturday. She died on Tuesday. She was in the last stages.

But I was able to be there for him and for her, and I was there when the priest came and did the sacrament. They did the sacrament of marriage, and I was their witness. It was just really cool. And I heard some things from her that I didn't understand until later…that she was okay. She was ready to go. I didn't realize that message she was giving me until much later.

The next day I held her children when they said goodbye to her. While that was happening, I realized I was the only one left in the room. Her husband and our other friend had left, because they couldn't handle it. I could.

I had a lot of conversations with God that night like…I don't want this. I don't want to be able to handle this. I could, and I did, and it was holy ground.

Dottie found out she has a very powerful gift. She is able to empower people in the most difficult situations. Bubbly, funny, youth leader Dottie is also a calm, strong, deeply caring influence when people need her the most. It might not be the gift she would have chosen for herself, but it is holy ground. Now, Dottie works as a chaplain at Porter Hospital.

Then, another empowering opportunity showed up in Dottie's life. Again, it was not what she expected.

Dottie is an avid runner.

"Actually, running saves my soul," Dottie laughed. "I worship a lot on the run, me and my dog...and the prairie dogs...and the rattlesnakes...and the coyotes."

One year in December, Dottie was reading Runner's World magazine—one of her favorite publications. In their December issue, they have something called "Heroes of Running" where they highlight between six and ten runners who are doing great things in the world. Heroes of Running can be world-class athletes or everyday people doing things through running to make the world a better place. Dottie told us about a short article on a Hero of Running that changed her life:

> This woman, Lisa Shannon, was a hero of running. By a runner's definition, she wasn't really a runner. She probably ran maybe ten miles a week, you know, maybe three miles at a time. Whatever. I think she's an IT person by training. You know, corporate woman with a job, running on the side. She saw Oprah talking about what was happening to women in the Congo, and she was devastated.
>
> So with a trainer she decided to run thirty miles at one time and sponsor one woman for every mile she ran. That was her goal. She trained, and she called on her friends. A sponsorship for one woman was about $300.
>
> That was her goal, and she did it. She raised $30,000 for the women in the Congo. Through her vision, her dream, and her efforts, the Run for Congo Women was born.
>
> She was it. She was the Run for Congo Women in 2006 in Portland. And she was featured as a Hero of Running. I kid you not, it was this tiny little article, but it hit me. I said I can do that.
>
> I called my girlfriend Paula, and I said did you get your Runner's World? Usually we sit down and read it from cover to cover the moment we get it. It's sort of a treat, like, oooh, I can read that tonight after the kids go to bed. Mommy is going in her room under the comforter. You can't disturb her for an

hour. Don't mess with her until she's done reading her Runner's World. I don't do that anymore, but I used to.

Paula agreed that the Run for Congo Women was a great idea, and they should do it. (Dottie thinks she was just being nice at the time and didn't realize Dottie was serious.) Dottie emailed Lisa Shannon right away, and Ms. Shannon gave her two or three names of other women in the Denver area who had expressed interest.

"So I called one of the names, Jen Parsons. Jen said yes, I think we can do this. Do you want to meet? Jen wasn't even a runner at the time. She had a one year old and a two-and-a-half year old, so we were on different ends of the parenting spectrum."

A tiny article in Runner's World set the whole thing in motion. Two women with nothing much in common, other than a desire to help other women, connected. That's all it took. The Run for Congo Women was born in Denver.

"Honestly, I have to say it took both of us to do it, because I would have quit long ago," Dottie admitted. "Jen had the passion to keep going, but she had no idea how to do a run. I had the organizational skills and understood how to run, but I needed her passion to keep the momentum going. We worked really hard that first year. It was like we had to invent the wheel, which we really didn't, but we did."

> *In everyone's life, at some time, our inner fire goes out. It is then burst into flame by an encounter with another human being. We should all be thankful for those people who rekindle the inner spirit.*
> —Albert Schweitzer

The first Denver Run for Congo Women took place in 2007. Paula was behind the scenes support, and Jen and Dottie were out in front making things happen. The details were mind boggling—everything from police support to the number of port-a-potties they needed for the event.

"It was that article that triggered it," Dottie shook her head in disbelief. "And then having somebody else with the same passion. We could feed off each other. When one of us wanted to quit, the other would somehow have all the passion. So we carried each other along, having the goal that our first priority was education and our second priority was raising money through the race. As long as we stayed focused on that, we could keep going when things got hard."

> *I learned about Congo, widely called the worst place on earth to be a woman. Awakened to the atrocities—millions dead, women being raped and tortured, children starving and dying in shocking numbers—I had to do something.*
>
> —Lisa Shannon

The Run for Congo Women is part of a larger organization called Women for Women International, founded by Zainab Salbi. This organization supports women in war-torn regions with financial and emotional aid, job-skills training, rights education, and small business assistance so that they can rebuild their lives.

Statistics on their website in the fall of 2010 stated that 9,324 women are actively participating in Women for Women International's year-long program of empowerment; 31,000 women have participated in the program since it was started in 2004. The results are nothing short of miraculous. In 2008, 86 percent of the participants reported having improved their economic situation; 88 percent of the women expressed an increase in self-confidence; and 83 percent reported that they now have a greater knowledge of their rights.

As their website states, Women for Women is changing the world—one woman at a time.

And Dottie is part of that change.

Once again, Dottie turned to her favorite people in the world—the youth. The cross-country team at her kids' high school is her number-one source of volunteers for the Run for Congo Women in Denver each year. Dottie's goal is education, so she gives the teens a quiz at the end of the day to earn their volunteer service hours.

"They always panic when I say okay, quiz time," Dottie laughed. "The ones who have done it for three years are like no, no, no. It's a group test. It's okay. We know the answers."

Every year since Dottie started the Run for Congo Women in Denver she says she's going to quit. Every year she complains. Every year her husband, John, says, "You're not going to do this next year, right?"

But every year she does it again.

Why?

Because it makes a difference—it makes a huge difference in the lives of the women from the Congo.

Women for Women International funnels the money earned through this event directly to the women in the Congo—they get every cent. This is why Dottie, Paula, and Jen come back and get involved every year. Every year, the number of women they are able to sponsor goes up. Every year they know they're in the right place.

Dottie has experienced another small miracle as a result of her efforts to organize the Run for Congo Women. As she has gotten to know many of the men and women who come to run in the event, she has found out that they often have two reasons for volunteering. One is to help the women in the Congo, and the second is to heal themselves. Many of the participants have their own story of abuse. This run is a way for them to stare down their past, to heal the pain and rise above it by reaching out to another who has experienced the same.

"I hear them. They've shared their stories with me," Dottie told us. "When we can heal ourselves, then we can heal the world. When participants in this event learn to run, they learn to find strength in their body. When they find strength in their body, they realize they have strength in their soul."

Toward the end of the interview, Dottie told us about one woman from the Congo and how a few words from her transformed everyone who participated in the Run for Congo Women in Denver that year:

> Annie came from the Congo in 2009. We met her in May. Annie is stunningly beautiful. She had on one of her full African dresses when we met. She was just beautiful. We talked to her a little bit, and we asked her if she would come to our run and speak. She said no. She said I'll come, but I don't want to speak. We said okay.
>
> She had the hardest time understanding what we did. She couldn't grasp why people here cared enough to do something for people they never met, for people half a world away. I mean, that was what she couldn't get her head around. I'm sure she totally didn't get the running thing, either. She kept asking, why do you do this? You don't know me.
>
> Anyway, Annie came to the Run for Congo Women in Denver this year. She lives with a host family in Aurora and is learning English. She also speaks French and a Congolese dialect. When we talked to her in May, we had a full conversation with her in English. It blew me away how fast she's learning. She's healing physically; she's healing emotionally. She spends a lot of her time with legal services just working on getting a job and a green card.
>
> So Annie came to the run. Her therapist had registered to run, which is very cool. And then Annie agreed to speak the week before and tell her story. I think at first she intended to tell it in English, but she couldn't. So they wrote it out, and she said it in French, and her therapist stood next to her and translated.
>
> I stood there in the crowd listening to Annie, and everybody was crying—I mean bawling. It's not a sob story. It's a hope story. But everybody was bawling.
>
> I thought to myself, all right. I'll do it next year. Annie is just one reason why.

> I want to help women who have been abused, to help women have a voice, to empower women. I do believe that is the way to peace. If the balance of power is more equal, I think there will be less to fight about.

Of course, the one constant in life is change. Recently, Dottie stepped down as co-director of the race, but she remains active in the Run for Congo Women. She told us in an email about this transition.

> Sometimes you have to know when to let go and allow others move a project forward. I continue to take part in the run as a volunteer. It was interesting this year to go "just" as a volunteer, but the rewards were the same; my passion to help is the same. Our dream was to outgrow our original venue, and that happened. The race has moved to Washington Park. The best part is more volunteers stepped up to fill my place, and part of my job went to paid professionals.

Whether she is taking part in the Run for Congo Women, working with youth, or offering comfort to hospital patients and family, Dottie is a constant source of strength, hope, and empowerment.

> *When we quit thinking primarily about ourselves and our own self-preservation, we undergo a truly heroic transformation of consciousness.*
> —Joseph Campell

Lessons from the Lakota

The Lakota tribe has a rich and often heartbreaking history. Sitting Bull was a Lakota, as was Crazy Horse and Red Cloud. There were 20,000 Lakota in the mid-eighteenth century, and the Lakota people are part of seven related Sioux tribes spread across North America. There are nearly 70,000 Lakota in the United States today, and over 20,000 of them still speak their ancestral language. Their story continues to hold heartbreaks and triumphs.

The Lakota people deserve an important chapter in the narration of a land we now call the United States. Native Americans roamed the plains long before Lewis and Clark made their famous expedition and white people followed to explore the West. Encounters between whites and Native Americans during those times were often adversarial.

Hundreds of years later, Bob and Phyllis Rodgers from Mason City, Iowa made their own expedition, and they experienced firsthand how times can change and people who were once adversarial can become friends. They were part of a mission trip to the Rosebud Reservation in 2005, and an admiration of the Lakota people blossomed into a transformation of head and heart that is evident today as they plan their fifth trip back to see their friends, the Lakota.

We interviewed Bob Rodgers in the early winter of 2009 and discovered more about what made him decide to volunteer on the Rosebud Indian Reservation. This down-to-earth gentleman explored his own spiritual transformation as it related to volunteerism when he answered our questions.

We asked Bob first if volunteerism had always been a part of his life, and his immediate answer was no. However, we found out as the questions progressed that he had an active volunteer spirit from a very young age. He mentioned that in high school he had really wanted to join the Peace Corps and travel the world helping people in troubled countries. Instead, he volunteered for the draft in 1968, and that took him on a different path to help people in need. But his ability to reach out to others extended even further back, as we found out in the answer to our next question.

When we asked him when he first discovered the joy of helping others, Bob's response was a typical Iowa shrug of the shoulders. Lending a hand was so much a part of his life that he didn't consider it special:

> I think good deeds have always been part of who I am. I have always given up my chair to someone else who needs one. I

> don't mind giving up my place in line if someone else seems to be in more of a hurry than I am.
>
> When I was about twelve years old, I had earned some money, and at that time, I could not think of anything that I needed, so I gave it to the church. My mom made a big deal of that; I really don't know why.

We asked him next if there was a specific person who encouraged him to volunteer.

> I think that person would have to be my mom. She encouraged us by example. She always made sure everyone was taken care of before she would consider her own needs. She was very active in our church and made sure her kids had a chance to know the way of our Lord. She was a very wise and caring person.

Bob didn't realize how his mother's actions and his own simple good deeds were shaping him into a person who was willing to go even further to connect with something greater than himself. Or maybe he did see it. Bob obviously understands the concept of *MORE than me*.

Bob's journey from donating his earnings to the church at age twelve to volunteering with the Lakota tribe years later is an interesting tapestry of singular events. He gave us an important thread when he talked about Dr. Rev. Jo Watkins, the associate pastor at First United Methodist Church in Mason City.

In 2005, Pastor Jo was trying to put together a mission team to go to the Rosebud Indian Reservation in South Dakota, and her enthusiasm for the project was catching. A partner in this mission trip was the Tree of Life Ministry, a multi-denominational, cross-cultural organization that hosts volunteer groups year around on the Rosebud Reservation and the Crow Creek Reservation. They are a relief agency, not a religious organization, and they have been very active on the reservations since 1985. One of the exceptional aspects of the Tree of Life Ministry is that they strive to respect the wisdom, common sense, traditional values, and sovereignty of the people they serve.

Both Bob and his wife, Phyllis, decided to go, and they had an incredible experience that is difficult for them to put into words. Not only did they enjoy the work, but they got to know and admire the Lakota people. Additionally, they grew together as a couple when they were able to share this experience.

"We both enjoy helping other people," Bob told us. "This trip gave us time together to do just that."

Bob had already gone on a couple of mission trips with the Appalachia Service Project at that point, and he yearned to do more. Their first trip to the Rosebud Reservation in 2005 filled a growing desire to help others on a larger scale. It was a short trip, and only about six or seven volunteers (including Bob and Phyllis) went with Pastor Jo. But those six or seven people came back and told their friends and family members about their experience, and soon the tapestry started to take shape. Pastor Jo provided an opportunity for volunteers to get a taste of what mission work was like. Trips like that have the power to change lives.

People continued to go year after year, and the numbers have grown. This year has been no exception. Around forty people had already signed up for the 2010 trip when we talked to Bob. Flexible dates have given more volunteers an opportunity to participate, as well. Some are going for an entire week; others will be there Monday to Thursday; and a third group will volunteer Wednesday through Sunday.

Bob explained to us that the short trips allow volunteers to try something new without committing an entire week of vacation time. If they like the experience, they will come back for more. Bob knows that one trip is all it will take.

"So far no one has disliked what they were able to accomplish. Everyone has benefitted from spending time with the Lakota people on the Rosebud Reservation."

The convenience of these mission trips has certainly done a lot to reel in potential volunteers—but it is the connection with humanity that keeps them coming back year after year.

"I tell people that mission work can be as big or little as they want it to be," Bob said. "A volunteer project can be as short-term as being a coffee host or a greeter at church on Sunday morning. It can also be a month-long trip to Africa. The first option takes little time and no money; the second takes a large investment of time and money."

But they both count. They both connect the volunteer to something bigger than themselves.

When one woman expressed interest in the mission trip to the Rosebud Reservation, she told Bob that she was hesitant because she didn't think she had any talents to contribute. The woman was elderly and almost blind.

Bob knew otherwise.

He explained to her that some of the volunteers enjoy visiting the nursing home on the reservation and spending time with the residents. It is a wonderful way to learn from the Lakota, experience their culture, and talk one-on-one with people who have several generations of memories to share. She took the trip in 2010.

Bob is obviously an inspiration to many volunteers, but what kinds of projects have inspired him over the years?

His answer turns right back to the Lakota tribe.

The project that has meant the most to him has been his involvement in building the Sicangu Lakota Youth Center. The youth center was inspired by Noella and Shane Red Hawk, Native Americans who returned to the reservation to help with the serious issue of troubled youth. They saw a great need for Lakota culture education and suicide prevention. They also wanted to help increase the percentage of students who graduated from high school and provide a safe haven for youth. The project was a huge undertaking, and it has taken three long years to complete. There were many different strands that came together to help bring it to fruition: the help of the Tree of Life Ministry, extensive fundraising, lots of prayer, and loads of elbow grease.

The Sicangu Lakota Youth Center is now almost complete. It will offer high school GED classes; accreditation courses; Lakota culture classes; and counseling services as needed. The youth center will even house a restaurant called the Buffalo Jump Grill, where youth will have an opportunity to learn a trade and earn money.

Bob could not praise the project leaders enough:

> It is my opinion that Shane and Noella have a great plan to educate and change the feeling of hopelessness shared by many young people on the reservation to a feeling of HOPE. They will be able to work with youth before they fall into the traps that their parents and families have known. It is a good way to secure the future of their culture.

The issues that face the Rosebud Reservation are not small. The suicide rate on the reservation is eight times the national average; they currently have a high school graduation rate of 30 percent; unemployment is a staggering 70 percent; and diabetes tops that number at 80 percent. Rosebud is one of the poorest counties in the United States.

After hitting us over the head with those sobering statistics, Bob told us another story about his journey with the Lakota tribe:

> Another project that I just kind of fell into was wheelchairs for the Rosebud Reservation. One day while I was working at a nursing home in southwest Iowa, I noticed that they put three wheelchairs out by the dumpster. Two of them looked as if they were in pretty good shape, and the other just needed a tire. I asked if I could take them, and they said yes, so I loaded them up and called Russell from the Tree of Life to see if there was a need for wheelchairs. He told me they were like gold on the reservation.

Bob's wheelchair project started about three weeks before our interview, and he had already come up with almost forty wheelchairs, thirty walkers, twelve canes, and four power chairs. It's amazing what a keen eye and a few phone calls will do.

Bob and Phyllis built a relationship with the Lakota people when they were on the Rosebud Reservation. They connected to something bigger than themselves and learned many valuable lessons from a culture that was once foreign to them. That translated into continued action. They didn't forget the Lakota, even when they were back home in Iowa. Bob's new wheelchair project is a perfect example of that. Their bond held firm, and when we talked to them, they planned to return to the reservation again in the summer of 2010 to continue to strengthen that bond.

Bob admitted in his interview that the new wheelchair project was already bigger than he could handle. He didn't have room to store the equipment or the time to make the needed repairs. But he commented that it is a great problem to have, and he had no doubt that he would find someone to help him.

We asked Bob if lending a hand to someone in need has changed his life.

He is certain it has. But he's not sure what happened first: was it spiritual growth that led to helping more people; or did he grow spiritually as a result of lending a hand?

That's a very good question.

Bob then told us another story that has stuck with him over the years:

> I was on a trip to Kentucky with the Appalachia Service Project. We were working on a young couple's home. They had two young girls, and the sisters had been sleeping on the couch in the living room, because there was only one bedroom in the house. Our project was to add on a bedroom for the girls. As we worked, we got to know these two sisters, and we were really happy to be doing this for them. It was so amazing and rewarding to see the looks on their faces when

we showed them the finished room. We all cried—and most of the crew was made up of men.

Bob returned once again to the Rosebud Reservation for his final story:

> A family on the Rosebud Reservation needed help boarding up their living room window. It had been broken months before, and now it was the dead of winter. They had a young child, maybe six or seven years old, who had just come home from a stay in the hospital with a terrible illness. His bed was in the living room. It was the opinion of the group that this child should never have left the hospital, but we all know that in some areas of the country this does happen. Between the crying and the grateful smiles, we knew the parents were very glad we were there to help. We were glad we were there, too.
>
> As I have gotten older, I have felt my spiritual beliefs grow. I have also felt a stronger need to do more to help others. By doing the mission work that I do, I receive far more from one trip than I could ever give back when I help someone else. It's hard to describe how it makes me feel. I don't do it for recognition. It just makes me feel good.

Bob Rodgers has discovered the gift of stepping outside of himself. He has physically and emotionally felt the benefits of helping others, and it inspires him to do more. A spiritual path and the ability to reach out and help someone in need are intertwined. But we don't need to unravel a tapestry that is as rich as Bob's to understand that each feeds the other. The colors deepen with every action he takes, and the weave is stronger as he explores his spiritual beliefs more deeply. Bob and Phyllis, the Lakota people of the Rosebud Reservation, the Tree of Life Ministry, Pastor Jo, and the First United Methodist Church in Mason City were all separate entities at one time. They aren't any longer. They have intertwined to create a beautiful and lasting gift for our humanity.

Now, Not Later

Andrea Juncos is a member of the board of directors of a group called Girls Write Now, an outstanding volunteer organization in New York City that empowers young women through writing. Professional writers and teachers offer to coach these young women. They help them hone their writing skills and develop incredible friendships in the process.

There is a long waiting list to get into this exceptional program. In fact, Girls Write Now received the prestigious Coming Up Taller Award in November of 2009. Youth and adult representatives of the program traveled to Washington, D. C. and accepted the award from First Lady Michelle Obama.

We were privileged to interview Andrea Juncos through email. Since she is obviously an excellent writer, we decided not to tinker with her answers. Instead, we'll give them to you straight. Here is our conversation as it unfolded over the Internet:

Has volunteerism always been part of your life? Have you been involved with other non-profit organizations or projects?

Yes. I've been involved with volunteer projects for most of my life. I went through twelve years of Catholic school, and service was always strongly emphasized, even as part of the curriculum. In high school, I was in the Community Service Corps, where we ran activities like Operation Santa Claus and food and clothing drives. In college, I tutored elementary school kids at the YMCA in Chester, PA, which I absolutely loved.

Also, I studied abroad in Ireland for a semester, and I joined the university's branch of the Vincent de Paul Society; a group of us used to visit a home for people who are developmentally challenged, and we basically just hung out with the residents there, playing games, even dancing to music. The point was to be active and engaged with the residents. It was a lot of fun.

When I came to New York after college, I wanted to get involved here, and there are so many opportunities. I was also trying to figure out what kinds of positions interested me professionally. I joined Girls Write Now almost immediately, because it was the perfect merging of all of my interests—education, writing, and the empowerment of girls.

I also volunteered for a while at the International Center in Manhattan, which provides a wide range of services to immigrants. I was a "conversation partner"—paired with immigrants who were learning English. One woman was from Japan, another was from Taiwan, and I talked to each of them one-on-one for an hour a week, helping them with their English conversation skills. I learned so much!

When did you first discover the joy of volunteering or simple good deeds?

Two experiences come to mind. One is the tutoring I did in college with elementary school kids in Chester, PA, who were involved with the YMCA's afterschool program. I helped the kids with their homework assignments, which they were required to do before running off to the gym to play basketball.

I had a real soft spot for one kid. His name was Michael, and he was in third grade at the time. I used to help him with his math homework, and he struggled with it. I tried to think of creative ways to explain the concepts to him, and after a while he really started to catch on and improve. It made me feel like a million bucks to help him.

The other experience would have to be my first job. This is probably going to sound made up, but my first job, which I held for four years as a teenager, was working at a nursing home and retirement community for Catholic nuns. I can't say it was volunteering because they did pay me, but it's definitely where I learned how great it feels to help someone.

Nuns are people just like anybody else, and I loved the little old ladies of Camilla Hall. I worked in the kitchen and in the dining room, kind of like a waitress. Over four years I got to know many of the nuns very well, and in many cases, they were lonely and didn't have much going on outside of their daily routines. Some of them were very ill or frail. In the dining room I helped them get their food, carried it to the table, I brought them their drinks, and so on. They were always so grateful for the help.

They really enjoyed the company of a high school student. They asked me all about my life, boyfriends, teachers, friends, family—everything. There was one nun named Sister Leonard who I got to know pretty well. She used to ask me to help her organize her room sometimes, put things away, and help her get around. She was very frail. She just liked to listen to my stories. It felt really good to make her happy and listen to her talk about her life, too. I certainly have many hilarious stories from my four years there, but it was probably the first place I really learned how rewarding it feels to help somebody out and to brighten their day—even through simple little tasks like carrying someone's plate to the dinner table or listening to them share a memory.

Was there a specific person who encouraged you to volunteer?

Definitely my mother, Maureen Juncos. She was one of eight children in an Irish Catholic family. They grew up relatively poor in St. Paul, Minnesota. She and my dad, who is from a small town in Argentina, both came from humble beginnings, and I know they wanted my brothers and me to appreciate what we had and learn the value of giving to others. My mom never wanted us to be spoiled or feel entitled; my own family has never been wealthy, but we grew up with much more than either of my parents had as children, and I think they never wanted us to take that for granted.

One year at Thanksgiving, my mom signed us up to serve the turkey dinner at a soup kitchen. I was probably about ten years old. I remember my brothers and me complaining beforehand, the way kids do, about not wanting to go to the shelter for Thanksgiving. I was probably just intimidated because I didn't know what to expect or what the people would be like. But once we were there, we all had fun. It was a great experience.

I saw all these people who were just so grateful to have somewhere to go on Thanksgiving. Everyone was in such a good mood, happy to be around people and to have a delicious meal to enjoy. And they definitely got a kick out of us kids, the youngest members of the kitchen staff. I don't even remember what I was serving at the counter, but it made me feel good. After we served the food, we sat down and ate with everyone. I was struck by how crowded it was, because I didn't have a concept of homelessness or poverty being so close to home.

It felt like a wonderful way to spend Thanksgiving, with so many people who were thankful for that meal and our helping out. I remember feeling silly that I had complained about having to go there because there were all these people there that didn't have a choice. And they were having a blast. I'm really grateful to my mom for taking us there.

Why did you decide to get involved with Girls Write Now?

About a year after graduating from college and moving to New York, I was looking for something to do in addition to my job. I wanted to get involved in some kind of volunteer activity, so I started looking on idealist.org. Girls Write Now was the perfect match for me; it combines all of my interests—writing, teaching, mentoring, and empowering young women. My major in college was English literature and education. The job I had after graduation, which I really enjoyed, was doing editorial work for a nonprofit organization dedicated to advancing women in business.

I wanted to tap into the education side of my interests more and work directly with students. The more I learned about GWN, the more I wanted to be involved. I was excited about the opportunity to be a mentor to a young writer, to help her build confidence and skills, and to encourage her (although, at the time I was pretty insecure myself and not sure how much I could offer in terms of professional experience only a year out of college).

I've always been interested in both writing and teaching, and GWN has allowed me to do both. At that time, I really hadn't had much formal instruction in creative writing, so I was excited to learn about new and different genres at the writing workshops and to get experience teaching as well. (The mentors lead the monthly writing workshops on a rotating basis.)

I was also really excited to work with high school girls! In college, I took an interest in adolescent psychology, especially around self-esteem issues for teenage girls. I think adolescence is a tough and critical time, especially for young women, and it's important for them to have encouragement and support for their unique interests and talents. For my senior thesis, I actually created an English curriculum for high school girls aimed at addressing female body image in literature and popular culture. I've had a chance to draw on it a bit over the years at GWN.

On top of all that, when I joined GWN, I was relatively new to New York and wanted to meet new people and build a network among a community of talented women writers.

I have changed jobs a couple of times since I moved to New York City, but am still with Girls Write Now. It has been the most consistent and rewarding thing I've done since I moved to New York. Joining the organization was one of the best decisions I've ever made.

What have been some of the highlights of your experience with Girls Write Now?

I was a mentor for seven years with GWN, from 2002 to 2009. During that time, I had the pleasure of being matched with five talented and amazing young women, many of whom I am still in touch with today. Every single one of them inspired me enormously and taught me something about myself.

The way our program works, mentor-mentee pairs meet on a one-on-one basis to work on writing; do fun activities or outings together; and of course, chat and get to know each other. I have many highlights, so it's hard to pick. Here are a few that stand out:

My first year mentoring, I was pretty insecure about what I could offer to a teenage girl. I was so young myself and I didn't really have much experience mentoring. (On top of that, my mentee was a star basketball player who towered over my 5'1" frame, and people often mistook her for the mentor!)

My mentee, whose name is also Andrea, really needed help with the college application process, and she wasn't getting much support at her school. I spent a lot of time helping with her college essay, and she really valued and appreciated my feedback. It made me feel like a million bucks to know I helped her through some part of that extremely complex process. She went on to a great college where she absolutely thrived.

Fast forward seven years. Last summer, Andrea invited me to see her in a spoken word performance here in New York, and I invited the mentee I was matched with at the time to come with me. It was a great experience to see my former mentee performing on stage—she was so poised and eloquent and bold—and for my current mentee to see her and meet her. I was so proud! It was a great night (although it did make me feel pretty old).

I've really enjoyed the collaborative writing I've done with my mentees. For the last several years, we've had a "pair reading" where each mentor-mentee pair co-writes a piece together or writes two pieces on the same topic. One year, my mentee Pearl, who moved to the U.S. from Vietnam, wrote a piece about sitting at the dinner table with her family and what a typical meal was like—everything from what kind of food they ate to the conversation. It was a great short memoir piece, and it inspired me to write about a dessert my mother used to make and how my dad and I learned how to make it more recently now that my mom is gone (she passed away when I was nineteen).

Pearl and I each read our pieces about food and family at the pair reading. We were extremely nervous but did a great job, and it was a powerful experience to share our personal family memories with each other and the rest of the GWN audience.

My most recent mentee, Mona, who I was matched with for three years, is also extremely creative and clever. We had a blast writing our pair pieces for the reading. One year, she had the idea for us to write a poem that was a conversation made up entirely of tongue twisters. (She is very original!) We sat in Barnes and Noble with a book of tongue twisters, a rhyming dictionary, and a thesaurus.

Over the course of a few sessions, we created a piece that was clever, funny, and extremely hard to recite without messing up!

At the reading, we were sure we would stumble over our tongue twisters, but we made it through perfectly and the audience loved it.

Another year, Mona had the idea for us to write a poem that has a different meaning depending on whether you read it from the top down, or the bottom up (based on how the words and lines were structured). She was inspired by a poem written by a Brazilian poet, which she translated from Portuguese and we used as a model. Our piece, called "Pendulum Poem," was a challenge to write but it turned out really well. It has to do with whether or not there is such a thing as an original piece of writing, or if everything has already been done, and what the value of writing is either way. We read it at the pair reading, each of us reading from a different starting point—the first line or the last line—and everyone really enjoyed it.

Another mentee of mine, Jenny, who is from the Dominican Republic, invited me to her high school to see her perform in a poetry slam. She got the idea to have the slam from Girls Write Now. At that time, she went to an excellent international school in Manhattan, where all the students are immigrants. She organized the whole event, and several students performed original pieces (to a supportive and engaged audience), and a few teachers were the judges.

In front of her whole school, Jenny stood up and read a very powerful and personal piece. She is absolutely fearless and a real leader. It was an awesome experience to come into her school and see her in that environment among her friends and teachers.

Pearl (my mentee from Vietnam) also went to an international school in Brooklyn, and she invited me to her end-of-the-year talent show, where students performed different skits, dances, and musical pieces, many of which were related to the culture of their home countries. Pearl performed a dance number with some friends, which was great, and I got to meet her dad. In both cases, it was wonderful to be invited to see my mentees perform something at their schools.

I could go on and on about my experiences with each mentee, but I'll stop there.

Other highlights include:

The workshops – I have learned so much about so many different genres at our writing workshops. Some of my best writing has come out of the workshops. I never used to think of writing as a communal activity, but being a part of GWN has shown me how productive and inspiring it can be to sit in a room full of talented and creative women, all quietly writing away in their journals. And we often share our work aloud, which is scary but exhilarating. It has helped me to take risks in my writing and try new things and get valuable feedback from others.

Workshop guests – We have tremendous guest speakers who come to our workshops to give "craft talks." Some that stand out from the last several years are Victoria Redel, who taught us how to write beautiful and accessible poetry about our everyday experiences; and Nahid Rachlin, who spoke to us about her book Persian Girls, a memoir about two sisters growing up in Iran. Both were inspiring in their own way and really broke down their process for us, which was very helpful to mentors and mentees alike.

The community – I have met so many amazing people through my experience at Girls Write Now—talented and accomplished writers (some of whom have mentored me), inspiring young women, dedicated teachers and administrators, selfless volunteers, and tireless and ingenious staff members and program leaders. I have made many close friends and hope that my former mentees know that they can always call on me for insight and inspiration—I'll definitely be calling on them!

Do you have any specific stories to share about how Girls Write Now has shaped your life?

Girls Write Now has come to be a big part of my life, and it has really helped me grow a great deal over the years—personally and professionally. In general, all of the roles I've had within the organization have pushed me to take risks and challenge myself, all within a supportive and encouraging environment that really values individuality and creativity. And I believe that is exactly what we are trying to provide for all of our participants.

When I joined the organization, I was young and insecure about my ability to mentor. But I have been very blessed with positive role models in my life, including my mother, and I wanted to pass on that experience of having someone guide and encourage you and push you to take risks and accomplish things you never thought you could.

As a writer, I know very well how difficult it is to share your work with someone else and to believe that what you're writing is something others will want to read. Even successful writers have those voices in their heads that tell them their work isn't any good or worth reading. And when you add the challenges of adolescence on top of all that, the need for encouragement is even stronger!

So I know how important it is to give young writers encouragement and constructive feedback. Working with my mentees and seeing concrete evidence of their progress—in terms of finishing or improving a piece, getting a piece published, standing up in front of a room full of people to share their work, getting into college, or simply accomplishing some goal that they worked hard towards—has shown me that I can really have an impact, and that I'm a role model even when I don't realize it.

I have helped some of my mentees deal with personal challenges—which are bound to come up when you're engaged in something as personal as writing, or even just in getting to know someone—and in each case, I have had the full support of the organization and its resources to help me figure out how best to address my mentee's and my concerns. These experiences have taught me that every teenager, every person really, faces challenges at different points in their life that they need support for, and I've learned how to handle a range of situations that come up and how to ask for support when I need it.

This year, I'm taking a break from mentoring. I joined the board of directors and am still on the organization's Program Advisory Committee, working on mentee enrollment strategy. I do miss the mentoring, but it's very exciting for me to take on a new role within the organization and contribute at a different level.

Besides, I still feel like a mentor to my past mentees. My most recent mentee, Mona, lives in Massachusetts now (Mount Holyoke bound!). We still talk often and she sends me writing to look over and comment on. I am so happy to continue to serve as a resource for her on everything from writing to college to apartment living to boys to life in general.

Since I worked with Mona longer than any other mentee, we have a pretty close relationship, and it's very important to me. I remember being struck when she would say things to me like, "Well I remembered that you said this . . ." or "I decided to do that because I remember what you told me about your experience." I realized: this girl is really listening to what I say! And she is internalizing a great deal of it. This initially both flattered and scared me, because I realized I better be careful about what advice I give and what ideas I bring to the table.

When Mona graduated from the program last year, she asked me very sincerely if I could still be her mentor even though she was leaving Girls Write Now and moving away. I didn't hesitate and responded instantly, "Of course!" Many of the relationships that are built in this organization are lasting, and that has been very rewarding for me.

Something else that has been rewarding is making connections between GWN and other parts of my life. For example, I wrote an article for work about Annette Gordon-Reed, the author of Pulitzer-Prize winning book *The Hemingses of Monticello: An American Family*. Annette is a professor at the law school where I work, and I wanted to write about her latest book for the magazine I edit. I had such a great experience talking to her about her craft, and I ended up telling her about GWN. She was really interested in the organization, and I later invited her to be the guest speaker at one of our public readings. The audience loved her. And I got the chance to introduce her at the event. She talked very openly and candidly to our mentees about her career path, and the mentors and mentees were all really inspired. It was a great feeling to bridge those two worlds of my job and Girls Write Now.

Has your work with Girls Write Now improved your quality of life? If so, how?

GWN has definitely improved my quality of life. For me, Girls Write Now has been a constant source of inspiration and creativity. Every time I go to an event where our mentees are reading their work, I walk out of the room completely energized, and with several ideas for what I want to write about next. And at our workshops, there is such a strong sense of connection and support among all the members of the community.

The organization emphasizes a collaborative approach, so there is not a hierarchical model in which the mentors are the only experts in the room, imparting their wisdom to the mentees. We are all learning from each other's experiences, and all of those experiences are valued. And of course, my mentees have been bold, talented, motivated young women who've inspired me immensely! I have been so amazed at what they go on to do. These women are all going to be very successful one day, mark my words.

I feel much more knowledgeable because of my experiences at GWN. I've learned so much about writing, leadership, relationships, and about myself. I've been privileged to watch the organization grow over the last eight years, and I've grown along with it. I can definitely say I've gained much more confidence in myself as a writer, a mentor, and a leader.

The relationships I've developed have been the most rewarding part—and my network continues to grow. Now that I'm on the board, I'm meeting new people involved with that part of the organization. I also have a regular meet-up in Brooklyn with GWN mentors and staff members who live around me. We have so much fun! I recently moved to Brooklyn (after eight years in Manhattan), and I was pleasantly surprised to find that I have a built-in network of GWN people in my new neighborhood. Also, I belong to a writers group with two former GWN mentors. Our monthly meetings are a blast, and their feedback on my writing is extremely helpful.

If someone was considering volunteering for Girls Write Now, what would you tell them?

Apply today! This organization is absolutely amazing. Every person involved gets so much out of it. I always say, I wish there had been an organization like this around when I was in high school! But I'm so excited to be a part of it today.

The community is growing and there are many opportunities to get involved. We recently received the Coming Up Taller Award from the President's Committee on the Arts and the Humanities, presented to our executive director and one of our mentees by Michelle Obama herself! We are at a very exciting time in our history, positioned for tremendous growth.

We are all at a very exciting time in our history. Andrea Juncos, Dottie Mann, and Bob Rodgers are three people who are leading the way.

What will we make of this world if we work diligently to empower others, bring them hope, and encourage them to reveal their talents? How will that in turn transform us?

We can hardly wait to find out.

15

It's in Your Job Description

"Why am I not doing this full-time?"

That's what a lot of people end up asking themselves once they start experiencing the joy of volunteering on a regular basis.

We talked to a couple of women who asked that question, did a little soul searching, and then took action. They turned their passion for volunteerism into a full-time job. Now, they live a life that asks them to continuously step out of themselves and into humanity…and they're loving every minute of it.

Women Reading Aloud

Listening, writing, and reading aloud: they are three very powerful ways to connect to a greater humanity. Julie Maloney has found inspiration by giving them equal value in Women Reading Aloud.

"Listening is one of the greatest gifts we can give to each other."

That was just one of the phrases that lingered long after our interview with Julie Maloney in the fall of 2009. Listening is a gift. What a wonderful point! Throughout this book we have been learning about so many different ways in which we can connect with humanity. Until this interview, it didn't dawn on either one of us that listening is one of the best ways to connect. It requires no action, no special tools, and no exceptional talent. On the other hand, it is active. It is a precious gift to listen; and so many people need to have their voices heard. It honors them in a simple and powerful way. When was the last time we made it our job to listen?

Julie Maloney understands the power of listening. She also understands the power of writing and reading aloud. These actions helped her to cope when she was diagnosed with cancer—twice—and she turned her revelation into a non-profit business called Women Reading Aloud.

Julie Maloney has always been an artist. She performed professionally as a dancer in several modern dance companies in New York City. Later, she became the artistic director, choreographer, and principal dancer of the Julie Maloney Dance Company, a successful endeavor that thrived for thirteen years. Artistic expression was her life and her passion.

But when Julie turned thirty-eight, her dance career came to a halt. She found herself living in the suburbs of New Jersey with three small children, floundering to find self-expression and weighed down by a crippling desire to reconnect with the freedom she had known in the arts. She fell into a deep depression.

In the midst of her darkness Julie reconnected with the arts. She stretched a hand out to humanity through writing and photography. The lights came back on, and Julie felt vibrant and alive again.

In 2000, Julie was diagnosed with breast cancer. The radiation and other treatments sapped her energy once again, but a voice deep within told her that she needed to move forward, keep a positive attitude, and hold on to her power. Writing helped give credit to that voice within.

The following is a poem Julie Maloney wrote while battling cancer:

UNTITLED

> *it comes like a wave*
>
> *hard at first*
>
> *then soft*
>
> *cancer*
>
> *whipping across my face*
>
> *like wet wind*
>
> —Julie Maloney, from *Private Landscape*

Her words are strong, stark, and truthful. Those words gave her new energy to fight back and embrace life.

Julie Maloney beat cancer, and in 2003 she started a non-profit organization called Women Reading Aloud to share the power of the writer, the reader, and listener with other women. Julie decided to hold the first event in her home. It would be an intimate gathering of twelve women sharing their joys, sorrows, worries, frustration, and triumphs with each other through the written and spoken word in the form of poetry, memoir, and fiction.

Julie was brimming with excitement as the inaugural event drew closer. However, three weeks after the press releases went out, Julie was hit once again with bad news. Her breast cancer had returned. Would she be forced to cancel?

"The show must go on!" Julie laughed. "I didn't cancel it; I wore a wig. It was very important to me."

The first gathering of Women Reading Aloud was a profound experience for all who were in attendance. The twelve women split into two groups and read their work. They listened, provided feedback, and treated each other like the authentic artists they were. At the end of the day, no one wanted to go home.

Julie realized immediately that she was on to a good thing—an intense opportunity was blooming right in her living room, and she had to let it grow. The energy from the first meeting of Women Reading Aloud carried Julie through her second set of cancer treatments. Between treatments, she planned more events. There would be workshops, retreats, special events, and speakers. She would find ways to let the women stay longer.

She also wrote a book of poetry in the middle of all this called *Private Landscape*. It is a beautiful testament to her journey. Julie was staring straight into the face of death, but she was bursting with life.

It was thrilling for Julie to see women discovering their voices as writers. Writing is a tool, and Julie knew it needed to be nurtured. She brought in more speakers and trained with a poet in Scotland to learn about techniques to encourage the writers who took part in Women Reading Aloud.

Julie also learned the Amherst Writers and Artists Method founded by Pat Schneider in Massachusetts and used the method at every event. It is a process built on positive feedback only.

Another woman named Julie—Julie Genovese—attended her first WRA workshop in the spring of 2005, and she wrote to us about her experience and how the Amherst Writers and Artists Method affected her as an artist:

> The masterful part of this method is that the critique in our circle was to answer two questions: what stays with you, and what is working in this piece. This positive, wise, and enlightened process encourages freedom and exploration. We can try out and expose new material without fear of judgment or criticism, and we will continue moving into the areas that are ringing true. The positive feedback sets an upbeat, supportive, and relaxed atmosphere. Julie's series gives the writer permission to open up, jump in, and trust the process of tuning into our own distinct and worthy voices.
>
> The WRA community beautifully supports us as writers and as women. It encourages the exploration of all that we are—past, present, and future. Each of our lives has provided endless and inspiring material that we can excavate

> and share through our writing. It is thoroughly soul-satisfying!

The method worked, and Women Reading Aloud grew. It has become a strong organization dedicated to the power of the writer's voice. Workshops, conferences, and retreats load the WRA calendar, and women need to sign up quickly, because the popular events fill up fast. The first retreat, held at a bed and breakfast on the Jersey shore in 2009, sold out almost immediately, as did the subsequent retreat in 2010. Julie continues to give workshops in her home—and she still has to practically kick the women out the door at the end of every session.

Another participant, Patricia McKernon Runkle, wrote to us about how a chance meeting with Julie turned into an unexpected, joyful journey of discovery.

> My first contact with Julie Maloney was at a poetry gathering. I had moved to New Jersey three months earlier from Minnesota, where I had lived for twenty-one years. The move was unexpected and challenging. Julie gave me a warm welcome, asked me about my interests, and offered to connect me with someone who had similar interests. I didn't know it then, but in this chance meeting, Julie demonstrated the essence of Women Reading Aloud: creating community among women to foster writing.
>
> The following spring, I took Julie's eight-week workshop series. I was apprehensive about reading my raw writing aloud—no chance to ponder or edit—but I quickly discovered that other writers in the group were open and receptive. The positive focus of the Amherst Method helped and so did Julie's gift as a group facilitator and community builder.
>
> WRA has helped me relax about sharing my writing, especially when it's fresh. I've gotten better at ignoring my internal editor. Now she joins the party! While she's counting

the strawberries at the food table, I can mix with my pals. Win-win.

Are all of the women who attend these events published authors or budding novelists? Absolutely not. All types of writers are welcome. Attendees have included financial advisors, stay-at-home moms, playwrights, CEOs, teachers, novelists, poets, and psychologists. It doesn't matter what they call themselves in the outside world. Women Reading Aloud welcomes every writer of every genre at every level. When they enter a WRA workshop, they are all writers. They are united in purpose: to discover their voice, to listen, and to be heard. That is empowering.

Julie Maloney has embraced humanity by forming this organization that promotes communication and respect. She has recently taken her mission one step further—or maybe it is full circle. Julie now gives workshops at the cancer center where she received chemo treatments. They are listed as healing workshops, but Julie treats the participants the same way she treats the women in WRA workshops. They discover that they are writers; they have a voice, and they can use that voice to fight cancer. The healing workshops bring life to a deadly serious disease.

Julie told us that she knows the healing workshops are successful because the writing is magnificent, and the patients leave feeling renewed.

"They leave glowing," Julies told us. "I can see it in their eyes."

A patient asked her in a recent workshop, "Is every workshop this special?"

Yes. Absolutely.

When two or more people reach out to one another to share their stories and listen—truly listen—the word special doesn't even cover it.

Julie has seen the workshops at Women Reading Aloud and the Carol G. Simon Cancer Center change people's lives. She lives her passion today through the organization she founded, and she uses that passion to connect with a greater humanity.

"They know they have found a community of people who share a common interest," Julie said. "And yet, they are still able to celebrate their individuality. They support one another while they discover the artist within."

Julie gives equal value to the writer, the reader, and the listener. In doing that, she exemplifies the mission of this book: to celebrate humanity and all of our connections. There is a give and take when we reach out to one another. The giver receives as much as the person who receives gives. We are connected in a circle, not a straight line. And that is a very powerful bond that should be nurtured and held dear. Julie Maloney understands that. She is a survivor, an artist, a teacher, a mother, wife, and a friend. She listens with intensity and speaks with grace, and she has made it her job to connect with those around her.

Her Little Warriors

"I started volunteering like many people start," Barbara Creed told us in an email interview in the spring of 2010. "I did it because I had to. In order to get confirmed in the Catholic Church, you are required to do community service work."

Thank you, Barbara, for bringing right out into the open the fact that most of us don't start volunteering because we're perfect, spiritual, always selfless individuals. We do it because our parents drag us there, a friend talks us into it, a co-worker bugs us until we finally sign up, or it's a prerequisite for something else we really want. Thank goodness motives don't count, or many of us would be in serious trouble.

So the Catholic Church got Barbara on the right road. What kept her on that road?

It's pretty simple. She liked it.

Barbara chose to do her community service work for confirmation at a nursing home where her mom worked as the activity director. Much to her surprise, Barbara ended up doing many more hours of service work than were required. She discovered somewhere during her first few visits that she really actually enjoyed it. Helping others wasn't a chore. It was fun.

Barbara told us that her parents were active volunteers in their church and community, so they provided terrific examples of stepping out of oneself and into humanity. Nevertheless, she believes that the desire to help others is innate—it's a need that comes from within. It might not have mattered at all that Barbara's parents were good role models. She has always had a desire deep within to reach out.

Barbara remembered another volunteer experience that left a mark on her soul. It was a week trip to the Appalachian Mountain region of West Virginia. A group from the church Barbara attended in college went to help clean up a halfway house for battered women and do a little handiwork.

"At the time, I didn't understand what it meant to be poor," Barbara wrote. "I left grateful for what I had and also with a strong desire to do more to help."

Every time Barbara has participated in a volunteer activity, she honors that desire within her to reach out and connect with others. Each time she steps out of herself and into humanity, she is somehow right with the world, part of something big, something special.

"Volunteering has made me a better person," Barbara told us honestly. "How? I'm not exactly sure. But it makes life not all about me."

As an adult, Barbara had an opportunity to experience volunteerism from the other side. Her husband is a U.S. soldier, and he spent significant time deployed in Iraq. This took a pretty big toll on their children, as well as on Barbara. Then, when her husband returned from Iraq, the family had to move from Virginia to California. Barbara knew her kids were feeling nervous and unsettled. She heard about the Little Warriors Surf Camp—a camp to help the youngest warriors: children from military families.

Study after study shows that military children have greater stresses in their lives than children in families that do not deal with deployments. They worry about mom or dad getting injured or dying in the line of duty. Little Warriors Surf Camp gives each child a day to become one with the ocean (I feel the ocean can be therapeutic) and learn a new sport. It's a way for these children to escape and find a happy place.

My children took part in the camp last summer. Their dad had just returned from a deployment in Iraq, and we had just moved from Virginia to California. It was a hard deployment; my middle son was well aware of the causalities of the war and knew that his grandfather's plane was shot down in Vietnam. He thought his dad would be next. On top of that, we had this impending move to California when my husband returned.

My children were not happy about what life had handed them. I feel the surf camp was a turning point in our move to California. My oldest, Caroline, was surfing almost immediately. Although Bart, my ten year old, was a little slower to learn to surf, he was able to get up on the board and enjoy the day. Each left with a surfboard to practice their skills whenever we go to the beach.

The Little Warriors Surf camp is a non-conventional way for children to get away from it all. It's a camp that has laughter all around and a sense of accomplishment for each child who attends. It's a great confidence builder.

Barbara's children left the camp with a new sense of hope and happiness, but Barbara left the experience with something, too. She was so impressed by the program and the larger organization, Freedom Is Not Free, that she felt a familiar tug deep inside. She wanted to become a part of this worthy cause.

When we asked Barbara why she decided to work full-time at Freedom Is Not Free rather than volunteer, her answer was again, "Because I had to."

Barbara needed the money.

When her children participated in the Little Warriors Surf Camp, Barbara was looking for a job. She is a teacher by trade, and because of the economic downturn, many teachers in California were being laid off. It made it difficult for this new resident to find a position. On top of that, she had let her teaching certificate expire when working as a stay-at-home mom to care for her children.

While Barbara watched her kids participating in the Little Warriors Surf Camp, she began to see exactly what Freedom Is Not Free was all about. Barbara started to joke with members of the organization that she wanted to take over the executive director job at this place.

A few months later, Barbara received a startling phone call. It was Jay Kopelman, Executive Director of Freedom Is Not Free.

Had someone taken her joke seriously and called the boss?

Mr. Kopelman's first question to Barbara was did she still want his job.

> *Freedom Is Not Free is a mission driven organization dedicated to assisting wounded service members and their families, and the families of the fatally wounded. We fulfill our mission in the following manner: Freedom Is Not Free makes grants to Purple Heart recipients and their families to meet their immediate financial needs, including but not limited to the expenses associated with medical care, travel, home modification, and paying bills. We support community projects for wounded veterans and provide support and healing activities for families of wounded service members, particularly their children.*
>
> —Mission Statement for Freedom Is Not Free

We'll let Barbara finish the story:

> I never did take Jay's job, but I did start to work at Freedom Is Not Free as the development director. The job has become so

much more than a means to earn money. It is a way to give back to the men and women who serve our country. Freedom Is Not Free helps service members that truly need help, whether it's a young service member who was burned in Iraq from IED and needs financial help, or creating a "spa day" for caregivers of wounded service members, or to provide a surf camp for the youngest warriors—children of service men and women.

Funny how things work out, isn't it?

Barbara feeds the desire deep within her to reach out to others, and she also has a great job so that she can continue to help support her own family.

We asked Barbara if her new connection with Freedom Is Not Free has improved her quality of life. Here was her response:

> It has made me a more compassionate person. I have more empathy. Everyone needs help at one time or another. We are all humans trying to survive n this world.
>
> I don't necessarily volunteer or work at Freedom Is Not Free to make my quality of life better, though. I know that many people who volunteer say that it has changed their lives. In the beginning that was probably true for me. But as I continue to help, it has become something different. I want to improve someone else's quality of life. Listening to someone who doesn't have anyone to talk to in a nursing home or playing bingo with them, tutoring at-risk kids, teaching middle school girls in a housing project to cook, helping do repairs on the roof of someone's house because they can't afford to do it on their own, painting the inside of a Head Start building—these are a few ways that I have made someone *else's* life better, not my own.

It looks like Barbara lives in that final, all-encompassing circle of humanity. She gets that she has a very important job here on earth, and that is to strengthen the circle, to be of service to others, whether she knows them or not.

Finally, we asked Barbara what she would tell someone who is thinking about volunteering but is still on the fence.

> GO FOR IT! My feeling is if you have time to watch an hour of TV then you have an hour to volunteer. I suggest starting small, volunteering for an hour at a time, and make sure it's a good fit for you. Also, volunteer with a cause you are passionate about. It's never too late or too early in life to become a volunteer.

Both Julie Maloney and Barbara Creed have taken their desire to help others to a new level. They turned an inner nudge, a passion, a desire into a lifetime of service.

Have you ever considered making a career out of service to others?

What would it be like to wake up in the morning and know that no matter what happens at work, you have helped another human being? Your entire job is to make someone else's life better.

Our guess is that even a bad day would be pretty great.

16

Volunteers Matter

No matter how big and powerful government gets, and the many services it provides, it can never take the place of volunteers.

—Ronald Reagan

HERE IS AN ODD BIT OF TRIVIA: DURING THE YEAR WE SPENT WRITING THIS book, we heard the starfish story no less than seven times—from parents, pastors, friends...random people on the street. For some reason, it kept coming up. Finally, we decided it might not be a coincidence.

Do you know the story?

Once upon a time, there was a wise man who used to go to the ocean to do his writing. He had a habit of walking on the beach before he began his work.

One day, as he was walking along the shore, he looked down the beach and saw a human figure moving like a dancer. He smiled to himself at the thought of someone who would dance to the day, and so, he walked faster to catch up.

As he got closer, he noticed that the figure was that of a young man, and that what he was doing was not dancing at all. The young man was reaching down to the shore, picking up small objects, and throwing them into the ocean.

He came closer still and called out "Good morning! May I ask what it is that you are doing?"

The young man paused, looked up, and replied, "Throwing starfish into the ocean."

"I must ask, then, why are you throwing starfish into the ocean?" asked the somewhat startled wise man.

To this, the young man replied, "The sun is up and the tide is going out. If I don't throw them in, they'll die."

Upon hearing this, the wise man commented, "But, young man, do you not realize that there are miles and miles of beach and there are starfish all along every mile? You can't possibly make a difference!"

At this, the young man bent down, picked up yet another starfish, and threw it into the ocean. As it met the water, he said, "It made a difference for that one."

The tale is adapted from *The Star Thrower*, by Loren Eiseley, who was an anthropologist, but it pops up all over the Internet and in speeches and conversations in various forms. It makes one very true, universal, beautiful point. You matter.

You don't have to be brilliant, talented, or loaded to make a difference in this world. You just have to be there for someone (or something) else.

Maybe when you have considered volunteering in the past, a feeling of powerlessness stops you from following through. What difference can one person make in the grand scheme of things? There is so much need in this world that sometimes it seems ridiculous to think that your contribution will change it.

If you have experienced this feeling, we encourage you to think about the starfish. You can make a difference in the life of at least one other individual today. You have the power to do that. It may not look like you are a significant force for change in the ocean of need that surrounds us, but you are significant in the world of that person.

We decided to dive a little further into this question of whether or not volunteers matter, and we discovered some awesome statistics.

According to the U.S. Bureau of Labor Statistics, 63.4 million people in the United States volunteered at least once in 2009. That's 26.8 percent of the total population and an increase of 1.8 million from 2008. Can you imagine what we could accomplish if we upped our numbers to just half of the population?

According to the Corporation for National and Community Service, volunteer time in 2009 added up to about 8.1 billion hours. Those hours are worth $169 billion!

Think about the organizations that couldn't operate without volunteer power—hospitals, teen centers, churches, colleges, blood banks, fire departments, shelters. These entities are central to the health and wellbeing of our communities, and they simply would not exist without volunteers.

You matter. If you take steps to volunteer today, you will be counted. You will make a difference in this world, and you have no idea what ripple effect you might cause in the ocean of need.

It Made a Difference to That One

Mark Wiitala has volunteered most of his life. We asked him if he is part of a legacy of volunteering, and he had numerous stories to tell us. Mark's great aunt Polly made a pretty big impression on him at a young age. He remembers hearing stories about her acts of kindness during the Great Depression. Aunt Polly would feed anyone who came knocking on her door and offer a little bit of extra money or clothes, too, if she had them to spare. Some relatives thought that made her an easy mark for people wanting to take advantage, but her experience was far from negative. Her life was full and happy when she reached out almost daily to people in need.

Mark also remembers another aunt who influenced him. She was always working on several volunteer projects at once, many of them through a local 4-H club. He recalls that her hands never stopped moving, and he marveled at her energy level. When she sat down to watch TV with her family, she had a sewing project on her lap.

Mark himself has spent most of his volunteer hours in the Boy Scouts or at church, and the legacy continues. After a recent holiday season, Mark and his son recycled Christmas trees in Medina, Washington with his son's Boy Scout troop. The legacy of service has passed through him to his children.

However, it was Mark's retelling of an experience with Eagle Outreach Ministries that highlighted for us exactly how much a single volunteer act matters. Mark and his wife, Carol, and her daughter, Tessia, are active in Overlake Church in Redmond, Washington. They have taken part in numerous volunteer activities through their church—some exciting and some as mundane as sharpening pencils for the pews. But when Mark walked us through one day they spent volunteering around the holidays, it took our breath away. The simple act of visiting one family was magical.

"Carol told me they would have refreshments," Mark joked. "Maybe that encouraged me to take part in this project in the first place. I was starved after a long day of work, and I loved those little weenies they served at the orientation meeting."

Mark then went on to describe a massive volunteer effort. His stomach may have led him there, but his heart suggested he follow through. Eagle Outreach Ministries is dedicated to supporting the children and families of inmates to ensure every child knows love. One of their largest ministries is a partnership with the Prison Fellowship Ministry's Angel Tree Christmas program. Mark, Carol, and Tessia would be hand-delivering gifts to the children of inmates and every family member in the caregiver's home.

A few weeks after the orientation meeting, the morning kick-off at the church was a worker-bee moment for everyone. One group brought loads of unwrapped gifts they had purchased. Then, a second group created labels with the addresses of recipients. The next group tallied up the items and wrapped them; and a final group placed the appropriate gifts in large, black garbage bags for delivery to each home.

From that point, Mark, Carol, and Tessia had the assignment of taking the giant gift bags to five homes. Mark's simple, straightforward account best describes what happened next:

> I remember driving up to the first home. It appeared fairly nice on the outside and reasonably well kept. I guess I was expecting the slums. When we went into the home, there was evidence of good times gone badly. The first thing I saw was a large projection TV that overpowered the modest living room. It didn't work. There was a Christmas tree with a couple of presents, and the house was very clean. I noticed various electronic gadgets around the home, but they were all broken.
>
> The grandmother and mother (the wife of the inmate) were very gracious and offered us some cider as we sat and talked for awhile. The grandmother told us that her son would not get out of prison for another ten years. It was clear that the family was declining financially. I was pretty sure the beat up car in the driveway wasn't running, and I thought to myself that if we hung around much longer I was going to have to start fixing things. As we talked, the teenage son and younger daughter of the inmate slowly came out of their rooms and joined the group.
>
> We didn't talk about their troubles much at all. The grandmother was good spirited and humorous. Instead, we shared stories about the good times—happy Christmases we all remembered in the past. Pretty soon, we were back in our Honda minivan checking out the MapQuest map to find our next location.

Mark, Carol, and Tessia spent a brief moment with that family, but they made a connection that altered them all. They made a personal, face-to-face difference to that one family in need—and the family in turn brightened the lives of Mark and his family.

We asked Mark if volunteering has shaped his life, and here was his answer:

> It has shaped my life. It's a gut check. No matter how bad I think my day has been, there are so many people out there who have different—and most likely worse—problems than I do. Money is such a worry if you have a family. We all know that. I often think about how the families we met are doing between events and fundraisers. It amazes me how they are able to survive.
>
> I think we are all closer to homelessness or financial ruin than we realize. It's so easy to have a blooper in life. When we reach out to help those in need, I think we are doing what we should be doing to protect our tribe.
>
> I feel a lot happier around the time that I volunteer. It makes me feel good that I have the physical body to do it and some money to give...and I think it does make a difference to me and to my community. If I didn't volunteer, I would probably buy too much stuff, and then I would waste all my time maintaining all that stuff. It's much more rewarding to spend time with others, to do a little bit to improve their lives. I think it's human nature to take care of *all* the members of our tribe.

Mark, Carol, and Tessia made a difference to that family in Washington the day before Christmas. Their actions counted, and their own lives are better as a result.

> *Very often people who step outside of themselves and begin helping others wind up getting better more quickly. They become part of the larger world. Their own problems no longer fill it up.*
>
> —Dr. Daniel Gottlieb

From the Perspective of a Starfish

Now we'd like to talk about another guy named Mark. He doesn't know Mark Wiitala, but they were both at our wedding. (This book is turning into our very own version of the Kevin Bacon Six Degrees of Separation game.) Anyway, Mark Zwilling is very in tune with the value of volunteers. He holds the title of Director of Music and the Arts at our church, St. Andrew UMC in Highlands Ranch, Colorado. We originally interviewed him for this chapter because his entire program is built on the shoulders of volunteers, but we got an added bonus when we sat down with him to hear his personal story.

It is quite obvious that Mark loves his job. He mentioned several times during the interview that he could hardly wait to go to work every day, because he gets to do what he loves. One of the most interesting aspects of Mark's job is that almost his entire staff is made up of volunteers.

The Charles Wesley Choir is the biggest music group in the church with over one hundred singers, and it is the centerpiece of Mark's music ministry. Members of the choir sign on for a pretty hefty commitment—rehearsals at least once a week, singing at two or three services a Sunday, and three or four additional concerts per year. But when you look into the faces of the choir members, they're not exactly suffering. They have a wonderful time together and, even though they are quite a large group, they are tightly knit.

Mark gave us just one example of how Charles Wesley Choir members take care of each other as well as offering their gifts of song to the congregation and community. In 2009, the husband of one choir member passed away. The widow was a young woman who suddenly found herself alone raising a large family. But she wasn't alone.

Mark made one announcement to the choir about possibly raising some money or bringing one or two meals over to the young woman's home, and a tiny miracle began to form. Casseroles piled up and hundreds of dollars were donated within hours. The members of the choir were there when their sister in song was in need, and they continued to look after her as she walked through difficult days.

This example is one of the reasons why Mark loves his job.

"What I like about my job is every day I get to work with truly authentic people. I'm attracted to that. It inspires me," he told us.

We asked Mark about what it's like to manage a team of volunteers every day, and he had some interesting thoughts:

> People have no earthly idea the blood, sweat, and tears—and careful strategy—that go into keeping people active in our music and arts programs. It's not handed to you automatically. You have to show people that they are valued. What they are doing is really important.
>
> You also have to treat volunteers' time very carefully. Volunteers want to be totally on task and doing what they're volunteering to do the moment they are engaged until they leave. That is really important for choirs or anything. You have to treat their time like it's gold, and it is. I try to always start and end rehearsals on time. Time is a commodity—that's what volunteers are giving you. You must respect it.

Mark knows that volunteers matter, and he considers them priceless gifts to his music ministry every day. The volunteers know that Mark matters, too. He is an incredibly talented and inspiring musician, and we often take for granted that he was always destined to be right where he is. What we didn't know about Mark until our interview was that he's also a starfish.

Mark almost took a much different path in life. Thank goodness, one music store owner in Albuquerque, New Mexico recognized Mark's hidden passion for music and threw him in the water.

From a very young age, Mark was captivated by music. His mother remembers him playing the coffee table when he was around five years old, moving his fingers across the wood as if he was playing the piano along with songs on the radio. But music was not encouraged in the Zwilling household. Both of Mark's brothers were into sports, and his parents steered all of their kids toward talents that would lead to stable and respectable careers. Music didn't make that list.

Nevertheless, Mark was continually drawn to it. When he was around thirteen years old, he begged his mom to stop in a music store when they were out shopping for school clothes. She reluctantly agreed to go in for a few minutes. The owner of the music store could see immediately that Mark was enthralled with everything he saw. He asked Mark if he would like to take piano lessons, but the answer from his mother was no. Mark's parents believed there were more appropriate things for a young man to be doing.

That's when the music store owner became that young guy on the beach. He took Mark aside and told him that he would offer him a job in the music store. The man made up the job on the spot, but Mark didn't know that.

When Mark showed up on the first day, his primary task was to go into one of the studios and play the piano as long as he wanted. Then, he would clean. Every Friday, Mark was allowed to go to the cash register and receive five dollars, and that five-dollar bill went directly down the street to piano lessons with a local teacher.

A perfect stranger committed one random act of kindness, and a new musician was born. Mark's talent continued to grow through high school, and when his parents sat down with him his senior year and asked him what he would like to major in when he went to college, Mark didn't hesitate to reply—music.

That answer didn't go over too well. By the way, Mark doesn't blame his parents at all for wanting him to take a safer route to a career. Parents want to protect their children, and they just didn't see how he could make a living as a musician—especially since they had no idea how many hours he had been practicing at the music store over the last few years. They explained to him that they could not pay for college if he was going to major in music. They would happily pay for a more appropriate degree.

Mark was devastated. He went back to the music store and told the owner about his parents' decision. Then another little miracle occurred. The music store owner picked Mark up again and lobbed him right back in the ocean. He made a deal with Mark. He would pay for Mark to study with a concert pianist for six months and learn the pieces he needed to audition for college. If he got in, great. If he didn't, maybe he should take his parents' advice and try a different major. Mark took the music store owner up on his deal and studied diligently for six months.

The day of the college audition arrived. Mark was nervous, but in the end he felt pretty good about how it went. However, when the list of scholarships was posted, Mark didn't see his name. He shuffled away from the crowd and was just about to leave the building when one of his friends yelled out, "Hey, Mark, way to go!"

Mark's name was not within the list of scholarship winners, it was on the TOP of the list. He had been awarded a full scholarship for four years!

Mark described what happens next as a made-for-TV movie. Someone from the music office found him and said he had a phone call. Mark couldn't imagine who it might be. He was four hours away from home at the university. The voice on the other line was unmistakable—it was the music store owner. He and his wife had driven four hours to the college to take Mark out for a celebratory dinner.

When Mark met the couple in front of the music building he said, "Wait a minute. How did you know I would win?"

"We didn't know," the music store owner replied with a grin. "We thought you'd need a good meal either way."

A single act of kindness from one music store owner in Albuquerque made a huge difference to Mark—and Mark hasn't forgotten it. He paid it forward through hard work in college and he has since created a wonderful career rich with beautiful music.

Right from the start, Mark got involved in church music. Shortly after he started music lessons, Mark took a job as the music director/organist at the Air Force base chapel near his home. Throughout his college years he had a church job, too, and was even a boarder at the pastor's house—going out with him on many late-night calls to parishioners. Church and music were constants in Mark's life from the moment he put his fingers on the keyboard.

After graduating from college, Mark found that his hard work paid off. He was flooded with opportunities to work as a musician. Mark even tapped into some star power, working with Michael Crawford for a period of time as his music director for a show in Las Vegas. That was about the time Mark's parents realized maybe he had some musical ability. After all, Michael Crawford was the first Phantom of the Opera—and more importantly, he had been on Johnny Carson!

One day, Michael Crawford invited Mark to be the music director for his upcoming PBS tour. It was the job of a lifetime, but Mark turned it down. Actually, Michael Crawford turned it down for him. He saw the look of hesitation on Mark's face and said, "Mark, your heart is in the church, isn't it?"

Mark had to agree.

From then on, Mark focused on a music career in the church. Millions have been touched by Mark's music all over the world. He inspires hundreds of volunteers every day, and they in turn inspire him. That's what happens when you throw one starfish into the ocean of opportunity.

Would you like to be that young man on the beach tossing starfish into the ocean? Can you imagine how light your heart would feel if you knew you made a difference in the life of just one other person? You can do that today. You matter.

17

FOLLOW YOUR PASSION

THE NUMBER-ONE BIT OF ADVICE WE HEARD DURING OUR INTERVIEWS WAS "follow your passion."

Find something you absolutely love to do or something that really stirs you up inside and use it to connect with humanity.

There are millions of ways to lend a hand. Why pick something you hate or something that you only find mildly interesting?

Choose something that excites you—something that keeps you up at night thinking about it or wakes you up early in the morning to take action.

No one said you have to experience drudgery when you volunteer.

Look for the things that give you butterflies instead.

So what are you passionate about? What brings you to life?

Don't ask yourself what the world needs. Ask yourself what makes you come alive, and then go do it. Because what the world needs is people who have come alive.
—Dr. Howard Thurman

We give Dr. Thurman a virtual high-five for this tremendous quote. We liked it so much that we decided to do a little research on this brilliant man. We found out more about Dr. Thurman through a PBS special called This Far by Faith, a six-hour series that examines the African-American religious experience through the last three centuries. The series highlights connections between faith and African-American cultural values.

Howard Thurman was raised in Florida by a grandmother who was a former slave. He grew up to become an ordained Baptist minister who made a strong impression on the world by expressing his passionate belief in overcoming persecution through peaceful means.

Dr. Thurman studied with Rufus Jones, a Quaker mystic; he met Mohandas Gandhi when he led the Negro Delegation of Friendship to South Asia; and his subsequent passionate writing and speaking was a huge influence on people like James Farmer (founder of the Congress of Racial Equality) and Martin Luther King, Jr.

Dr. Thurman's passion was to bring people of all ethnicities and backgrounds together in peace and faith, and he co-founded The Church for the Fellowship of All Peoples to ignite that passion that kindled within him. It was the first completely integrated church in the United States.

> *Do not be silent; there is no limit to the power that may be released through you.*
> —Dr. Howard Thurman

Dr. Howard Thurman followed his passion, spoke up about it, and look what happened! He became an integral, positive piece of national and world history.

You have no idea what will happen to you, too, if you follow your passions in life. In the very least, the experience will lead you toward the true joy of reaching out to others and connecting in a meaningful way.

Two people from our interviews stood out in this category of following one's passion in life. They had the nerve to do it, and their experiences have been impactful and extraordinary.

Take the Lead

Steve Farr (or "Stevie" as Kelly has called him since they were jumping out of haylofts on their grandparents' farm) is a humble, quiet guy with a wicked sense of humor. You have to pay attention, or his jokes will fly right by you. Stevie has also always had a gift when it comes to working with animals. From birds to dogs to horses, Stevie has that special "animal whisperer" talent that is so rare in humans. Animals just like him.

Stevie, an adult now, is a popular high school Spanish teacher who relates well with his students in the classroom or on spring break trips abroad. He is not a big fan of being the center of attention, though, so it took the input of the entire family sitting around the kitchen table to complete this interview.

Actually, it's fitting that everyone was there. Steve is fortunate to have the support and assistance of his parents, brothers, sisters, cousins, and friends who volunteer hours of their time in his new program.

But let's backtrack a little bit.

Steve has always had a volunteer spirit. As a youngster, he shared in his extended family's various volunteer tasks, mostly associated with church and 4-H. His grandparents started the first horse 4-H club in Ashtabula County, Ohio. Steve spent much of his youth showing horses and mucking stalls at the county fairgrounds. It was through these unassuming activities that he developed a deep love of horses—a love that was grounded in his family's history. In 4-H, members are required to do some type of volunteer work each year, so Steve and his sister and brothers took on a variety of volunteer activities growing up.

But as an adult, Steve discovered a new opportunity to combine his teaching skills and his love of horses into one. His discovery ignited a passion for reaching out to children with developmental delays who also love horses but never thought they could learn to ride.

Steve heard about a group called Therapeutic Riding of Erie County, Pennsylvania (TREC) and decided to find out more about them. Therapeutic riding programs are designed for children and adults with physical or mental disabilities. The results are amazing. They range from a broad smile of satisfaction across the face of a child while experiencing the movement of the horse to substantial physical benefits to the muscles of people with diseases like cerebral palsy. Therapeutic riding can help improve balance and coordination. It can also increase concentration and self-esteem and has shown particularly great success with autistic children.

As Steve said in an interview with the Ashtabula Star Beacon back in 2007, "They learn to take charge of something other than just themselves. It's something they can do and be proud of and have fun at the same time."

It was obvious to Steve after just one session with TREC that he had found his niche. He volunteered with TREC and wasted no time in becoming certified by the North American Riding for the Handicapped Association (NARHA). Steve then started to make plans to open his own program in northeast Ohio. As soon as he was certified, he founded Take the Lead Therapeutic Riding.

Take the Lead started as a small business, and it was an immediate success. It was open to individuals with developmental delays ages four and up. Steve guessed correctly that there was a strong need for therapeutic riding in the area, and he saw the sessions fill up quickly. Classes are limited in size by NARHA standards, and there are a lot of expenses that go into training and buying the right horses and providing proper safety equipment. Steve's goal is to change Take the Lead from a for-profit business to a non-profit, so that he will be eligible for grant funding that will help him increase the scope of his mission and include more kids (and adults).

Steve also spends a lot of time at the racetrack.

No, he doesn't have a gambling problem, and he's not hoping to win big so that he can fund Take the Lead. Steve buys retiring racehorses and retrains them to work as gentle, mellow mounts at Take the Lead Therapeutic Riding.

Steve loves to share his passion for horses with children with developmental delays. He feels privileged to witness in every session the favorable changes in those who are given this opportunity. The children shriek with laughter and blossom in confidence. Their parents beam from the other side of the fence as they watch their kids make physical and emotional connections that have previously been difficult for them.

It's not just the kids who are having fun. Take the Lead has become a place for their parents to socialize and recharge, and Steve is seeing a change in them, too. They have developed a network of friends facing similar challenges. Hope blooms inside and outside the ring.

> *No hour of life is wasted that is spent in the saddle.*
> —Winston Churchill

Steve soon learned that he needed additional volunteers who enjoy children and horses and feel comfortable with both. He trained "side walkers" to lead the animals and hold the children safely in place with belts. Many of Steve's family members were quick to offer their enthusiastic services. Neighbors and aides from Happy Hearts School (for the developmentally disabled) in Ashtabula County also came to assist. Most of his volunteers have had experience around horses or ponies—all are willing to learn more. Their positive attitudes and giving hearts make it easy for them to develop fast friendships with the riders. Many of them were sitting around the kitchen table during this interview.

Ruth Farr (Steve's mother, a primary school principal):

> Wonderful friendships develop when you volunteer. As for Steve's program, it's so rewarding to help the children—it lifts my spirits! As I drive home smiling, I think of the unabashed things the kids say out of pure joy and innocence...the simple things they appreciate and find amazing, like the birth of a baby pony. Some of the children are very bright, yet they'll never experience what typically developing children do because of their physical limitations. This program helps fulfill some of their dreams. They make new friends there, too. The kids are fun—we love them!

Ruth's parents were active volunteers. Throughout her life, she has followed their example as a 4-H member and leader; Sunday school and vacation Bible school teacher; provider of food for funerals; waitress in the Grange food stand at the county fair; and chauffeur for elderly friends, taking them to the grocery store and doctors' appointments. Ruth continually steps out of herself and into humanity.

Julia and Todd Pew (Steve's sister and brother-in-law):

As parents of young children, Julia and Todd have a lot of experience volunteering in their children's sports and school activities. But they find a new and different kind of fulfillment in their participation in Steve's riding school. Todd, like Steve, is tall and strong and can help lift a child onto the horse. Julia is an experienced equestrian and an elementary school teacher who understands the fears of children around large animals. As a side walker, she gently calms and comforts them.

Connie Farr (Steve's sister-in-law):

Although Connie's experience with horses is in its early stages, she is a dedicated side walker with a wonderful sense of humor. Her husband, Tommy (Steve's brother), often volunteers in the program, too.

Connie says she was thirteen years old when her cousin encouraged her to volunteer at the Ashtabula County Nursing Home. She visited with the elderly, went on day trips with them, and helped them with small tasks. Connie mostly enjoyed just talking and laughing with them. She felt good about helping people and making them happy, and she learned from them, too. Connie eventually made a career of caring for the elderly.

LuAnn and Kelly Fischer (Steve's cousins):

LuAnn and Kelly also come from this family of 4-Hers who were active in volunteer service work. They are experienced equestrians who are comfortable assisting as side walkers or doing anything Steve requests in the equestrian setting. They enjoy interacting with the children and parents, and they feel a strong personal satisfaction from their involvement with Steve's program.

> *I pledge my head to clearer thinking*
>
> *My heart to greater loyalty*
>
> *My hands to larger service*
>
> *And my health to better living*
>
> *For my club, my community, my country, and my world.*
>
> —4-H Pledge

Take the Lead is most definitely a group effort. Steve must have been dancing on the inside as everyone around the table talked about how it has enriched their lives—but he'll never let on. Steve was the spark, and now everyone is alight with a passion for helping children learn to ride horses and experience a new kind of freedom and happiness.

Roots and Shoots

"About the time I wrote my symphony, I had a meeting that would change the course of my life."

What?!

That was one of first few lines we read in an email from young Mitch Paine of Lincoln, Nebraska.

Who is this child prodigy? Have we stumbled upon the next Mozart?

Well, it turns out he's a firecracker. Mitch Paine is a young man on a mission. We get the feeling he never sits still for very long, either, and we thoroughly enjoyed getting to know him. That chance meeting he mentioned resulted in a passionate response and produced a young activist who is making a difference all over the world—but especially in his own community.

When Mitch was in middle school and high school, music was his passion. He played a number of instruments and even started writing music. He formed a string quartet in the eighth grade that was soon booked for weddings, retirement parties, and church services all over town. The performances were purely volunteer, and Mitch discovered just how powerful music is as he watched it bring joy to people's lives with every event.

Mitch was also a member of the Lincoln Youth Symphony (playing viola), and during that time he wrote a two-movement symphonic piece on the theme of racial discrimination. The first movement depicts a meeting between two strangers and is filled with turbulent chords and adversity. The second movement reveals understanding. The two people learn about each other and understand that even though they look different, they are really very similar and both part of the same community of people on earth.

The conductor of the Lincoln Youth Symphony asked Mitch to conduct his composition on a concert. As he stood in front of the eighty-piece orchestra, Mitch grew in an instant. He rooted himself to the ground and shot up like Jack's beanstalk, thriving in the light of encouragement and passionate creativity.

"This leadership experience greatly affected how I participated in all of my other volunteer activities throughout the following years," Mitch told us. "I found that I could make a small change in the world through my music."

That was the spark.

Now, for the flame.

When Mitch was in the midst of writing his symphony, the lighter fluid showed up in his home town—it came in the form of a petite woman with a powerful message—Jane Goodall.

Many of us know Jane Goodall as the "chimp lady." She is one of the foremost experts on chimpanzees in the world. Jane Goodall is probably best known for her forty-five year study of wild chimpanzees in Gombe Stream National Park in Tanzania, but she is also a leading champion of conservation and animal welfare issues. She founded the Jane Goodall Institute, which is dedicated to these important pursuits.

If you ever have an opportunity to hear Jane Goodall speak, we highly recommend it. We heard her give a talk a couple years ago on the University of Denver campus, and she was stunning—so small and so powerful—she is one of the most captivating speakers either of us has ever heard.

Evidently, Mitch had the same reaction.

Mitch and his mother attended a lecture given by Jane Goodall at Nebraska Wesleyan University. Here is how he described the evening:

> After her lectures, Jane Goodall always does a book signing and stays until every single person has gotten a signature. My mother and I went to the lecture together, and afterwards we waited for a little bit at the very back of the line. One of the staff people told us that the signing would last for a couple hours. He suggested we come back, and then we wouldn't have to wait in line. So after two hours, we came back and found the auditorium completely empty.
>
> We searched all over the place and finally we came across Jane and a few of her associates eating dinner in a small art gallery in the building. We poked our heads in and asked if she would sign one last book. She obliged, probably quite annoyed that we had found her, but pleasant about it just the same. She asked me what grade I was in and what I enjoyed doing, as she completely stopped the meal to sign our books.
>
> I told her that I was really interested in dolphin training and wanted to work with dolphins on developing a common language between the two species. She was very interested in my love for animals and my future goals. (I obviously didn't follow through with those goals, because here I am in land-locked Nebraska!)

Mitch may not have developed a common language between dolphins and humans, but he did follow through on something else—getting involved in Roots & Shoots. During his brief conversation with Jane Goodall that evening, she encouraged him to join the program that she developed as part of the Jane Goodall Institute. In fact, she gave him a directive: create a Roots & Shoots group in your high school and report back. Mitch soon learned what Roots & Shoots was all about: young people changing the world through changing their own communities.

> *Roots creep underground everywhere and make a firm foundation. Shoots seem very weak, but to reach the light, they can break open brick walls. Imagine that the brick walls are all the problems we have inflicted on our planet. Hundreds of thousands of roots & shoots, hundreds of thousands of young people around the world, can break through these walls. We CAN change the world.*
>
> —Jane Goodall

Jane probably had an idea that she could count on Mitch, and she was right on target. He came to embrace her words and followed through by starting a Roots & Shoots program in his school. Knowledge, compassion, and action are the three steps that Roots & Shoots uses as a working model for all activities. The program encourages young people to find out what is happening in their communities.

Knowledge first.

Once they are informed, then they begin to develop positive, passionate attitudes toward changing their communities for the better. Finally, they take action.

That's exactly what Mitch did in his sophomore year of high school. Jane Goodall set him on fire with a passion for caring for all creatures, and he translated that passion into action. He joined a science focus program that was commonly known as Zoo School. It was housed (appropriately) in the Lincoln Children's Zoo.

"It was there at Zoo School that I gathered together a group of students to talk about Jane and her Roots & Shoots organization," Mitch wrote in his email to us. "I arranged to have a representative from South Dakota come down to Lincoln and chat with some of us, and we heard from her about the inspiration behind Jane creating Roots & Shoots. She talked a lot about the various projects all around the world that Roots & Shoots groups undertake. I was drawn to the organization and realized the potential that it had to work in Lincoln."

Next, Mitch elicited the help of his teacher, Sara Toren, and she was quite enthusiastic about the project.

"Ms. Toren was a science teacher at Zoo School, and experiential learning was an essential element of her teaching philosophy. She strongly encouraged us to help out at science fairs and other similar events and also to help in the zoo. Every spring, our Roots & Shoots group organized a spring clean up, where we helped the zookeepers clear out brush and get the zoo ready for opening day in April."

The kids were hands on. They even took part in various animal exhibits in the zoo. Mitch was fortunate to spend three years helping train two harbor seals, Pearl and Toney. This included feeding them and conducting a training routine for zoo visitors that included narration and music.

"Every time I volunteered with the seals, it was the best part of my day," Mitch recalled. "Working with such fantastic animals and dedicated zookeepers was an incredibly rewarding experience. Seals are very similar to dogs, but a little bit pickier...like a cat."

Mitch's senior year of high school was a blur of musical activities and preparations for graduation, but one of the highlights was that Mitch was invited to join the College Leadership Council, a group of college students who acted as an advisory team to the national Roots & Shoots organization and a resource for college groups around the country.

On their annual leadership retreat, Mitch fueled his passion by interacting with students from all across the country, learning how to become a better leader, and developing a deeper understanding of

Roots & Shoots. He also learned more about Jane Goodall and her mission in life to work for conservation and animal welfare. Disney World graciously partnered with Jane Goodall for the event, and Mitch met a lot of incredible people and heard stories that continued to fuel his fire. Disney World showed the students how they were "going green" in their theme parks, which was an added bonus to an extraordinary few days.

"At that retreat, I truly learned the power of young people," Mitch told us. "After hearing everyone's stories, projects, philosophies, and getting to know their personalities, I gained a lot of hope that we could transition into a better world, and the youth could lead the way."

On his trip home from that retreat, Mitch Paine had another life-changing meeting. He had a three-hour layover at Chicago O'Hare Airport before making it home to Lincoln, and while he was waiting to board his flight, an African man sitting next to him struck up a conversation. Father Nkyi was a priest at a parish in Omaha, but he was originally from Ghana. The chance meeting would change Mitch's life forever.

Mitch and Father Nkyi talked for three hours about Ghana, and when it was time for Mitch to board his plane, they exchanged contact information and agreed to stay in touch.

Mitch went back to Lincoln, and soon after, he and his best friend, Lauren Thompson, were students at the University of Nebraska-Lincoln (UNL), where they immediately started a new Roots & Shoot group and started petitioning to have Jane Goodall come back to Nebraska to inspire another assembly of young people to get involved.

Mitch and Lauren had a bit of a rocky start on campus.

"We found it hard to get people motivated to see the environmental issues that needed to be tackled. In Nebraska, there isn't striking environmental destruction, like rivers on fire or other environmental disasters," Mitch said. "Therefore, it's hard to get a core group of students (or people in general, for that matter) together to work on an issue. Often, it was just Lauren and me working on Roots & Shoots projects, but we still managed to get a lot done."

One of their big projects was to highlight the only endangered species in Lincoln, Nebraska: the Salt Creek tiger beetle.

That's a tough sell.

"The interesting thing about this beetle is that it exists only in Lincoln, Nebraska and nowhere else in the world," Mitch explained. "If anything was to bring this species away from the brink of extinction, it would be community-centered conservation—the essence of the Jane Goodall Institute and Roots & Shoots."

Mitch and Lauren doubled their efforts and built up public education on the beetle. They took photographs of the beetle on the salt flats and then put together posters with information about the tiger beetle and its importance to the ecosystem in and around Lincoln. They wanted to show Lincolnites that they really had something special there.

Some of the comments in response to newspaper articles on saving the Salt Creek tiger beetle were vicious. People weren't interested in spending money to save a bug. But Mitch and Lauren were undeterred.

They put up more posters in coffee shops and all around town and continued to spread the message. In fact, one of those posters still proudly hangs in one of the cafes.

Suddenly, Mitch had an opportunity to take his story of the tiger beetle to the international stage.

"I was invited by Roots & Shoots to speak on behalf of the organization at the United Nations International day of Peace on September 21 at UN Headquarters in New York City. I kept reading and rereading the email to see if it was true. I immediately said yes."

Mitch and Jane Goodall spoke on the environment and peace; and Ban ki Moon, Michael Douglas, Elie Wiesel, Princess Haya of Jordan, and three other students spoke about other aspects of peace. They stood before a group of about six hundred young people from every corner of the world.

"We all spoke about how every single person can make a small change with everyday acts. No action is too small, and everyone is important in making the world a better place. This is the most important thing that Jane and Roots & Shoots have taught me, and getting this message across to a large audience was a true privilege."

After returning from the UN, Mitch's passion for Roots & Shoots was white hot. He knew exactly what he wanted to do next: study in Ghana.

Mitch called up his friend from the airport, Father Nkyi, and told him of his plans. Father Nkyi invited Mitch to stay with his family for the first month and a half before school started, and Mitch gratefully accepted, as the cost to go over with a study abroad program was out of his reach. Father Nkyi's brother warmly accepted Mitch into his family for those months.

Soon after starting classes at the University of Ghana, Mitch began looking for opportunities to expand his Roots & Shoots activities to Africa. He found the perfect opportunity with an organization called Sun and Moon Turtle Foundation in Accra. We'll let Mitch tell the rest of the story in his own words:

> I rode down to Teshie, a small fishing village just east of the giant city of Accra, and met Emmanuel Kuhameh. We spent the evening chatting about sea turtle conservation and life in Teshie. I left his house feeling very inspired and ready to help.
>
> Over the course of the next four months, I helped Emmanuel at least twice a week. In Teshie, there are two main threats to sea turtles: fishermen catching the turtles (usually accidentally) in their nets out at sea; and unemployed men who pick up nesting turtles from the beaches at night. They sell the turtles in the market for traditional turtle soup.
>
> Emmanuel was working to solve both problems. He employed some of the men to bring the turtles to his house (instead of selling them), where he had enclosed an area of beach to allow the female turtles to lay their eggs in safety.

I helped with a solution to the fishermen catching the turtles in their nets, and I also helped Emmanuel start a Roots & Shoots group in Teshie.

Emmanuel even posed as a villager who eats turtles and hired a fisherman to purchase every turtle that came from the boats. Emmanuel would receive the turtles late in the morning and then hold them in his yard until late afternoon when it was safe to release them. He had to watch over them the entire time. Otherwise, passersby would pick them up and take them to the market. Emmanuel also had to keep pouring water on their shells to maintain their temperature. I would help him by coming to his house and taking care of the turtles during the afternoon. When we released the turtles, it was the most rewarding experience.

One time, Emmanuel called me very excited. He said that he thought he had a new species. In Ghana, the primary turtles that nest are olive Ridley sea turtles. I came down to his house immediately and agreed that we had a green sea turtle, which he had never seen before. We called a biologist from the University of Ghana, and he quickly came down and agreed that we had the first living specimen of a green sea turtle found in over five years in Ghana.

There had been a storm that day, but after we had finished talking, the sea was calm. When we finally released the green sea turtle, there was a magnificent sunset, and a small crowd gathered to watch the turtle swim away. We explained the different species to the local villagers who watched. They were almost overwhelmed to see this huge reptile out of the water.

As she swam away, the turtle seemed to say thank you.

In that moment, I knew I had made a difference in this country thousands of miles from home. At least I had changed the community of Teshie very slightly. I'll never forget watching those turtles swim out to sea and watching the Ghanaians smile as they looked on in wonder.

When Mitch returned to the United States, the passionate student became an activist. He realized that he could merge his Roots & Shoots activities with another volunteer interest: politics. Through his work with Roots & Shoots, Mitch realized that there was a niche he could fill, and that was working with and for the government on public policy as it relates to the environment.

Mitch wasted no time. He was elected to the Board of Directors of the Nebraska Sierra Club, which works primarily on legislative and election issues surrounding the environment, renewable energy, and sustainability; and Mitch also worked directly with the Nebraska legislature on bills that furthered these causes. Mitch even worked on campus to ensure that the student government focused on environmental issues.

The greatest danger to our future is apathy.
—Jane Goodall

From passionate student to activist, Mitch has grown into a positive force in his hometown of Lincoln, Nebraska, and he has no intention of slowing down. He thanks his volunteer activities, particularly with Roots & Shoots, for giving him direction and the fiery passion to lobby for various causes.

"I would venture to say that my volunteer activities take more time and have a higher precedence than my schoolwork," Mitch admitted. "I thrive on helping people and helping my community. I've never been able to sit back and simply watch an issue destroy some element of our lives. I speak up when there is new construction in Lincoln that's not sustainable; I write to the newspaper when an unfavorable comment about the Salt Creek tiger beetle is made; and I try very hard to make Lincoln a place that I want my kids to live in."

When we asked him about how Roots & Shoots has impacted his life and what he would tell other young people about volunteering, Mitch had the following to say:

I have met the most incredible and inspiring people through my volunteer activities. The friendships, networks, and communities I now consider myself a part of are priceless.

My advice to young people around the world is just get involved. No action is too small.

I repeat, no action is too small.

Something as seemingly insignificant as cleaning up a neighborhood park is a huge action and may really change someone's perspective on his or her community.

Also, I would hope that people really focus on their own communities. We need a global network of young people trying to make their own communities great places to be.

My last word of advice is never let someone tell you no. Too many times I have been told "no, we can't do that" or "it won't work here." In my experience, those naysayers are almost always wrong. I've been told many times on campus "recycling will never work," but this year we're seeing huge increases in recycling, just through education and inspiration. We have to start dealing with these issues now. Together, we can make a difference.

Honestly, we can't imagine anyone ever telling Mitch no.

Can you?

Follow your passions.

See where they lead you.

They might take you to turtles in Ghana, tiger beetles in Nebraska, or horse farms in Ohio. Wherever you go, the ride will be worth it.

You have the power to ignite a fire today and make the world a better place tomorrow.

Epilogue

These interviews have given us a jolt of optimism that no amount of caffeine could ever reproduce. It has been exhilarating to witness the great things that are happening all over the world...one person at a time. We truly hope the people in these pages have inspired you, too.

Think of all the opportunities we have—each moment of every day—to reach out and strengthen the circles that bind us together. You can be part of a change that helps us all evolve into a more caring community and world.

If you are still uncertain about your steps to volunteering or reaching out to someone in need, we encourage you to visit www.more-than-me.com. This website lists over one hundred opportunities that we will continue to update as people (like you) send us information. Take some time to browse around and follow the links to volunteer websites. Have fun searching for your next transformational experience.

We also encourage you to find a comfy chair and sit down with a notepad to answer the following questions:

- What are you passionate about?
- What social justice issues fire you up? Is there something you can do to right a wrong?
- What do you do for fun?
- Do you like to be around lots of people, or would you rather hang out with someone one-on-one?
- Have you said "someone should really do something about that" recently? Are you that someone?
- What age groups do you like to spend time with the most (children, teens, young adults, adults, the elderly)?
- Has someone recently asked you for help?
- Has someone recently asked you to join a volunteer activity?

- What makes you happy? Can you use it to reach out to others?
- Have you ever stepped out of your comfort zone? Do you want to give it a try?
- Are you sick of your job and looking for a change? (Volunteering is a great way to explore your gifts and talents in different areas—plus sometimes non-profits are hiring.)
- Is there a person or institution that has given you a hand in the past? What would be a great way to pay that forward?
- Has your quiet inner voice been making suggestions while you've been reading this book? Are you listening to that voice, or did you put it on mute?

Take the time to answer these questions thoroughly and maybe even journal a little bit about your thoughts. They may lead you on a new and exciting journey. It's your turn now to experience MORE.

Eric likes to tell a story about the first time he and Kelly climbed a 14-er together. (That's a mountain over 14,000 feet—for those of you who only know sea level.) To Eric, the story is endearing; to Kelly, it's a little embarrassing. They were a mere 500 yards away from the summit of Mt. Sherman in Colorado when Kelly stopped to take a breath. She looked around her and then burst into tears.

The mountain range that surrounded them stretched out for miles, the robin-egg blue sky was brilliant, and the air was crisp and clean. A sprinkling of hikers in front and behind them picked their way over the loose rocks to reach their destination. All of it created such a stunning picture that Kelly was flooded with a sudden wash of gratitude.

Eric thinks this story has a message—Kelly didn't shed a single tear at the summit. She was overcome with the beauty of it all before she ever reached the top.

That's exactly how life should be.

We are all in the middle. We're well beyond the starting gate, but we haven't yet reached the finish line—or the summit—of our lives. We're somewhere in the heart of our journey.

Don't wait.

Start now.

Step out of yourself.

No cats were harmed in the creation of this book.

4CatsInk.com

Made in the USA
Lexington, KY
22 December 2010